MVP Development for Entrepreneurs

Entrepreneurs' blueprint for defining problems, building MVPs, and iterating with lean principles

---

Dinker Charak

bpb

www.bpbonline.com

First Edition 2026

Copyright © BPB Publications, India

ISBN: 978-93-65896-404

To View Complete
BPB Publications Catalogue
Scan the QR Code:

Dedicated to

My mother, Phoola

About the Author

Dinker Charak is a seasoned product strategist and technology innovator with a career spanning diverse industries and disciplines. He brings deep expertise in data and AI, product management, asset-based consulting, and EEBO metrics, with a sharp focus on helping organizations build impactful, revenue-generating digital products.

Over the years, Dinker has developed software products for real-time operating systems, paperless workflows, home automation, and online video advertising—significantly shaping the early evolution of these markets in India. His entrepreneurial journey includes launching a messaging app for children. This experience offered him invaluable first-hand lessons in product-market fit, user behavior, and startup resilience—insights that directly inform the practical wisdom shared in this book.

Before transitioning into product leadership, Dinker contributed to high-energy particle physics research at globally renowned laboratories, including CERN in Switzerland and Fermilab in the United States. He holds a patent in advertising technology and has filed multiple provisional patents related to metrics and product innovation.

Dinker is also the author of multiple books on product management and development. He regularly shares his insights through his blog and often hosts his podcast as well. He actively mentors early-stage entrepreneurs and product managers through initiatives by NASSCOM and CIIE. He conducts workshops that bridge the gap between theory and practical application in building minimum viable products.

MVP for entrepreneurs is his latest effort to empower founders with a clear, structured approach to building what matters—without wasting time, money, or opportunity.

About the Reviewers

❖ **Anupam Sarsar** is an alumnus of Tezpur University and NITIE (now IIM Mumbai). Based in Mumbai, India, he works as a product manager in the banking and financial services sector. He has been instrumental in launching a payments bank and several large-scale applications across the insurance and mutual fund domains, working for various large entities in India. Outside of work, Anupam writes for his Medium publication, The Editors post, and enjoys watching lawn tennis in his leisure time.

❖ **Pankaj Sharma** is a seasoned business, product, and technology leader whose career spans early-stage and growth startups, mid-sized ventures, and Fortune-5 organizations across technology, healthcare, finance, and consumer domains. Drawing on more than a decade of experience, he has steered early-stage product launches through rapid iteration cycles, scaled platforms to unlock new revenue streams, and helped enterprises pivot toward more agile, outcome-driven models. As an investor and mentor, Pankaj has evaluated and guided multiple emerging startups, providing counsel on market validation, go-to-market planning, and team building to drive measurable traction and investor interest.

A lifelong learner, he continuously explores ideas at the intersection of leadership, innovation, and human behavior. Pankaj regularly shares insights with peer networks, contributes thought pieces on product management, and coaches young professionals to cultivate curiosity, resilience, and ownership.

❖ **Sarang** is a passionate product management professional and enterpreneur with over 14 years of experience in the IT/ITeS sector, delivering high-impact solutions for startups and Fortune 500 companies. He has led cross-functional teams through Agile and lean methodologies, championing MVP and MMP development that align with both user needs and business goals.

As a bootstrapped enterpreneur, Sarang spent over five years building ventures from the ground up - including an import/export business and a local cafe - where he practiced ideation, applied design and strategic thinking, crafted go-to-market strategies, developed user stories, experimented with price models, and validated product-market fit through real-time customer feedback. These experiences sharpened his ability to think creatively, act dicisively, and build customer centric products with aglity and purpose. Sarang is a certified scrum product owner and a lifelong learner with certifications in UX, AI, data science, and product management. As content creator, mentor, and an avid learner, he is inspired to share his knowledge and practicle insights to help others navigate their carrier or startup journey. His unique blend of technical acumen and enterpreneurial grit brings real-world clarity to the MVP process.

Acknowledgement

A product thinker's journey is one of transformation—from simply executing tasks to questioning why something needs to be done. My own journey from what to why has been shaped through collaborations with many remarkable individuals, and I want to take a moment to acknowledge them.

I have chosen to be expansive in my acknowledgments for another reason as well—I want readers to see that their entrepreneurial journey does not have to be a lonely one. We are all influenced by many people along the way. My hope is that by sharing my experience, others will feel encouraged to seek guidance and help as they navigate their own paths.

I am deeply grateful to Sagar Paul and Naren Nachiappan for their mentorship and the opportunities they provided. The most important lesson I learned from them was that any product, whether built by an entrepreneur or an enterprise, must create genuine value for the customer. While this seems like a simple concept, it remains one of the most challenging aspects of product development.

I want to thank Santosh Mahale and Sachin Dharmapurikar for our enriching discussions, which have broadened my perspective and deepened my understanding.

A special thanks to Sudhir Tiwari for asking questions so simple and obvious that answering them required me to study, analyze, think, and synthesize for days.

I appreciate Pranjal Dubey, who leads the Sant Singhji Institute of Science and Management in rural Madhya Pradesh, and Srijayanth, who runs the STEP program at Thoughtworks, for giving me the opportunity to interact with their students. Teaching them has been an incredible experience that has, in turn, brought me greater clarity.

I want to especially thank Piyush Purwar for his insights during countless video calls and airport lounge discussions.

I want to thank Akshata Gadigi, Bala Rajesh, Bismaya Kumar Purohit, Prakhar Jain, and Rituraj Gogoi, whose thought-provoking questions during NASSCOM ProductSkills mentoring sessions helped enrich this book.

A heartfelt thank you to Baargav Duggirala (then at NASSCOM CoE, Vizag), Deboleena Raha Das at NSRCEL (IIMB), Khushbu Gupta, Prashant Verma, Shreya Sharma at NASSCOM ProductSkills, Noopur Pathak, Priyank Pathak, Prashant MJ at Agile Network India, Eric

Batliwala, Supriya Nair, Susmita Ghosh at CIIE (now IIMA Ventures) for offering opportunities to share my learnings with product managers and entrepreneurs.

This book would not have been possible without the deep discussions I have had with Aditya Garg, Kartik Kannan, Mir Hidatayhulla, Nagarjun Kandukuru, Nittish Veeraputhirasamy, Prakash Kini, Prasanth Soman, Rajavel Manoharan, Sachin Sapre, Shree Damani, Srivats P., Sudarshan Purohit, Sudheer Hullemane, Suganth Chellamuthu, Sunil Shrivastava, Vaishnavi Nayaranan, and Vinay Panshadhari.

I am grateful to Abhishek Sharan, Harin Dave, Karan Arora, Linfeng Yu, Shankar Devraj, Sudhir Shetty, Vikram Sharma, and Walter Trotta for challenging me with complex, real-world enterprise problems. Many of the learnings shared in this book stem from the process of solving their unique challenges.

A special acknowledgment to my first startup team—Kanika Chopra, Piyush Trivedi, Sanjay Kumar, Saneef Ansari, Smita Kumari, and Wairok Makunga—for their dedication and collaboration. I want to thank Daljit Singh Charak, Dinesh Charak, Munish Jauhar, Naresh Goel, Navneet Gosal, Nitin Goel, Soumitra Bajpai, Sumit Garg, and Vikash Jain for believing in me. Though that entrepreneurial journey did not achieve commercial success, those three years were the most enriching and transformative of my life.

I appreciate Diaz Nesamoney, Amit Jain, Kshitij Shori, Parth Chandra, Sanjay Dahiya, Vikas Kotwal, and Vijayachandran Mariappan for their insights on why and how to build a product so valuable that customers are willing to pay the asking price.

Finally, I want to thank Anandhi Sarangan, Gerry Guglielmo, Margaret Votava, Michael Mathur, and Sharon Lackey, who, as my supervisors in my early career, consistently guided me to focus on outcomes over the mere completion of tasks.

Each of these individuals (and I am sure I missed some names, and apologies for that) has played a role in shaping my journey, and I am incredibly grateful for their support, wisdom, and influence.

I am also grateful to BPB Publications for their guidance and expertise in bringing this book to fruition. It was a long journey of revising this book, with the valuable participation and collaboration of reviewers, technical experts, and editors. Grateful to all the technical reviewers for taking the time out of their busy schedules to review the manuscript with such meticulous attention to detail.

Finally, I would like to thank all the readers who have taken an interest in my book and for their support, feedback, and reviews. Your encouragement has been invaluable.

Preface

Every entrepreneur starts with a spark—a brilliant idea that they believe can change the world. This is what Steve Jobs famously articulated as: *to put a dent in the world*.

It is that initial excitement, that *aha!* moment, the entrepreneur's enthusiasm that drives us to dive into the journey of building something new, something meaningful. As many seasoned entrepreneurs will tell you, a great idea alone is rarely enough to guarantee success.

The road from concept to reality is full of challenges, and the path goes through graveyards of startups that did not make it. In the US, 90% of startups fail . This number will be very similar in India, also.

The top reason is failure to find an adequate product-market fit. Product-market fit is the point at which a product satisfies a strong market demand in such a way that customers are willing to buy it, use it, and even recommend it to others.

The journey of transforming an idea into a tangible product is one of the most exhilarating yet demanding experiences in the entrepreneurial world. It is a process that requires not just creativity and passion, but also strategic thinking, rigorous planning, and, most importantly, a willingness to learn and adapt. The ultimate goal is to achieve the product-market fit. This is where the concept of the **minimum viable product (MVP)** becomes invaluable.

An MVP is not a stripped-down version of your final product; it is a powerful tool that allows you to test your ideas in the real world, gather crucial feedback, and make informed decisions about your next steps. It is about building something small, but useful for customers, that can validate your assumptions and help you understand whether you are on the right track.

But let us be clear: building an MVP is not about cutting corners, managing the scope of work, or rushing to market with a half-baked product. It is about being smart with your resources and focusing on the core features that will provide the most value to your customers. It is about understanding that the first version of your product is just the beginning, not the end. The goal is to create a version of the product that is sufficiently good to attract early adopters, yet flexible enough to evolve based on their feedback.

The biggest mistake many entrepreneurs make is assuming that their idea is flawless and that once it is built, customers will flock to it, but the reality is very different. No matter how much research you do or how confident you are in your concept, there will always be unknowns and variables you did not account for. That is why it is crucial to approach product development with a mindset of continuous learning and improvement.

This book is designed to guide you through the process of developing an MVP in a way that is both practical and strategic. We will explore the steps you need to take to identify and understand your customers' pain points, assess your market, prioritize opportunities, and generate solutions that are both innovative and feasible. We will also look into the importance of defining the right metrics to track your progress and ensure that you're moving in the right direction.

Throughout this book, we will emphasize the importance of iteration. Building an MVP is not a one-time task; it is an ongoing process of testing, learning, and refining. By adopting an iterative approach, you can continuously make small, manageable changes that lead to significant improvements over time. This not only increases your chances of success but also allows you to stay responsive to your customers' needs.

So, whether you are a first-time entrepreneur or a seasoned founder, a technology-first thinker or a business-first thinker, I invite you to join me on this journey. Together, we will explore how to take your idea from concept to reality in a way that is both efficient and effective—because in the world of startups, it is not just about having a great idea; it is about making that idea work.

Section 1: Discovery

Chapter 1: Understanding Customer Pain Points – This chapter guides entrepreneurs in identifying real customer problems using tools like Empathy Maps, user personas, interviews, and surveys. It highlights common startup pitfalls where founders overly focus on their ideas rather than customer needs and contrasts different entrepreneurial journeys—both technical and non-technical. It emphasizes that success starts with validated problems, not just great ideas.

Chapter 2: Market Analysis and Validation – Entrepreneurs learn how to assess the business opportunity around a validated problem. The chapter covers **Total Addressable Market (TAM)**, competitive analysis, regulatory considerations, and tools like pre-sales and landing pages to measure real demand. It provides a framework to understand market dynamics and buyer intent before investing heavily.

Chapter 3: Opportunity Prioritization – This chapter focuses on identifying the most promising problems to solve using frameworks like the value-complexity matrix and custom rubrics. Entrepreneurs learn how to align these problems with internal business goals to ensure resource efficiency and long-term strategic fit.

Section 2: Solutions

Chapter 4: Ideation and Solution Generation – Entrepreneurs are introduced to structured ideation techniques to move from problem to solution. The chapter warns against overattachment to initial ideas and encourages iterative thinking, creativity, and alignment with customer needs and insights.

Chapter 5: Problem-solution Fit – This chapter teaches how to validate whether the proposed solution meaningfully addresses the chosen problem. It introduces tools like the Value Proposition Canvas, **Jobs to be Done (JTBD)**, and prototyping to refine and evaluate fit before building an MVP.

Chapter 6: Defining Metrics – Entrepreneurs learn how to set actionable, goal-oriented metrics to track MVP success. The chapter emphasizes how metrics improve accountability, reduce bias, and align the team and stakeholders around shared outcomes.

Section 3: MVP Creation

Chapter 7: Building Successful MVP – The chapter explains how to distill the solution into a minimum viable product with just the essential features. It introduces various MVP types and prioritization techniques to help entrepreneurs validate assumptions efficiently while keeping development lean.

Chapter 8: Business Model Validation – Here, entrepreneurs explore how to validate pricing, revenue models, and cost structures using tools like the Business Model Canvas. Emphasis is placed on real-world experiments and feedback to discover a repeatable, scalable business model.

Chapter 9: Iterative MVP Development – The chapter details how to develop MVPs using Agile practices, breaking down work into iterations. It covers team roles, outsourcing vs. insourcing, and maintaining flexibility while building toward long-term scalability.

Chapter 10: Iterative MVP Testing – Entrepreneurs learn to use data-driven techniques such as A/B testing, heatmaps, and usability testing to refine their MVPs post-launch. This chapter emphasizes the importance of continuous feedback and learning loops.

Chapter 11: Fail-fast – This final chapter presents the Fail-fast mindset and tools to assess and manage risks early. It shows how embracing failure as part of the process helps entrepreneurs pivot quickly and avoid wasted effort, increasing their odds of success.

Coloured Images

Please follow the link to download the
Coloured Images of the book:

https://rebrand.ly/cf6c93

We have code bundles from our rich catalogue of books and videos available at https://github.com/bpbpublications. Check them out!

Errata

We take immense pride in our work at BPB Publications and follow best practices to ensure the accuracy of our content to provide with an indulging reading experience to our subscribers. Our readers are our mirrors, and we use their inputs to reflect and improve upon human errors, if any, that may have occurred during the publishing processes involved. To let us maintain the quality and help us reach out to any readers who might be having difficulties due to any unforeseen errors, please write to us at :

errata@bpbonline.com

Your support, suggestions and feedbacks are highly appreciated by the BPB Publications' Family.

At www.bpbonline.com, you can also read a collection of free technical articles, sign up for a range of free newsletters, and receive exclusive discounts and offers on BPB books and eBooks. You can check our social media handles below:

| *Instagram* | *Facebook* | *Linkedin* | *YouTube* |

Get in touch with us at: business@bpbonline.com for more details.

Piracy

If you come across any illegal copies of our works in any form on the internet, we would be grateful if you would provide us with the location address or website name. Please contact us at business@bpbonline.com with a link to the material.

If you are interested in becoming an author

If there is a topic that you have expertise in, and you are interested in either writing or contributing to a book, please visit www.bpbonline.com. We have worked with thousands of developers and tech professionals, just like you, to help them share their insights with the global tech community. You can make a general application, apply for a specific hot topic that we are recruiting an author for, or submit your own idea.

Reviews

Please leave a review. Once you have read and used this book, why not leave a review on the site that you purchased it from? Potential readers can then see and use your unbiased opinion to make purchase decisions. We at BPB can understand what you think about our products, and our authors can see your feedback on their book. Thank you!

For more information about BPB, please visit www.bpbonline.com.

Join our Discord space

Join our Discord workspace for latest updates, offers, tech happenings around the world, new releases, and sessions with the authors:

https://discord.bpbonline.com

Table of Contents

Section 1:
Discovery

CHAPTER 1
Understanding Customer Pain Points

Introduction

Identifying and understanding customer problems involves using tools such as the **Empathy Map** to step into the user's perspective and conducting diverse customer research methods, including interviews, surveys, sampling, and observational research. Additionally, creating detailed customer personas aids in gaining deeper insights into target users and their specific needs. This involves building and prioritizing personas to ensure a comprehensive understanding of customer pain points and preferences. It is also important to distinguish between perceived problems and actual pain points through validation methods. By utilizing these methods effectively, businesses can develop a clearer understanding of their customers' challenges and tailor their solutions accordingly.

Every product journey has a starting point, and for most entrepreneurs, it begins with an idea. They share this idea with friends and family, gathering a mix of feedback, some enthusiastic, some skeptical. However, true to their nature, entrepreneurs draw energy even from the naysayers and push forward. If the entrepreneur has a technical background, they might start building the product themselves, seeking help along the way. Eventually, the product is ready, and it is unveiled to the world. Then comes the wait. Sometimes there is a spark of interest, but often, even those who praised the idea do not actually adopt the product. Undeterred, the entrepreneur continues refining it, collecting feedback here and there, until, eventually, the momentum fades, the budget is exhausted, and conversations with VCs lead nowhere. The journey becomes a story told in hindsight.

For entrepreneurs without a tech background, the path is different but no less challenging. They search for a tech partner to bring their idea to life. Often, this tech partner wants a stake in the potential success, maybe even a co-founder role, which can lead to difficult conversations. Sometimes, they agree to build the product for a fee. The development process may go relatively smoothly, with a few changes along the way. However, when the product does not take off, the entrepreneur might blame the implementation, the design, or something else. Once again, the journey becomes a story, shared over coffee but not much else.

This scenario plays out time and again in cities and coffee shops everywhere.

However, the blame for these outcomes does not rest with the entrepreneur, the tech developer, the sales team, the marketing folks, or anyone else who was involved.

The real issue lies at the very start of the journey—the belief that the idea is what truly matters. Many entrepreneurs are so enamored with their idea that they keep it secret, afraid someone will steal it.

Successful entrepreneurs do a few things differently. They focus on two key things: they do not start with just an idea, and they obsess over the implementation rather than the idea itself.

Structure

In this chapter, we will cover the following topics:

- Understanding customer needs
- Importance of customer centricity
- Importance of user research
- Importance of a continuous feedback loop
- Importance of prioritization
- Identifying stakeholders
- Empathy Maps
- Value Stream Mapping

Objectives

By the end of this chapter, the entrepreneur will have learned how to effectively identify customer needs and translate them into clear problem statements. They will understand techniques for prioritizing which problem to address first, ensuring focus on the most addressable areas. Additionally, the reader will be able to identify key stakeholders—beyond just the end user—and apply tools like the Empathy Map to develop a deeper understanding of the emotions, motivations, and challenges faced by those affected by the problem. Finally, they will gain the ability to map the current customer journey as a flow of value, highlighting opportunities for improvement, identifying root causes of customer problems, and introducing innovation.

Understanding customer needs

People do not adopt a product simply because they are impressed by the entrepreneur's idea; they adopt it because it serves a purpose in their lives. Whether it solves a problem they are facing or offers a new opportunity, the value the product provides is what truly matters to them.

People adopt a product when they believe it will meet a need (*I need a way to easily track my daily expenses to manage my budget*), satisfy a want (*I want to see old movies during my hour long ride to office*), overcome a problem (*I am unable to discover what else is happening the field of my professional specialization across the globe*), an opportunity (*I can make money from hobby if I can connect with those who like what I make*), do something better (*I want to write emails that have correct grammar and are spelling mistake free*), do a chore faster and conveniently (*I need to order daily needs while working from home*).

To achieve this, it is essential to identify and understand customers on a deep level—to truly grasp what they want, need, or struggle with. This understanding is the cornerstone of creating a product that resonates with them.

An entrepreneur's journey begins with understanding customers' pain points.

This means going beyond assumptions and actively engaging with potential customers to uncover their challenges and desires. Understanding these distinctions—needs, wants, and problems—helps entrepreneurs position their product more effectively and communicate its value in the customer's terms. Employing techniques like user interviews, surveys, and observational research helps entrepreneurs empathize with users and gain a clear, detailed picture of their needs. Creating users' profiles or personas further enhances understanding of the target audience, allowing the product to be tailored to meet specific requirements.

By effectively employing these methods, entrepreneurs not only validate their ideas but also ensure that the product is designed with the customers in mind. This approach significantly increases the chances that the product will be adopted and valued by those it is intended to serve.

For example, *Tara*, a 36-year-old with extensive experience and expertise in her domain, is eager to embark on her entrepreneurial journey. She is passionate about several areas and wants to ensure she makes a well-rounded decision on which problem to tackle first. To do this, Tara begins by listing out a series of problem statements that have frequently crossed her mind, such as:

- Balancing work-life demands
- Issues with a reliable water supply
- Decline in community fitness due to the rise in personal fitness trends
- Shortage of public green spaces

- Limited availability of quality senior care services
- Inconsistent quality of consumer services
- Dependence on imported goods for quality
- Challenges in accessing affordable rural healthcare
- Managing noise pollution
- Concerns about personal and digital security
- Restrictions on farmers trading grain freely
- Lack of farm-to-table options

She soon realizes the list keeps getting longer and will need some first-level analysis.

Importance of customer centricity

A customer centric approach places the user at the heart of every decision. It is about creating a product that aligns with what customers value, rather than what the entrepreneur assumes they need or the perceived brilliance of their idea. This mindset not only increases the likelihood of the product being adopted but also fosters loyalty, as customers feel understood and valued when they see their feedback reflected in the product.

By being customer centric, the entrepreneur is not just building a product; they are building relationships with their users and regularly incorporating user feedback. These relationships are key to sustaining and growing the business over time. When customers feel that a product truly understands and solves their problems, they are more likely to become repeat users and advocates, spreading the word and driving organic growth.

Importance of user research

User research is the foundation of any customer centric approach. It involves actively seeking to understand the potential customer's behaviors, needs, motivations, and pain points. By engaging directly with potential users through interviews, surveys, and other research methods, valuable insights are gathered that guide product development.

This research helps validate assumptions, ensuring the product addresses real problems rather than hypothetical assumptions. It also aids in prioritizing features that matter most to customers, allowing resources to be focused on what will have the greatest impact. In short, user research reduces the risk of building a product that misses the mark and increases the chances of creating something that truly resonates with potential users. Without user research, entrepreneurs risk building solutions based on intuition rather than actual customer demand.

Importance of a continuous feedback loop

Building a **minimum viable product** (**MVP**) is not a one-time effort; it is an iterative process. This is where the continuous feedback loop comes into play. After launching the MVP, it is crucial to gather feedback from users and use that information to make informed decisions about what to improve, add, or remove.

A continuous feedback loop allows the product to be adapted based on real user experiences, rather than assumptions. It helps the startup stay Agile and responsive to customers' evolving needs, which is particularly important in the fast-paced world of startups. By regularly iterating on the MVP based on user feedback, the product is not only improved, but it also demonstrates to customers that their input is valued and that the entrepreneur is committed to delivering value by following the cycle of build-measure-learn.

Importance of prioritization

As an entrepreneur, it is unrealistic to try solving all problems at once. That is why it is crucial to focus on a specific, narrower problem statement that you can realistically address. Even within a well-defined problem, its implications may span multiple countries, regions, or markets. Additionally, the solution might benefit a diverse range of people in various ways. Attempting to address all these aspects from the start can overwhelm both the product and the development process. This often leads to feature bloat, diluted value propositions, and a loss of focus, especially harmful in the early stages of an MVP.

This is where prioritization becomes essential. At each stage of development, an entrepreneur must constantly prioritize and narrow their focus. By concentrating on the most critical problem for the smallest viable audience, you can create a product that effectively meets their needs. This approach not only simplifies development but also increases the chances of early success. As your product gains traction, you can then expand and refine it to address broader markets and larger populations.

Prioritization is not just a strategic choice; it is a practical necessity. By being disciplined about what to focus on first, you can ensure that your product solves the most pressing issues for your target audience, laying the groundwork for scalable success.

For example, Tara carefully analyzes each one, assessing her own ability to effectively address, bring customer-centricity, and be able to perform user research, she asks herself the following questions:

- *Am I passionate enough about this topic to work on this tirelessly for many years?*
- *Do I have deep awareness of the topic to discover a solution?*
- *Do I know ways to network with key people who can validate my solution?*
- *Do I know how to engage potential early adopters who will take a leap of faith?*

To streamline her prioritization process, she organizes her thoughts into a simple, structured table, shown as follows:

Problem statements	Passionate?	Aware?	Network?	Engage?
Balancing work-life demands	N	Y	Y	N
Issues with reliable water supply	N	N	N	N
Decline in community fitness due to rise in personal fitness trends	N	Y	Y	N
Shortage of public green spaces	Y	Y	N	N
Limited availability of quality senior care services	Y	N	N	N
Inconsistent quality of consumer services	N	N	N	N
Dependence on imported goods for quality	N	N	N	N
Challenges in accessing affordable rural healthcare	Y	N	Y	N
Managing noise pollution	N	Y	N	N
Concerns about personal and digital security	N	N	Y	Y
Restrictions on farmers trading grain freely	Y	Y	Y	Y
Lack of farm-to-table options	N	Y	Y	N
Navigating the complex taxation system	N	N	N	N
Bureaucracy in the healthcare system	N	N	Y	N
Accessibility and cost issues in urban healthcare	N	N	N	N
Limited quality leisure and recreation opportunities	Y	Y	Y	N
Educational pressure on children	N	N	Y	N
Concerns about digital privacy	N	N	Y	N
High real estate prices	Y	N	N	N
Inconsistent power supply	N	Y	Y	N
Social isolation in urban areas	Y	Y	N	N
Dealing with air pollution	N	N	N	N
Lack of marketplaces for local artisans	Y	Y	Y	Y
Challenges in finding reliable childcare services	N	N	Y	Y
Absence of skill-based microlearning opportunities	Y	N	Y	N
Complexity in investment and financial planning	N	N	Y	N
Difficulty planning sustainable travel	Y	N	N	Y
Lack of on-demand in-home vehicle maintenance services	N	N	N	Y

Problem statements	Passionate?	Aware?	Network?	Engage?
Poor quality of public infrastructure	N	N	Y	N
Growing environmental concerns	Y	N	Y	N
Concerns about food safety	N	N	N	N
Challenges in sustaining work from home	Y	Y	Y	N
High cost of quality online tutoring	N	N	Y	N
Traffic congestion and long commute times	Y	N	Y	N
Challenges in accessing reliable domestic help	Y	Y	Y	N

Table 1.1: Problem statement—Entrepreneur alignment matrix

As she went through this exercise, Tara quickly realized that although she had discussed and thought about many problems, she was truly passionate about only a few of them—those she could see herself dedicating the next five or six years of her life to solving. This insight helped her prioritize more effectively, focusing on the issues that resonated most deeply with her.

These two problem statements emerged as right fits, as shown in the following table:

Problem statements	Passionate?	Aware?	Network?	Engage?
Restrictions on farmers trading grain freely	Y	Y	Y	Y
Lack of marketplaces for local artisans	Y	Y	Y	Y

Table 1.2: Prioritized problem statement—Entrepreneur alignment matrix

Tara now had a more focused list to explore in depth. After further deliberation and seeking opinions and advice, she realized that the existing players in the farmer-related supply chain were well-established and resistant to change. Given this insight, she decided to concentrate on the problem statement, *lack of marketplaces for local artisans*, as the primary focus for her entrepreneurial efforts.

Identifying stakeholders

Identifying stakeholders based on a problem statement involves understanding who is affected by the problem, who is interested in solving it, and who can influence the outcome.

Grouping stakeholders based on their proximity to those directly affected by the problem helps organize engagement efforts more effectively, as shown in the following figure:

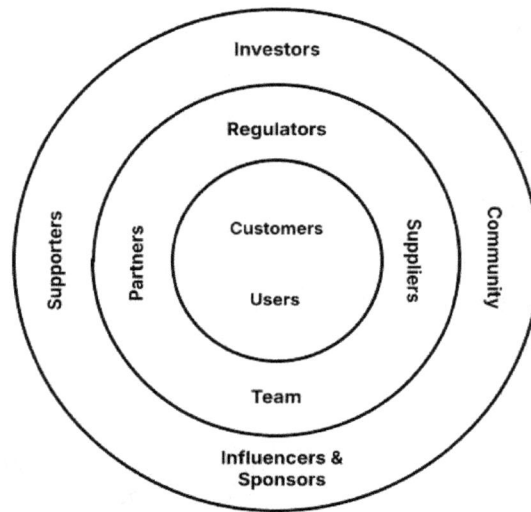

Figure 1.1: Product stakeholders

Understanding the power and influence of each stakeholder helps prioritize communication and involvement during product development.

Primary stakeholders

The first step in identifying primary stakeholders is to distinguish between users and customers.

Users, or **end users**, are the individuals or groups who directly experience the problem and will benefit from the solution. For example, if the problem involves healthcare access, the users might be patients or hospital staff who interact with the solution daily.

Customers, on the other hand, are the people or organizations who will pay for or adopt the product or service being developed to address the problem. In the healthcare example, the customers might be the hospital management that decides to procure and implement the solution.

In a **business-to-consumer** (**B2C**) scenario, where businesses sell products or services directly to individual consumers, the customers and users are often the same person. For example, when you purchase a product for your own use, you are both the customer and the user.

In a **business-to-business** (**B2B**) scenario, where businesses sell products or services to other businesses, the customers and users tend to be different people. For instance, in the healthcare example mentioned earlier, the hospital management might be the customer purchasing the solution, while the hospital staff and patients are the end users who interact with it.

Understanding this distinction ensures the solution is both desirable for users and viable for customers, an essential balance for successful product adoption.

Secondary stakeholders

Secondary stakeholders are those who support or influence the experience of primary stakeholders, the users and the customers.

Regulators can be government bodies, industry associations, or organizations that set the standards, regulations, or laws related to the problem area. They play a crucial role in ensuring that your solution complies with the necessary legal and regulatory requirements. For example, in the healthcare scenario, regulators might include health ministries or medical boards that enforce healthcare standards and policies.

Suppliers are organizations or individuals who provide the essential resources, technology, or services needed to develop and implement your solution. In the healthcare example, suppliers could be companies that provide medical equipment, software vendors, or pharmaceutical suppliers who contribute key components to the solution.

Partners are other organizations or entities that collaborate with you to support your activities and help bring your solution to market. These could include strategic alliances, joint ventures, or NGOs that share a common goal. In the healthcare scenario, partners might be technology firms, research institutions, or advocacy groups that help enhance and promote your solution.

Teams or employees are the internal stakeholders who will be directly involved in or affected by the solution's development and implementation. These could be your product development team, marketing department, or customer support staff, all of whom play a vital role in bringing your MVP to life and ensuring its success.

Support ecosystem

Influencers are individuals or entities with the ability to shape public opinion or impact the decisions of key stakeholders. These may include industry experts, media outlets, or thought leaders with a significant following who can lend credibility to your solution. Their endorsement can accelerate adoption by building trust with hesitant stakeholders or target customers. In the healthcare example, influencers might be well-known healthcare professionals, influential journalists, or prominent thought leaders who advocate for the innovative healthcare solution an entrepreneur is building.

Supporters are individuals or groups not directly affected by the problem but who have a vested interest in its resolution. These might include advocacy groups, NGOs, or community leaders who align with the cause and can provide valuable backing. For instance, in the healthcare scenario, supporters could be patient advocacy groups that champion better access to healthcare services.

Partner organizations, such as distributors, technology integrators, or strategic allies, extend the support ecosystem. Their collaboration may expand reach, enhance credibility, or streamline implementation.

The **community** consists of people who may come together to support the product because they are indirectly impacted by or interested in the problem. This could include local residents, social groups, or broader networks who see value in the solution. In the healthcare context, the community might be the residents of a particular area, or social groups concerned with improving healthcare access in their region.

Investors are individuals or entities that provide the financial resources needed to develop and scale the solution. They are crucial stakeholders who seek a return on their investment and often bring valuable expertise, connections, and guidance. In the healthcare example, investors might be venture capitalists, angel investors, or impact investors focused on funding innovative healthcare solutions that promise both financial returns and social impact.

Now that Tara has decided to focus on the *lack of marketplaces for local artisans* as the primary problem for her entrepreneurial efforts, she begins identifying the various stakeholders involved. Using the framework mentioned in *Table 1.1*, she identifies key stakeholders critical to her venture's success.

Taking a customer-centric approach, Tara chooses to prioritize her research on the primary stakeholders to refine and shape her MVP. She decided to hold off on engaging with investors for now, as she felt it was too early in the process and preferred to explore the possibility of starting with her own funds.

The resulting stakeholder map is shown in the following table:

Customers	Online shoppers Urban retailers Corporate buyers Exporters
Users	Local artisans Artisan cooperatives Middlemen or aggregators
Regulators	Ministry of textiles State handloom and handicrafts departments Ministry of company affair Income tax department
Suppliers	Packaging suppliers Logistics companies
Partners	E-commerce platforms Package delivery companies Payment providers Social platforms Corporate CSR initiatives
Influencers	Art and culture bloggers Instagrammers Celebrity endorsers

Supporters	Cultural preservationists Local community leaders Art and skills schools
Community	Artisan villages Cultural enthusiasts Cultural tourists
Investors	-

Table 1.3: *Stakeholder map*

Empathy Maps

Empathy refers to the ability to deeply understand and connect with the emotions, needs, and experiences of stakeholders. It involves the entrepreneur putting themselves in the shoes of the customers to truly comprehend their pain points, challenges, and desires.

One effective framework for capturing this understanding is the Empathy Map, a collaborative tool that entrepreneurs use to gain deeper insights into their stakeholders. The Empathy Map was developed by *Dave Gray*, founder of *XPLANE* in May 2021 as a method to foster collaboration and achieve a more profound understanding of users.

At its core, an Empathy Map helps entrepreneurs explore and articulate what users feel, think, and need. Typically divided into segments such as *says*, *thinks*, *does*, and *feels*, the Empathy Map provides a comprehensive view of user behavior and emotions, offering valuable insights that can guide product development and customer engagement strategies. Insights from Empathy Maps can directly inform MVP feature selection by highlighting the most urgent and emotionally resonant customer needs. The following figure shows the Empathy Map:

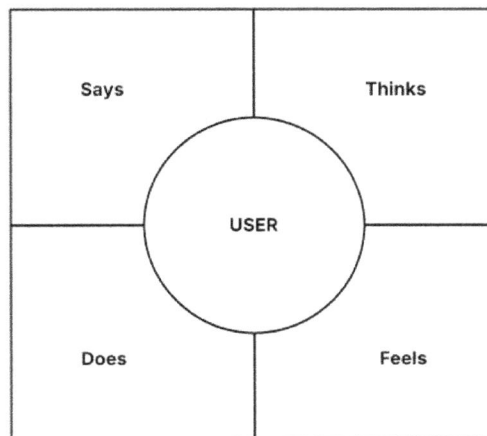

Figure 1.2: *Empathy Map*

Let us take a closer look at each section of the Empathy Map:

- **Says**: For an entrepreneur, what a user says provides an immediate feedback loop. These are the raw, often unfiltered comments that can highlight pain points, delights, or areas of confusion. It is crucial to note these down accurately without interpreting or paraphrasing, as they offer direct insight into the user's experience.

- **Thinks**: This component can be more challenging as it requires inferential understanding. Entrepreneurs must analyze what users have said, observed, or shared and deduce what might be running through their minds. This segment offers an invaluable glimpse into the user's expectations and preconceived notions.

- **Does**: By observing user actions, entrepreneurs can correlate behaviors with specific features or aspects of their product or service. Are users skipping a step? Do they repetitively engage with a particular workflow? This component reveals actions that can inform and enhance product capabilities.

- **Feels**: Emotions can range from frustration and confusion to joy and satisfaction. By empathizing with users' emotions, entrepreneurs can gain deeper insights into their needs, motivations, and expectations. This understanding allows entrepreneurs to design solutions that resonate with users on an emotional level, creating a more engaging and meaningful experience.

The Empathy Map often reveals contradictions between what a user says and what they do or feel. This helps entrepreneurs move closer to genuine user understanding. It reinforces the importance of truly knowing your user, a critical element in developing a successful MVP.

Tara is focused on addressing the *lack of marketplaces for local artisans*. She utilized the Empathy Map to deeply understand the experiences of online shoppers in metropolitan areas who are eager to buy from local artisans but are struggling to do so. She also connected with artisans across various locations to empathize with their challenges and needs.

After gathering insights, Tara summarized her findings by creating two Empathy Maps—one for online shoppers and another for local artisans, capturing the key emotions, thoughts, and behaviors of both groups.

The following table is an example of Tara's Empathy Map for online shoppers:

Says	Thinks
I want to buy unique, handmade items, but I can't find reliable platforms.	Are these products truly handmade, or are they mass-produced?
It's hard to tell if the products are authentic.	I hope my purchase helps the artisan directly.
Shipping takes too long, and I'm not sure about the quality.	Is the price I'm paying fair for both me and the artisan?
I love supporting local artisans, but I wish it was easier.	I wonder if there's a platform that guarantees authenticity and quality.

Does	Feels
Spends time browsing multiple websites but often leaves without making a purchase.	Frustrated by the lack of trustworthy platforms to buy authentic handmade products.
Reads reviews and looks for certifications to ensure authenticity.	Disappointed when products do not meet expectations in quality or delivery time.
Shares potential finds with friends or on social media, seeking opinions before purchasing.	Eager to support local artisans but feels uncertain about how much of their purchase actually benefits them.
Abandons the cart if the delivery time is too long or if trust in the platform is low.	Satisfied and happy when they find a genuine, high-quality product that supports local artisans.

Table 1.4: Example Empathy Map

The following table is an example of Tara's Empathy Map for local artisans:

Says	Thinks
It's hard to find reliable buyers for my artwork.	How can I get my artwork in front of people who like buying handmade goods?
I want to sell online, but I don't know how.	I need help to showcase my artwork and tell its story.
I struggle with getting noticed.	
Managing courier and returns are too complicated for me to handle.	Am I selling my artwork for less money?
	I wish I had more support with courier and customer questions.
Does	**Feels**
Sells at local markets and relies on word-of-mouth for business.	Overwhelmed by the complexities of online selling and logistics.
Attempts to use mobile but finds it challenging to attract buyers.	Isolated from larger markets and unsure how to expand.
Participates in artisan fairs but struggles with scaling beyond that day's sales.	Frustrated by the lack of direct access to customers who value their craft.
Tries to handle shipping independently, leading to breakage, delays and customer complaints.	Hopeful when they hear success stories of other artisans who have connections that help them.

Table 1.5: Example Empathy Map

Value Stream Mapping

For an entrepreneur, it is crucial to thoroughly understand their users. Empathy Maps help develop a deep understanding of the users whose problems the entrepreneur is trying to address.

Another key aspect of understanding users is grasping their current journey. This journey is the process users undergo in which they encounter the problem defined by the entrepreneur. This is the journey that needs to be addressed—whether it is to be modified, shortened, made faster, simplified, or even completely circumvented.

Value Stream Mapping (**VSM**) is an excellent framework for these scenarios.

VSM is a visual tool used to analyze and map out the sequence of steps a user takes to complete a task or achieve a goal, including the flow of information and materials. It is a lean management technique that helps entrepreneurs visualize, analyze, and improve user journeys by highlighting inefficiencies, bottlenecks, and non-value-adding activities.

By mapping out the current journey of users, especially the stages where they encounter the defined problem, entrepreneurs can gain a clear understanding of which steps are essential, which create friction, and where improvements can be made. This enables better decision-making around optimizing operations, reducing cost or time, and increasing the value delivered to users.

The value in this context refers to the benefit or worth that the customer receives and is willing to pay for. A VSM breaks down the entire journey into individual steps, helping to identify the value that each step adds toward delivering the final cumulative value to the customer.

Through this process, entrepreneurs can gain a deeper understanding of the underlying why behind the problem statement they are addressing as they understand the flow of value better.

Here is how VSM can help:

- **Identify waste**: VSM helps identify non-value-added activities, delays, and inefficiencies within current processes that can be eliminated or streamlined.

- **Optimize processes**: By mapping out the current state of the value stream, entrepreneurs can design an improved future state that optimizes flow and reduces lead times between each step.

- **Enhance customer value**: The ultimate goal is to increase the value delivered to customers by ensuring that every step in the process contributes to meeting their needs and expectations. Entrepreneurs can design a future state where each step delivers more value.

- **Discover alternatives**: By mapping out the current state of the value stream and asking key questions like *Why is this step needed?* and challenging underlying assumptions, entrepreneurs can discover new, shorter, and more efficient value streams that can replace the existing ones.

By mapping out each step of the process, VSM helps identify bottlenecks, delays, or unnecessary steps in the user journey. This allows entrepreneurs to streamline their product or service to deliver value more efficiently. In doing so, entrepreneurs can create a more streamlined, customer-centric solution that directly addresses user pain points, ultimately leading to a more effective and successful MVP.

Generating Value Stream Map

VSM visually represents the sequence of activities a customer undertakes to achieve a goal. While traditional lean methodology includes a detailed library of symbols and complex representations, entrepreneurs can benefit from a simplified version focused on understanding customer pain points.

Creating a VSM helps visualize where friction occurs in the user journey, allowing entrepreneurs to focus their efforts where they can deliver the most value.

Entrepreneurs can take the following steps to create a VSM, ensuring that they can effectively map the problems their customers encounter:

1. **Form a small working group**: The process begins by discussing the high-level steps with the customer. From these discussions, other key participants who can provide insights into the process and effectively highlight the problem statement are identified. For an entrepreneur, the working group size can remain small, focusing on bringing together all relevant participants within the process.

   This approach ensures open communication, preventing information from slipping through the cracks. While larger enterprises might prefer a group size of around 10[1] entrepreneurs can tailor the group size to the number of participants directly involved in the flow.

2. **Kick-off the process**: Once this working group is identified, assemble them for the value mapping session.

   Even if the session's purpose was discussed during the recruitment phase, it is essential to spend a few minutes at the beginning reiterating the problem statement. The entrepreneur should explain why they believe they can solve this problem and how the group's input will deepen their understanding of the current process, allowing them to identify inefficiencies and waste.

3. **Documenting the current state map**: To create a current state map, the entrepreneur should start by walking through the flow with the customer, interviewing them and other participants about their actions at each step. This can be illustrated using a simple flowchart with boxes and arrows, as shown in the following figure:

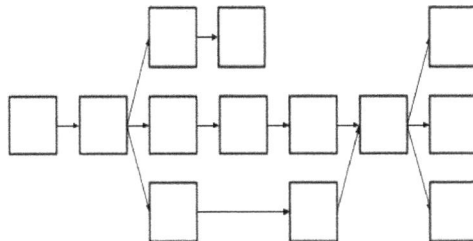

Figure 1.3: *Simplified view of a Value Stream Map*

---

1 Value Stream Mapping Tutorial - What Is VSM?, n.d.

Entrepreneurs often struggle with determining the level of detail needed. They should begin with a high-level overview of the value map and iteratively dive deeper. This approach ensures the mapping is neither too broad—where no new insights are gained—nor too detailed—where the big picture is lost.

4. **Analyze and reassess the current state map**: A list of questions should be prepared to ask about each step in the process. These questions should be simple and jargon-free, ensuring they are easily understood by all participants. Not every question will apply to each step, but they will help explore the purpose, identify problems, and consider improvements.

    The key questions to consider include:

    - **Purpose of each step**:
        o *Why is this step necessary?*

    - **Problems in each step**:
        o *Are there inefficiencies in this step?*
        o *Are there bottlenecks?*
        o *Are there known or unpredictable delays?*
        o *Are there any wastes?*

    - **Improvement possibilities**:
        o *Is there a better way to accomplish this step?*
        o *Can the cost of this step be reduced?*
        o *Can the duration of each step be reduced?*
        o *Can the value delivered by this step be increased?*
        o *Is there an alternative approach to this step and subsequent steps?*

5. **Creating the future state map**: Using insights gained from the previous steps, the entrepreneur should start incorporating the participants' suggestions to develop a future state map that outlines a more efficient process flow.

6. **Revisiting the future state map**: After thanking and possibly compensating the participants for their time, the entrepreneur should continue refining the flow. Feedback on the improvements should be sought from the same participants or other subject matter experts.

The primary goal is to understand the customer's pain points. It is crucial not to become too attached to the future state map as the final solution. Instead, it should be seen as an evolving tool, with the final solution potentially being a refined or reimagined part of this map.

The ultimate outcome is a deep awareness of customer pain points, helping the entrepreneur focus on solving the right problem and avoiding the pitfall of falling in love with an idea rather than addressing the customer's real challenges.

To benefit from the simplified Value Stream Mapping method, Tara followed the following steps to create a VSM, ensuring she could effectively identify and address the problems customers encounter:

1. **Form a small working group**: To effectively map out the value stream for both the online shopper (*Shobha*) and the local artisan (*Prabhu*) in a single session, Tara invites a diverse group of participants who can provide valuable insights into the entire process, from production to purchase.

2. **Tara includes the following**:

    o *Elisa*, a friend who works for an e-commerce platform, brings her expertise in online marketplaces and product listings.

    o *Lalu*, a logistics/shipping expert she connected with on *LinkedIn*, who can offer insights into the challenges and opportunities in product delivery.

    o *Chandan*, Elisa's colleague, who has experience as a customer support specialist and is currently on a break, provides a perspective on customer interactions and issue resolution.

    o *Danish*, a digital marketing specialist, she met at an industry event, who can discuss strategies for promoting artisan products and attracting customers.

    o *Pascal*, a student at a leading design school with an interest in packaging and branding, can contribute ideas on how to enhance product presentation and protection during transit.

    This well-rounded team will help Tara gain a comprehensive understanding of the value stream, ensuring that both the shoppers' and artisans' experiences are thoroughly mapped and optimized.

3. **Kick-off the process**: Tara booked a meeting room for the entire day at a centrally located co-working space, making it convenient for everyone to attend. She ensured the space was well-stocked with essentials, including plenty of drinking water, snacks, and mobile phone charging cables. For lunch, she ordered vegetarian thalis from a popular nearby restaurant.

    She also made sure there were ample sticky notes and whiteboard markers to last through the day. Additionally, she planned to take photos of the maps they created to keep a record of their work.

    To express her gratitude, Tara prepared thank-you envelopes containing Amazon and Flipkart gift cards for each participant as a small token of appreciation for their time.

When everyone had arrived, she kicked off the session with a quick recap:

Thank you all for being here today! First off, I want to say how excited I am to have each of you here. After many years of a successful professional career, I've decided to dive into something I'm really passionate about, building a startup that addresses the lack of marketplaces for local artisans.

The goal of this startup is to create a product that brings real value to both online shoppers and local artisans. To make that happen, I'm working on an MVP, and part of that involves understanding the entire journey—from the moment a piece of artwork is created to when it finally lands in the hands of an online shopper. That's why we're all here today.

We'll kick things off by mapping out a very high-level flow of this process, and then we'll dig deeper step by step until we've identified the major inefficiencies and issues.

Before we dive in, I want to make sure everyone feels comfortable. Please feel at home—grab some water or snacks whenever you need a break. Let's keep things light and collaborative—be nice to each other, avoid speaking over one another, and don't hesitate to get up and add a sticky note to the whiteboard.

Alright, if everyone's ready, let's get started! And don't worry, there are no wrong ideas—just opportunities to improve. Plus, if anyone comes up with a brilliant idea, I promise not to take all the credit... just 90% of it! [She winks.]

4. **Documenting the current state map**: It took Tara a couple of days to document and synthesize the discussion. The group successfully mapped out the steps and identified key issues, but they ran out of time before they could develop a future-state solution. Tara was not too concerned, though—her primary focus was on uncovering pain points rather than rushing into solutions.

She summarized the process as a table where each row represented a step in the process:

1	*Prabhu* designs and crafts a handmade item (e.g., pottery, jewelry, textile).	**Time taken**: 1-2 weeks depending on the complexity of the product. **Inefficiencies**: Manual production process can be slow; lack of tools or resources can extend production time. **Bottlenecks**: Limited access to high-quality materials; production delays during high-demand periods.
2	**Product documentation and photography** *Prabhu* documents the details of the product (materials used, dimensions, care instructions) and takes high-quality photographs.	**Time taken**: 1-2 days. **Inefficiencies**: Poor lighting or inadequate photography skills can result in unappealing images. **Bottlenecks**: Lack of access to professional photography equipment or skills.

3	**Product listing on e-commerce platform** *Prabhu* or the platform uploads the product information and images onto the e-commerce site.	**Waste**: Time spent re-entering data or correcting errors in listings. **Time taken**: 1 day. **Inefficiencies**: Platform interface may be complex, leading to errors or repeated entries.
4	**Product marketing and promotion** The product is promoted through various digital marketing channels (social media, email newsletters, search engine ads).	**Waste**: Ineffective ad spend, low **return on investment (ROI)** on certain marketing channels. **Time taken**: Ongoing process, with initial setup taking a few days. **Inefficiencies**: Poor targeting, ineffective ad creatives, and low engagement rates. **Bottlenecks**: Delays in marketing campaign approvals.
5	**Customer browsing and discovery** *Shobha*, the online shopper, browses the platform and discovers Prabhu's product.	**Waste**: Time customers spend searching for products and leaving without purchasing. **Time taken**: Varies, typically 5-10 minutes per session. **Inefficiencies**: Poor search functionality, lack of filtering options, slow loading times. **Bottlenecks**: Overcrowded marketplace, making it hard for customers to find specific products.
6	**Customer decision-making** *Shobha* evaluates the product by reading the description, examining photos, checking reviews, and comparing prices.	**Time taken**: 1-3 days on average, depending on the product. **Inefficiencies**: Lack of clear, persuasive information; negative reviews or unclear pricing. **Bottlenecks**: Complicated comparison processes, distrust due to lack of authenticity assurance.
7	**Customer adds product to cart** *Shobha* adds the product to her shopping cart.	**Waste**: Time wasted if the customer abandons the cart. **Time taken**: 1-2 minutes. **Inefficiencies**: Poor cart design, hidden costs (e.g., shipping) appearing late in the process.
8	**Order placement and payment** *Shobha* completes the purchase by entering payment information and placing the order.	**Waste**: Abandoned transactions due to complex or slow payment processes. **Time taken**: 2-5 minutes. **Inefficiencies**: Complicated payment processes, limited payment options, or unresponsive payment gateways. **Bottlenecks**: Payment gateway failures, security concerns, lengthy payment verification times.

9	**Order notification to artisan** *Prabhu* receives an order notification from the platform.	**Waste**: Delays in notification leading to slow order fulfilment. **Time taken**: Instant (automated notifications). **Inefficiencies**: Delays in notification if systems are not integrated. **Bottlenecks**: Manual processing delays.
10	**Product packaging** *Prabhu* packages the product securely for shipping.	**Waste**: Excessive packaging materials, time spent finding appropriate packaging. **Time taken**: 1-2 days. **Why necessary**: Protects the product during shipping and enhances the unboxing experience. **Inefficiencies**: Inadequate packaging leading to product damage, excessive packaging costs. **Bottlenecks**: Delays due to lack of appropriate packaging materials or equipment.
11	**Shipping and delivery** The product is picked up by a logistics provider and shipped to *Shobha*.	**Waste**: Time lost during transit, products getting lost or damaged. **Time taken**: 5-7 days on average. **Inefficiencies**: Inefficient routing, delays, or unreliable shipping partners. **Bottlenecks**: Customs delays, logistics mishaps, and remote delivery locations.
12	**Order tracking by customer** *Shobha* tracks her order through the platform's tracking system.	**Waste**: Customers repeatedly checking tracking information due to poor updates. **Time taken**: Ongoing until delivery. **Why necessary**: Provides transparency and reassures the customer during the delivery process. **Inefficiencies**: Inaccurate or delayed tracking updates.
13	**Product delivery** *Shobha* receives the product.	**Waste**: Returns or exchanges due to damaged products or incorrect orders. **Time taken**: Depends on location; 5-7 days from shipping. **Inefficiencies**: Mis deliveries, damaged goods, or delivery to the wrong address. **Bottlenecks**: Failed delivery attempts, or lack of proper delivery instructions.

14	**Customer feedback and reviews** *Shobha* provides feedback and possibly writes a review of the product and her experience.	**Waste**: Lack of feedback if the customer does not leave a review. **Time taken**: 5-10 minutes for the customer. **Inefficiencies**: Low response rates, lack of incentives to leave feedback.
15	**Customer support (when needed)** If there is an issue, *Shobha* contacts customer support for assistance.	**Waste**: Time wasted on unresolved issues or repeated calls. **Time taken**: Varies depending on the complexity of the issue. **Inefficiencies**: Poor response times, ineffective problem resolution. **Bottlenecks**: Understaffed support teams, complex escalation processes, and lack of training for support staff on nuances of handmade artwork-based commerce.
16	**Payment to artisan** The platform processes the payment and transfers funds to *Prabhu* after deducting any fees.	**Waste**: Delays in payment processing, unnecessary fees. **Time taken**: 1-2 weeks post-sale. **Inefficiencies**: Delays in processing payments, lack of transparency in fee deductions. **Bottlenecks**: Payment system failures, manual processing delays.
17	**Replenishment and inventory management** *Prabhu* updates his inventory and decides whether to create more products based on sales data.	**Waste**: Overstocking or stockouts, time spent manually tracking inventory. **Time taken**: Ongoing; varies based on sales volume. **Inefficiencies**: Inaccurate inventory tracking, delays in replenishing stock. **Bottlenecks**: Manual inventory processes, unpredictable demand patterns.
18	**Post-purchase engagement** *Shobha* may be targeted for future marketing campaigns based on her purchase.	**Waste**: Missed opportunities for future sales or customer retention. **Time taken**: Ongoing, with initial follow-up within a few days post-delivery. **Why necessary**: Helps build customer loyalty and drives repeat purchases. **Inefficiencies**: Generic follow-up messages, lack of personalized engagement. **Bottlenecks**: Limited customer data, ineffective communication strategies.

Table 1.6: Example Value Stream Map

Tara now feels she has gained a deep understanding of the customer pain points and has moved beyond a surface-level grasp of the issues surrounding the lack of marketplaces for local artisans.

Actions for the entrepreneur

1. Prioritize among various problem statements based on your passion for the topic, your depth of awareness to discover a solution, your ability to network with key people who can validate your solution, and how effectively you can engage potential early adopters willing to take a leap of faith.

    Prioritize among various problem statements based on:

    a. Your passion for the topic.

    b. Your depth of awareness and capability to discover a solution.

    c. Your ability to network with key individuals who can validate the solution.

    d. Your effectiveness in engaging early adopters willing to take a leap of faith.

2. Identify key stakeholders and map their current (as-is) value stream.

Conclusion

Building a successful product is not about having a brilliant idea; it is about deeply understanding and solving a real customer problem. Entrepreneurs often get caught up in the allure of their idea, assuming that is what will lead to success. However, what really matters is how well the product addresses the pain points and needs of its users.

For entrepreneurs developing an MVP, this approach of empathy, research, and iteration ensures that the product will be aligned with real customer needs, increasing the chances of success in the market.

As Tara's journey highlights, the path from idea to product involves prioritizing customer-centricity, conducting thorough user research, and developing a continuous feedback loop.

In the next chapter, the entrepreneur will learn how to analyze and size the market.

Join our Discord space

Join our Discord workspace for latest updates, offers, tech happenings around the world, new releases, and sessions with the authors:

https://discord.bpbonline.com

CHAPTER 2

Market Analysis and Validation

Introduction

Once an entrepreneur has identified and gained a deeper understanding of the customer pain point, they are passionate about solving. The next step is to research the business opportunity. This includes assessing whether a significant portion of the market shares the same pain point and determining if there is a large enough audience willing to pay for a solution.

Assessing the target market's size and viability requires determining the **Total Addressable Market** (**TAM**) and validating access to it. Identifying trends, competitors, and potential barriers to entry is critical. This can be done using tools like the Competitor Analysis Canvas and by evaluating legal and regulatory obligations. To validate market demand, entrepreneurs can employ strategies like pre-sales, landing pages, and pre-bookings to measure customer interest and willingness to pay. Through thorough market analysis and validation, entrepreneurs can gain a clear understanding of market dynamics, the competitive landscape, and customer demand, leading to informed decision-making and stronger market entry strategies.

Structure

In this chapter, we will cover the following topics:

- Market opportunity analysis
- Market segmentation analysis

- Serviceable market analysis
- Trend analysis
- Competitive landscape analysis
- Porter's Five Forces
- In-depth competitor analysis
- Understanding legal, regulatory, and compliance

Objectives

By the end of this chapter, the entrepreneur will have gained the skills to assess the size and viability of their target market by calculating the TAM and validating their access to it. They will learn how to analyze market opportunities, perform serviceable market and segmentation analysis, and identify trends, competitors, and entry barriers. Additionally, the entrepreneur will be equipped with primary and secondary research techniques, including interviews, focus groups, surveys, and tools like the Competitor Analysis Canvas and Porter's Five Forces. They will also understand how to research legal, regulatory, and compliance obligations. Finally, the reader will learn how to validate market demand through the development and testing of a value hypothesis, using methods such as landing pages, pre-bookings, and customer surveys to inform their market entry strategies.

Market opportunity analysis

The term **market** refers to the entire ecosystem in which a product exists, encompassing potential customers or consumers who have a need or desire for the product or service, along with the ability and willingness to pay for it. It also includes competitors, distribution channels, suppliers, and external factors such as regulations and economic conditions that influence both demand and supply.

Market opportunity analysis involves evaluating the potential of a new product or service within a given market. Entrepreneurs assess factors like customer demand, competition, industry trends, and potential barriers to entry. This analysis helps determine whether a viable business opportunity exists and whether the market has enough growth potential to support the new venture.

Total Addressable Market

The first step in analyzing market opportunity is to quantify the market. Entrepreneurs need to answer the question, *If we sold this product to every potential customer, how much revenue could we generate?* This helps estimate the maximum potential for growth, commonly referred to as the TAM.

The simplest way to calculate TAM is by multiplying the total number of potential customers by the **average revenue per user** (**ARPU**).

TAM = Total potential customers × Average revenue per user (ARPU)

This gives a clear estimation of the market's total revenue potential if the product reaches every customer.

Understanding the TAM is crucial for entrepreneurs, as it helps determine whether the market for the problem the product aims to solve is large enough to justify the investment of time, money, and effort. Investors also place significant importance on TAM to gauge the potential return on their investment. A large TAM signals a substantial growth opportunity, making the business more appealing to investors seeking high-growth ventures.

Ultimately, before entering a new market, entrepreneurs use TAM to assess whether the opportunity is worth pursuing. If the TAM is too small, they may decide to shift their focus to a more promising market.

Let us consider Tara's example to understand TAM:

After identifying several potential problem statements she could address as an entrepreneur, Tara zeroed in on one she felt deeply passionate about. She chose a problem where she could develop genuine empathy for those experiencing the pain and actively engage not only with them but also with others in the ecosystem to gain a deeper understanding. Tara gathered various stakeholders involved in the prioritized problem statement and mapped their journeys. To further assess the scope of the problem and determine if building a financially viable product was feasible, she proceeded to calculate the market size to understand how many people were affected by the issue.

Tara found a study estimating that India's upper and middle segments of the middle class made up 30% of the population in 2021, when India's total population was 140 crores. This meant there were potentially 42 crore customers. Another study found that the average online shopping spend was INR 1,587. Tara estimated that, on average, shoppers would be willing to spend this amount twice a year on handcrafted products made by local artisans. Based on this, she calculated an ARPU of INR 3,174 annually.

Applying the formula for TAM:

TAM = 42 crores × INR 3,174

With a TAM of *INR 1,33,308 crores*, Tara realized that this was a large enough market to justify building a viable product to address the problem.

Market segmentation analysis

Market segmentation analysis is the process of dividing a broad market into smaller, more defined segments based on shared characteristics, such as demographics, behaviors, or needs. By targeting these specific groups, entrepreneurs can tailor their products, marketing strategies, and messaging to better meet the needs of each segment, improving the chances of success.

Demographic segmentation

Demographic segmentation divides the market based on identifiable traits of a population, such as age, gender, income, and life stage. This method helps businesses tailor their products and messaging to specific groups of people, recognizing that different segments may have distinct needs, purchasing power, and preferences.

Some common segments are based on:

- **Age groups**: 18-24, 25-34, 35-44, 45-54, 55+
- **Gender**: Male, female, others
- **Income levels**: Low, middle, high
- **Life stage**: Students, young professionals, parents, retirees

Geographic segmentation

Geographic segmentation categorizes the market based on physical locations or other geographic factors such as region, climate, or urban vs. rural settings. This allows companies to adapt their offerings to local conditions, cultural differences, or logistical requirements.

Some of the common segments are based on:

- **Regions**: North America, Europe, Asia, Africa, South America, Australia
- **Climate zones**: Tropical, dry, temperate, cold
- **Urban vs. rural**: Metropolitan areas, suburbs, rural areas

Psychographic segmentation

Psychographic segmentation focuses on the personal traits of consumers, such as their values, lifestyle, and attitudes. It explores the psychological aspects that influence purchasing decisions, providing insights into how people perceive and prioritize different products.

Some common segments are based on:

- **Risk tolerance**: Conservative, moderate, aggressive
- **Financial goals**: Retirement, wealth accumulation, daily expense
- **Lifestyle**: Tech-savvy, traditional, eco-conscious
- **Values**: Financial independence, social responsibility

Behavioral segmentation

Behavioral segmentation divides the market based on consumer behavior patterns, such as how frequently they use a product, their loyalty, or how they engage with specific features. This helps businesses identify and target customers based on actual usage and buying behavior, allowing for more personalized marketing strategies.

Some common segments are based on:

- **Usage rate**: Heavy, moderate, occasional users
- **User loyalty**: Loyal users, switchers, new users
- **Feature adoption**: Users who utilize all features, users who use only basic features, users who use specialized features

Need-based segmentation

Need-based segmentation groups customers based on their specific needs or challenges that the product or service addresses. This method ensures that businesses focus on delivering tailored solutions to different segments, which may prioritize collaboration, scalability, customization, or regulatory compliance.

Some common segments are based on:

- **Collaboration needs**: Organizations looking for a product for team collaboration
- **Scalability needs**: Organizations looking for a solution that can grow with them
- **Customization needs**: Organizations desiring a high level of customization
- **Compliance needs**: Organizations in highly regulated industries

Firmographic segmentation

Firmographic segmentation applies to B2B markets and categorizes companies based on characteristics such as industry, company size, revenue, or location. It helps businesses tailor their offerings to the needs of organizations with different operational scales, financial capacities, or geographic presence.

Some common segments are based on:

- **Industry**: Manufacturing, retail, healthcare company size: small, medium, large (200+ employees)
- **Annual revenue**: Less than $1M, $1M-$10M, over $10M
- **Geographic location**: North America, Europe, Asia-Pacific

It is common during market segmentation for a product to address multiple segments, each defined by different criteria.

Let us consider Tara's example to understand these segmentations.

Tara reviews various market segmentation approaches and narrows her focus to the segments that not only experience the pain described in the problem statement but are also lucrative and accessible enough to prioritize.

As expected, the segments she narrowed on are multiple segments across multiple segmentation criteria:

- **Demographic segmentation**:
    o **By age groups**: 25-34, 35-44, 45-54
    o **By gender**: Male, female, others
    o **By income levels**: Middle
    o **By life stage**: Young professionals, parents, retirees
- **Geographic segmentation**:
    o **By regions**: Across India
    o **By population density**: Metropolitan, urban, rural
- **Behavioral segmentation**:
    o **By user loyalty**: Will try new things

Serviceable market analysis

Once the TAM has been identified and the market segments defined, the next step is to refine the TAM to reflect the portion of the market the product can realistically serve.

Serviceable available market

The **serviceable available market (SAM)** is the subset of the TAM that a product can realistically serve, factoring in geographic, technological, or product limitations that may limit access to the entire TAM.

SAM analysis should also consider the entrepreneur's own limitations, such as geographical reach, customer preferences, or the ability of building and nurturing relationships that can provide support, opportunities, and resources to grow a business (networking).

Market segmentation provides clarity on what percentage of each segment (segment factor) the product can address, which is rarely 100%.

Formula for calculating SAM is TAM multiplied by what percentage of population across each segment is available for servicing.

$$SAM = TAM \times Relevant\ market\ factor(s)$$

This refinement makes the TAM more actionable, helping the entrepreneur focus on a realistic market opportunity.

Now, based on publicly available data, Tara determined that over 40% of India's population is under 25 years old, and 6.9% is aged 65 and above. From this, she estimated that approximately 53% of the population falls within the age group relevant to her product. Thus, the demographic segmentation factor was set at 53%.

She also found a study showing that around 36% of India's population lives in urban areas, leading to a geographic segmentation factor of 36%.

With these factors, Tara calculated the SAM for her product:

$$SAM = INR\ 1,33,308\ crores \times 53\% \times 36\%$$

This yielded a SAM of INR 25,435 crores. Tara was excited to see that this still represented a substantial market opportunity, making the case for building a viable product to address the problem even stronger.

Trend analysis

Now that the entrepreneur has a clear understanding of the market they want to focus on, the next step is to identify patterns or shifts within that market over time, a process known as **trend analysis**. Entrepreneurs use trend analysis to spot emerging opportunities, better understand market dynamics, and anticipate changes that could impact their business. Staying aware of trends is crucial for ensuring that the identified problem remains relevant and that the envisioned product is competitive and aligned with market needs. Being proactive about trends helps entrepreneurs stay ahead, reducing the risk of creating something that the market may no longer require.

Identifying trends

Identifying trends requires an exploratory research approach for entrepreneurs. This involves using **primary research,** where firsthand data is gathered directly from the SAM through surveys, interviews, focus groups, or observations to learn what products they currently use. In addition, **secondary research** is crucial, involving the analysis of existing data from sources such as web searches, industry magazines, research reports, and public data. By combining both approaches, entrepreneurs can gain comprehensive insights into the trends.

Primary research

We have all experienced being approached by businesses asking for our input—whether through surveys at a mall, a quick feedback form after a purchase, or a phone call asking about our experience with a service. This is primary research in action, method businesses use to gather direct insights from their target audience. As entrepreneurs, primary research can be an invaluable tool to collect firsthand data for a variety of objectives, whether it is understanding customer preferences, validating a product idea, or assessing market needs.

When conducting primary research, it is essential to follow best practices to ensure the data collected is both reliable and gathered ethically. Here are some key guidelines to keep in mind across all primary research methods:

- **Define objectives clearly**: Before beginning any research, it is important to clearly define the purpose and objectives. Determining what needs to be learned will guide the questions and ensure that the data collected is meaningful and focused.

- **Take comprehensive notes**: During interactions, taking detailed notes is essential, and when possible, recording the conversation (with consent) is recommended. Recording ensures accuracy and allows for capturing non-verbal cues and other subtle insights that may otherwise be overlooked.

- **Ensure informed consent**: It is crucial to ensure that participants fully understand the purpose of the research, how their information will be used, and any potential risks. Obtaining written or verbal consent before beginning ensures that participants are comfortable and informed.

- **Maintain confidentiality**: Protecting participants' privacy is a priority. Their data should be stored securely, and any quotes or information used from the research should be anonymized unless explicit permission is granted. Maintaining confidentiality fosters trust and upholds ethical research practices.

- **Be respectful of time**: It is important to adhere to the agreed-upon duration for the interaction. While participants may be willing to continue beyond the allotted time, being mindful of their schedules and respectful of their time is essential.

Next, let us explore the various methods available for applying these practices and gathering useful data.

Risk of leading questions

Leading questions are questions that subtly suggest or imply a particular answer. They often guide the respondent toward a desired response, intentionally or unintentionally. For example, instead of asking, *what do you think of this feature?* A leading question might be, *don't you think this feature is useful?*

Entrepreneurs should avoid leading questions because they can distort the feedback process and give biased results. The purpose of gathering feedback is to understand the genuine thoughts, preferences, and concerns of the target users. Leading questions can mislead respondents into providing answers that align with the entrepreneur's assumptions rather than their true opinions.

This can lead to flawed insights, misguided product decisions, and ultimately, the development of an MVP that does not truly meet the needs of the customer. Instead, entrepreneurs should ask open-ended, neutral questions that allow for honest, unbiased responses, giving them a clearer picture of user needs and preferences.

Risk of observer effect

The **observer effect** refers to the phenomenon where the presence, biases, or subtle cues of an observer unintentionally influence the behavior of those being observed. A famous example of this is the story of *Clever Hans*, a horse in the early 1900s that appeared to perform complex arithmetic by tapping his hoof in response to questions[1].

Hans's owner, *Wilhelm von Osten*, believed the horse had extraordinary intelligence. Hans would seemingly solve math problems and answer questions with amazing accuracy. However, psychologist *Oskar Pfungst* conducted a series of experiments and discovered that Hans was not actually solving the problems. Instead, he was reacting to subtle, often unconscious cues from his owner, such as changes in posture or facial expressions, which signaled when Hans should stop tapping his hoof.

When these cues were removed, by hiding the answer from the owner, Hans's accuracy dropped dramatically. This demonstrated that Hans was not performing complex arithmetic but simply responding to non-verbal signals from the observer.

This classic case highlights how the observer effect can skew research findings, even if the observer has no intention of influencing the outcome. It is a reminder for entrepreneurs conducting user research to be mindful of their own presence and potential impact on participant behavior.

Interview

We have all participated in more than a few interviews, whether from one side of the table or the other. **Interviews** are one-on-one conversations designed to gather in-depth qualitative insights. To maintain the quality of the information collected and the integrity of the research, entrepreneurs should follow these best practices:

- **Choose the right interview type**: Select between structured (fixed questions), semi-structured (flexible guidelines), or unstructured (open-ended conversations) depending on the research objectives.

- **Script development**: Prepare a list of questions or key topics to maintain consistency across interviews.

- **Pilot testing**: Conduct a test interview to refine your questions and approach before the actual session.

- **Establish rapport**: Start by introducing yourself, explaining the purpose of the interview, and making the participant feel comfortable.

---

1 Ferguson, Philip M.. "Clever Hans". Encyclopedia Britannica, 7 Oct, 2019, **https://www.britannica.com/topic/Clever-Hans**. Accessed 23 Feb, 2024.

- **Stay neutral**: Avoid leading questions that might bias responses. Keep a neutral tone to ensure honest, unbiased answers.

- **Practice active listening**: Focus on the participant without interruptions and be open to exploring follow-up questions beyond your script.

- **Encourage openness**: Use open-ended questions to elicit detailed responses. Phrases like *Can you tell me more about that?* encourage deeper insights.

- **Be adaptable**: While a script helps, flexibility in your approach allows for valuable, unexpected insights to emerge.

- **Ask for clarification**: If a response is unclear, ask for further explanation to ensure accuracy.

- **Conclude properly**: Thank the participant, invite any questions, and explain the next steps in the research process.

- **Post-interview reflection**: After each interview, take a few minutes to reflect on key insights or surprises, noting areas for future exploration.

By following these best practices, entrepreneurs can gather the valuable qualitative and quantitative information needed to inform and shape their MVP development.

Focus groups

When an entrepreneur is trying to gather insights from a diverse group of potential users or stakeholders, **focus groups** can be a highly effective tool. A focus group is a small, guided discussion with selected participants used to gather opinions, feedback, or insights about a product, service, or idea. Imagine you are testing a new app concept designed to help local artisans reach a broader audience. A focus group could bring together a small group of potential users—artisans, online shoppers, and even logistics experts- to discuss their experiences, needs, and pain points in real-time. The entrepreneur listens and observes, gathering qualitative insights that are hard to capture through surveys or one-on-one interviews.

Here are some best practices to consider when conducting focus groups:

- **Participant selection**: Choose participants who represent the diversity of your target audience. However, ensure enough homogeneity in demographics or experiences to make participants feel comfortable sharing their thoughts.

- **Moderator skills**: Select a skilled moderator who can facilitate the discussion, keeping it on track and encouraging everyone to participate. The moderator should remain neutral and avoid steering the conversation.

- **Preparation of discussion guide**: Develop a set of open-ended questions or topics to guide the discussion, but allow flexibility for unplanned yet relevant topics to emerge.

- **Logistics and setting**: Choose a distraction-free, comfortable location. Arrange seating to foster open discussion, such as in a circle or semicircle. Depending on the objectives, participants may be asked to face the moderator to minimize influence from each other's body language or facial expressions. Ensure recording equipment is set up and functional.

- **Set ground rules**: Start by establishing basic ground rules like speaking one at a time, respecting differing opinions, and maintaining confidentiality within the group.

- **Manage group dynamics**: To promote engagement, use icebreakers or techniques like having participants write opinions on sticky notes to ensure quieter members are heard. If a disagreement arises, the moderator can call a timeout or use techniques like **Enough, Let's Move On (ELMO)** to keep the discussion productive. In extreme cases, disruptive participants may be separated.

- **Stay neutral**: Avoid leading questions or showing any approval or disapproval to maintain genuine responses.

- **Duration**: Focus groups typically last 60 to 90 minutes.

- **Thank participants**: Recognize participants' contributions and offer incentives or compensation if applicable.

From a focus group, entrepreneurs can expect rich, qualitative data that offers valuable insights into user motivations, pain points, and expectations. These insights help refine the product and guide future iterations. However, while focus groups provide a deep understanding of user perspectives, the results should be seen as directional rather than definitive, making them useful for identifying trends but not for drawing final conclusions.

Observations

Imagine an entrepreneur observing how users interact with an app in a coffee shop or watching artisans use a new tool in their workshop. These scenarios help gather insights that go beyond what users might say in an interview or survey. **Observational research** focuses on watching and recording user behavior in their natural environment, providing raw, unfiltered data that can be crucial for understanding how a product is used in real-life settings.

Here are some best practices for conducting observational research:

- **Choose the appropriate observation method**: Decide whether to use participant observation or non-participant observation. In participant observation, the observer is actively involved in the activity. In non-participant observation, the observer simply watches without taking part. Each approach has its own advantages, depending on whether the situation calls for deeper involvement or objective detachment.

- **Minimize observer effect**: The presence of an observer can sometimes alter participant behavior. To reduce this effect, be discreet, use unobtrusive methods, or allow participants time to adjust to the observer's presence.

- **Maintain objectivity and neutrality**: It is important to avoid letting personal biases influence observations. Entrepreneurs should document findings without preconceived notions, ensuring they capture genuine behaviors.

- **Document context**: Pay attention to the environment, time of day, and any other factors that might affect user behavior. This context can provide additional insights and a deeper understanding of the actions being observed.

- **Stay adaptable**: Field research can be unpredictable, so it is important to stay flexible. If the environment or situation changes, adapting the observation plan ensures valuable data is still collected.

Observational research is particularly valuable for entrepreneurs looking to understand how users experience a pain point in real-world settings or to identify behaviors that users may not consciously recognize or articulate. It is especially effective for gaining insights into workflows and pinpointing issues that may not surface through direct questioning.

By directly observing users, entrepreneurs can uncover hidden pain points and unexpected use cases that might otherwise go unnoticed. This approach often leads to actionable insights that can refine product development and enhance the user experience, ensuring the MVP truly addresses the needs of its target audience.

For example, the **Follow Me Home (FMH)** program, initiated by *Intuit* co-founder *Scott Cook*, is a customer research approach where company representatives observe how customers use their products in real life[2]. The idea behind FMH is to step into the customers' shoes and understand the full picture of how they interact with and run their businesses using the company's products.

This method provides invaluable insights into customers' experiences, challenges, and preferences without any preconceived assumptions. It is particularly useful for businesses offering tangible products or services, as it involves a simple setup with an interviewer and a note-taker. The real-life observations gained through FMH help improve products and services, emphasizing the power of direct customer observation in driving meaningful product iterations.

Surveys

When entrepreneurs are looking to gather a broad range of opinions, behaviors, or preferences from a larger population, surveys are an essential tool. Whether they are trying to validate an idea, understand user preferences, or identify market gaps, surveys offer a structured and efficient way to collect both quantitative and qualitative data.

Designing an effective survey requires thoughtful consideration to ensure results are accurate and meaningful. Here are some key practices for creating a survey:

---

2 Rathjens, Lisa. "Why every company should be doing a Follow Me Home". Intuit Developer, 21 Jan, 2021. **https://blogs.intuit.com/2021/01/21/why-every-company-should-be-doing-a-follow-me-home/**. Accessed 23 Feb, 2024.

- **Define objectives clearly**: Establish clear goals before starting the survey. Understanding your purpose will guide the types of questions asked and help focus on collecting relevant data.

- **Keep it short**: Respect respondents' time by keeping the survey concise while still gathering essential data. Shorter surveys increase completion rates.

- **Use simple and clear language**: Avoid jargon or overly complex language. Ensure that all respondents can easily understand the questions, regardless of their background.

- **Avoid leading questions**: Ensure questions are neutral. Instead of *Don't you think our app is helpful?*, ask *How would you rate the usefulness of our app?* to avoid influencing responses.

- **Offer a range of response options**: For multiple-choice questions, provide enough options so respondents can accurately reflect their opinions.

- **Include open-ended questions sparingly**: Use open-ended questions when seeking detailed insights, but limit their use to avoid overwhelming respondents and creating too much data to analyze.

- **Randomize answer choices**: To reduce order bias, randomize the order of answer choices to ensure more accurate data.

- **Ensure anonymity and confidentiality**: Assure respondents their answers will remain confidential and explain how their data will be used. This builds trust and encourages honest responses.

- **Avoid double-barreled questions**: Split questions that ask about more than one issue, like *How satisfied are you with our product's price and quality?*, into two separate questions.

- **Use a logical flow**: Start with general questions, then progress to more specific ones. Grouping similar questions helps respondents stay focused.

- **Include a mix of question types**: Use a variety of question types, like multiple choice, Likert scale (e.g., *strongly agree* to *strongly disagree*), and ranking, to gather different types of information.

- **Pre-test your survey**: Conduct a small test run to identify any issues with question clarity or survey functionality before sending it to a larger audience.

- **Be mindful of demographics**: If demographic data is important, include questions on age, gender, location, etc., but be respectful of privacy concerns.

- **Include a progress indicator**: For longer surveys, show respondents how far along they are to reduce abandonment rates.

- **Thank respondents**: Always thank participants for their time and consider offering incentives if appropriate.

Surveys are particularly useful when the goal is to gather data from a large number of people or when entrepreneurs need to make data-driven decisions regarding features, user preferences, or potential market trends. The results of a well-designed survey can provide a clearer understanding of customer needs, behaviors, and preferences, offering valuable guidance for the development and refinement of the MVP.

Likert scale

When gathering feedback or assessing stakeholder opinions, entrepreneurs often need a way to measure subjective responses in a structured and quantifiable manner. A practical tool for this purpose is the Likert scale, which allows respondents to express varying levels of agreement or disagreement on a given topic. This method is particularly useful for understanding sentiments, preferences, or satisfaction levels.

Developed by psychologist *Rensis Likert*[3] in 1932, the Likert scale typically offers a range of options—often from *strongly disagree* to *strongly agree*—enabling respondents to share their attitudes or experiences in a more nuanced way. This structured approach makes it easier to interpret and analyze the feedback, providing actionable insights.

For entrepreneurs developing an MVP, Likert scales can be highly effective in user surveys, product tests, or feedback sessions. For example, asking users how satisfied they are with specific product features on a scale from *very dissatisfied* to *very satisfied* can highlight areas that need improvement. Similarly, gathering stakeholder feedback on product development priorities using this scale ensures alignment and uncovers potential concerns early.

Likert scales come in various forms, depending on the information needed. Some common five-point scales include:

- **Satisfaction**: Very dissatisfied, dissatisfied, neither, satisfied, very satisfied
- **Likelihood**: Very unlikely, unlikely, neutral, likely, very likely
- **Concern**: Very unconcerned, unconcerned, neutral, concerned, very concerned
- **Agreement**: Strongly disagree, disagree, neutral, agree, strongly agree
- **Frequency**: Never, rarely, sometimes, often, always

Sampling

When conducting surveys, an essential step in gathering reliable insights is the process of sampling. Sampling involves selecting a subset of individuals from a larger population to represent that group in the research. This method allows entrepreneurs to gain valuable information without needing to engage the entire population. Here is why sampling is so powerful:

---

3 Jamieson, Susan. "Likert scale". Encyclopedia Britannica, 23 Feb, 2024,
 https://www.britannica.com/topic/Likert-Scale. Accessed 30 Mar, 2024.

- **Representativeness**: A well-chosen sample accurately reflects the characteristics of the broader population, ensuring that the insights gathered are relevant and applicable to the target market.

- **Cost-effectiveness**: Surveying an entire population can be prohibitively expensive and time-consuming. Sampling offers a practical solution by focusing resources on a smaller, manageable group while still providing meaningful data.

- **Time efficiency**: Sampling allows entrepreneurs to collect data quickly, enabling faster decision-making, which is crucial during the MVP development phase when time-to-market is critical.

- **Accuracy and reliability**: With proper sampling methods and statistical techniques, the data gathered can be highly accurate, allowing entrepreneurs to make informed decisions based on solid insights.

- **Mitigating bias**: Sampling reduces the risk of relying on the opinions of a select few, such as the **Highest Paid Person's Opinion** (**HiPPO**), by ensuring the selected group is representative. This helps avoid drawing skewed or inaccurate conclusions.

By leveraging sampling effectively, entrepreneurs can streamline their research process and obtain actionable insights without unnecessary complexity or cost.

Common sampling methods

When conducting surveys, selecting the right sampling method is crucial to ensure that the results are both representative and aligned with the survey's objectives. Entrepreneurs have several common sampling techniques to choose from, each suited to different types of research:

- **Simple random sampling**: Every individual in the population has an equal chance of being selected. **Example**: A company launching a new smartphone feature randomly selects 1,000 users from its entire user base to gather unbiased feedback.

- **Stratified sampling**: The population is divided into non-overlapping groups, or *strata*, and a random sample is taken from each stratum. **Example**: A music streaming service seeking to improve its playlist algorithm divides users by age and randomly selects participants from each age group to ensure balanced feedback.

- **Cluster sampling**: The population is divided into clusters, often based on geography, and a random sample of clusters is chosen. Every individual within those clusters is then surveyed. **Example**: A retail chain opening a new store layout selects 5 random stores and surveys all customers from those locations.

- **Multi-stage sampling**: This involves selecting clusters, but instead of surveying every individual in the chosen clusters, a sample is taken from within those clusters. **Example**: An online grocery service first selects cities, then neighborhoods within those cities, and finally surveys a subset of households.

- **Systematic sampling**: Individuals are chosen at regular intervals from a larger population. **Example**: An e-commerce platform surveys every 50th customer after a purchase to gather insights on a new checkout process.

- **Convenience sampling**: Participants are selected based on their ease of access. **Example**: A SaaS company gathers feedback from trade show attendees who visit their booth because they are readily available and willing to participate.

- **Judgment or purposive sampling**: Individuals are handpicked based on specific criteria or knowledge. **Example**: An enterprise software company selects experienced IT managers to provide feedback on a new admin dashboard due to their familiarity with the product.

- **Quota sampling**: Similar to stratified sampling but based on a fixed number or quota from each group. **Example**: A fitness app collects feedback from 100 users at each fitness level—beginner, intermediate, and expert, until they reach the set quota for each group.

By choosing the right sampling method, entrepreneurs can ensure that their research gathers insightful and actionable data while remaining cost-effective and efficient.

Sample size calculation

When determining the appropriate sample size for a survey, entrepreneurs need to consider several factors to ensure the results are both reliable and meaningful. These factors include the study's objectives, the level of precision desired, and the diversity within the target population.

To calculate the ideal sample size, statistical formulas are typically used to ensure the sample is large enough to yield statistically significant results. While larger samples generally provide more accurate data, it is essential to recognize that after a certain point, the benefits of increasing the sample size diminish, and the additional cost and effort may not justify the minimal gains in accuracy.

For practical reference, here is a table that estimates the number of respondents needed to achieve a 95% confidence level with a 5% margin of error, which is common in survey research:

Population size	Sample size
100	80
1,000	287
10,000	370
100,000	382
1,000,000	385
100,000,000	385

Table 2.1: Suggested sample size based on population to survey

As seen in the table, for large populations, the sample size stabilizes around 385 respondents. This is based on **Cochran's formula**[4], a well-known method for sample size calculation. Entrepreneurs can also use online calculators provided by platforms like **SurveyMonkey**[5] to quickly estimate sample sizes for their specific research needs.

Secondary research

Often referred to as desk research, secondary research involves analyzing existing data rather than generating new information. Entrepreneurs use this approach to gather insights from a wide variety of sources, making it a highly efficient method for understanding market conditions, competitor strategies, and industry trends. By tapping into available resources, entrepreneurs can build a comprehensive understanding of their target market and competitors without the time or expense associated with primary research.

Here are several common methods entrepreneurs can use for secondary research:

- **Industry and market reports**: Consulting reports from firms like *Gartner* or *Forrester* helps entrepreneurs understand the competitive landscape, market leaders, and industry trends.

- **Company publications**: Annual reports, product whitepapers, or investor documents can provide insights into a company's financial health and product strategies.

- **Government and institutional databases**: Regulatory and compliance information from government sites can be critical for industries like fintech or healthcare.

- **News and media outlets**: Tech publications like *TechCrunch* offer real-time updates on product launches and industry shifts. Monitoring these sources helps entrepreneurs stay current with market developments.

- **Trade journals and magazines**: Publications focused on business domains or technology are excellent for tracking industry trends.

- **Literature review**: This involves reviewing academic and industry-specific publications to gain insights into best practices, trends, and emerging technologies. Entrepreneurs might use databases like *Google Scholar* or *IEEE Xplore*.

- **Historical records**: By analyzing archives or competitor histories, entrepreneurs can understand how markets and products have evolved over time. *Crunchbase* provides company histories and funding details for competitors.

- **User forums and communities**: Online platforms are valuable for identifying common pain points or challenges users face.

---

4 Cochran's theorem. (n.d.). Wikipedia. Retrieved September 14, 2024, from **https://en.wikipedia.org/wiki/Cochran%27s_theorem**
5 Free Online Sample Size Calculator (Full Guide and Examples). (n.d.). SurveyMonkey. Retrieved September 14, 2024, from **https://www.surveymonkey.com/mp/sample-size-calculator/**

- **Product sites**: Platforms like *G2 Crowd* aggregate user reviews, helping entrepreneurs assess customer satisfaction with various products and gauge market response to similar products. In cases of mobile apps, reviewing the Apple App Store or Google Play Store under similar categories will help surface similar products, along with user ratings and reviews.

- **Competitor analysis**: Reviewing competitors' feature lists, FAQs, and customer reviews can offer insights into product positioning. Entrepreneurs can also compare traffic data on platforms like *SimilarWeb*.

Entrepreneurs should use secondary research to assess market viability, understand the competitive landscape, and gain insights into customer needs. It is especially useful for identifying gaps in the market or trends. While secondary research offers a broad understanding, it may need to be supplemented with primary research for actionable, more specific insights.

Competitive landscape analysis

Evaluating the competitive landscape is essential for entrepreneurs as it provides a clear understanding of the market dynamics and reveals opportunities for differentiation. By analyzing competitors' weaknesses and strategies, entrepreneurs can identify gaps in the market where their product can stand out and offer a unique value proposition. Similarly, studying competitors' strengths offers valuable lessons on what works well and might be worth replicating. This insight helps shape critical aspects of product development, pricing, marketing, and overall business strategy, ensuring the startup addresses real customer needs and stands out in the market.

Interestingly, having competition is often an advantage for entrepreneurs. It provides the chance to learn from what predecessors have done right and, just as importantly, what they have done wrong.

Some entrepreneurs are excited when they believe they have little or no competition, viewing it as validation of their unique idea. However, this could indicate insufficient market research or that the problem being addressed is too niche or difficult for any product to have succeeded so far. In either case, careful competitive analysis is key to avoiding these pitfalls and refining the product approach.

Identifying competitors

When identifying which companies are part of the competitive landscape, entrepreneurs should consider multiple categories to get a full picture, such as:

- **Direct competitors**: Companies that offer a similar product or service and target the same customer base. Entrepreneurs must look for businesses solving the same problem in a similar way. For example, if the entrepreneur is developing a ride-sharing app, *Uber* and *Lyft* would be direct competitors.

- **Indirect competitors**: Companies that offer different products or services but address the same underlying need. These competitors may solve the problem differently. For example, a public transportation app is an indirect competitor to a ride-sharing service, as both help people get from point A to point B but with different solutions.

- **Replacement competitors**: Companies offering a product or service that customers may use instead of adopting a new solution. These might be outdated technologies or manual processes. For instance, for a digital bookkeeping startup, pen-and-paper accounting or Excel spreadsheets would be replacement competitors.

- **Emerging or future competitors**: Companies or startups entering the space who could potentially disrupt the market. Entrepreneurs must pay attention to industry news, funding rounds, or companies getting attention in early-stage startup competitions. Tech blogs, innovation platforms, and accelerators often feature new entrants.

- **Adjacent competitors**: Companies in related industries might expand their product line into the entrepreneur's space. Entrepreneurs must watch for businesses expanding their offerings into new verticals. For example, a payment processing company entering the point-of-sale hardware market could become a competitor to companies in that space.

- **Substitute competitors**: Companies that offer a completely different product but address the same customer pain point. Entrepreneurs must identify companies that provide alternative ways to solve the same problem. For instance, if the entrepreneur is building an online language-learning platform, physical language courses or language-learning books are substitute competitors.

- **Geographic competitors**: Companies that operate in the same or similar geographic market, often offering localized services. Entrepreneurs must consider both global players that operate in specific regions and local competitors serving a particular geographic area. Research regional market reports and directories.

- **Customer segment competitors**: Companies target the same customer segments with similar products, even if the features differ. If the entrepreneur is targeting a niche group, such as small business owners, other companies focusing on that demographic are relevant competitors, even if the product is not identical.

- **Competitors in different price tiers**: Companies offering products at different price points for similar solutions. Entrepreneurs must identify whether your product competes with premium or budget alternatives. For instance, a premium video streaming service competes with both low-cost and ad-supported options.

- **Technological competitors**: Companies that use different technologies to provide a similar solution. Entrepreneurs must watch for companies that offer different technical approaches to solving the problem. For example, one company might use AI-based analytics while another relies on traditional data processing.

- **Regulatory competitors**: Companies that meet specific legal or regulatory requirements that others do not, potentially offering an advantage. Entrepreneurs must understand which companies adhere to industry-specific standards or regulations. For instance, companies certified for certain healthcare or financial regulations might offer a competitive edge in those markets.

Let us consider the example of Tara. Like any savvy entrepreneur, Tara understood the value of learning from both her competition and her primary research. She carefully built a competitive landscape for her marketplaces for local artisans by categorizing and listing companies in each relevant segment. This allowed her to gain insights into the market, identify potential gaps, and position her product more strategically.

- **Direct competitors**:
  - **Etsy**: A global marketplace focusing on handmade, vintage items, and craft supplies.
  - **Craftsvilla**: An Indian marketplace specifically for ethnic products, including handmade goods from artisans.
  - **Jaypore**: A platform that focuses on artisanal and handcrafted products, with a special focus on Indian heritage.
- **Indirect competitors**:
  - **Amazon Karigar**: A section of Amazon that sells handmade products, though it lacks the artisan-focused community feel.
  - **Myntra**: A popular fashion and lifestyle e-commerce platform in India that may sell artisanal fashion products but is not artisan specific.
  - **Pepperfry**: A furniture and home decor e-commerce platform that features products from Indian artisans alongside mass-produced items.
- **Replacement competitors**:
  - **Local markets/fairs**: Artisans may rely on local fairs, markets, or exhibitions to sell their products directly.
  - **Boutiques**: Some artisans may sell their goods through local brick-and-mortar boutiques or stores.
  - **Social media (Instagram/Facebook marketplace)**: Artisans selling directly to consumers via social media platforms without using a formal e-commerce platform.
- **Emerging or future competitors**:
  - **Trezi**: A recently launched platform focusing on small local sellers and artisans, gaining traction in specific regions.
  - **GoCoop**: An emerging marketplace for artisans and weavers that aims to connect cooperatives with global buyers.

- o **Artisans' collective**: A startup that helps artisans from rural areas list their products online with a specific focus on sustainability.

- **Adjacent competitors**:
  - o **Shopify**: While currently a tool for building online stores, *Shopify* could expand its platform to better serve artisans with niche tools for handicrafts.
  - o **Flipkart**: As a large e-commerce player in India, *Flipkart* could create a dedicated section for handmade or artisan goods.
  - o **Paytm Mall**: Another e-commerce giant in India that could potentially create a dedicated space for local artisans.

- **Substitute competitors**:
  - o **Luxury boutiques/Designer brands**: Some customers might choose premium luxury or designer brands instead of buying from artisans.
  - o **Mass-produced alternatives**: Consumers may opt for mass-produced goods available on platforms like *Amazon* or *IKEA* as substitutes for handmade products.

- **Geographic competitors**:
  - o **IndiaMART**: Although primarily a B2B marketplace, *IndiaMART* features local sellers, including artisans.
  - o **Utsav Fashion**: An India-based e-commerce platform that focuses on ethnic and handmade goods, primarily in fashion.
  - o **Gaatha**: A niche platform focusing on handmade Indian crafts and promoting rural artisans across India.

- **Customer segment competitors**:
  - o **Fabuliv**: An Indian home decor brand offering products made by artisans.
  - o **The India Craft House**: An online platform targeting customers who are passionate about traditional Indian handicrafts.
  - o **Okhai**: A platform selling handmade, sustainable products, targeting socially conscious customers.

- **Competitors in different price tiers**:
  - o **Tjori**: A platform offering handmade products, targeting mid-to-high-end customers with premium pricing.
  - o **Fabindia**: Known for handmade and artisanal products, *Fabindia* operates at a slightly higher price tier.
  - o **Chumbak**: While not entirely artisan-based, *Chumbak* offers handcrafted items at relatively affordable price points, competing in the mid-range market.

- **Technological competitors**:
  - ○ **Meesho**: An online platform allowing individuals to resell products via social commerce, using a different model from traditional e-commerce.
  - ○ **Zepo**: An e-commerce platform providing small businesses, including artisans, with tools to create their own online store.
  - ○ **WooCommerce**: A plugin for *WordPress* that allows artisans to build and manage their own online stores, competing with centralized marketplaces.
- **Regulatory competitors**:
  - ○ **Etsy India**: Since *Etsy* is a global platform, they ensure that sellers comply with international trade regulations, giving them an edge in global reach.
  - ○ **Government-backed artisan platforms**: Platforms supported by governmental organizations (such as those under India's Ministry of Textiles) may have advantages in terms of regulatory compliance and access to grants or subsidies.

By understanding these competitors, Tara can better position her marketplace and identify opportunities for differentiation and growth.

Porter's Five Forces

The business world was introduced to Porter's Five Forces in a 1979 *Harvard Business Review* article[6]. This framework helps businesses assess the competitive dynamics of their industry.

It evaluates five key factors that influence profitability and competition:

- ○ **Threat of new entrants**: The risk that new competitors may enter the market, increasing competition and reducing profitability.
- ○ **Bargaining power of suppliers**: The influence suppliers have over pricing and availability of inputs, potentially impacting a company's margins.
- ○ **Bargaining power of buyers**: The ability of customers to influence pricing and demand better quality or service, affecting profitability.
- ○ **Threat of substitutes**: The likelihood that alternative products or services could fulfill customer needs, potentially reducing market demand.
- ○ **Intensity of competitive rivalry**: The level of competition between existing players in the market, impacting pricing, innovation, and market share.

An entrepreneur must recognize that they are the *Threat of New Entrants* to every established player. It is essential to understand how incumbents are building high barriers to protect themselves from disruption and learn how to navigate or overcome these obstacles.

---

6 Porter, Michael. "How Competitive Forces Shape Strategy, **https://hbr.org/1979/03/how-competitive-forces-shape-strategy** ." Harvard Business Review. March-April 1979. pp. 137-145.

Consider the following common *Threat of New Entrants* barriers an incumbent erects to keep a new entrant away and how an entrepreneur can break them:

- **Product differentiation**: Strong brands with loyal customer bases create barriers by restrictive IP protection or establishing their product or methods as de-facto industry standards, making it hard to create a differentiation.

  Breaking this barrier: Entrepreneurs can identify areas where customer preferences are shifting or where personalization and innovation might win over consumers dissatisfied with none, generic or mass-market options.

- **Capital requirements**: High costs for entering the market, such as purchasing equipment or building facilities, deter smaller or newer competitors.

  Breaking this barrier: Entrepreneurs can explore lean startup models, outsourcing, or partnerships to minimize capital investment and enter the market at a lower cost.

- **Access to distribution channels**: Existing companies that control key distribution channels limit the entry of new firms, as newcomers must create alternative methods to reach consumers.

  Breaking this barrier: Entrepreneurs can explore digital or direct-to-consumer strategies to bypass traditional distribution networks and tap into unmet demand.

- **Switching costs**: When customers face high costs, whether monetary or time-based, to switch from one product to another, it discourages them from trying out new entrants.

  Breaking this barrier: Entrepreneurs can offer incentives, better user experiences, or integration options that make switching less painful for consumers.

- **Supply-side economies of scale**: Firms that spread fixed costs over large volumes can produce goods more cheaply, making it hard for smaller players to compete.

  Breaking this barrier: Entrepreneurs can focus on small, premium segments where lower volume production does not disadvantage them or use technology to optimize production and reduce costs.

- **Demand-side benefits of scale (network effect)**: Products or services become more valuable as more people use them, making it harder for new entrants to attract users.

  Breaking this barrier: Entrepreneurs can tap into underserved groups or niches and build their own network effects by offering superior service or features.

- **Incumbency advantages**: Established companies benefit from brand loyalty, customer familiarity, and long-term relationships that are difficult to displace.

  Breaking this barrier: Entrepreneurs can disrupt by offering more personalized services, addressing frustrations customers may have with incumbents, or leveraging emerging trends to create fresh appeal.

- **Government policy**: Government regulations, such as patents, monopolies, or franchise requirements, create legal barriers to entry, protecting incumbents.

  Breaking this barrier: Entrepreneurs can work on innovative models that comply with regulations or challenge monopolies through legal means, or enter adjacent markets where regulations are less restrictive.

In-depth competitor analysis

Understanding the strengths and weaknesses of competitors is essential for entrepreneurs looking to make their mark. By taking a structured approach to evaluating competitors, businesses can uncover opportunities to differentiate their products and stand out in the market.

The Competitor Analysis Canvas, as shown in *Figure 2.1*, provides entrepreneurs with a structured tool for evaluating their competitors and finding opportunities to learn from their product. By systematically examining competitors' strengths, weaknesses, strategies, and market positioning, entrepreneurs can discover a niche in a crowded market.

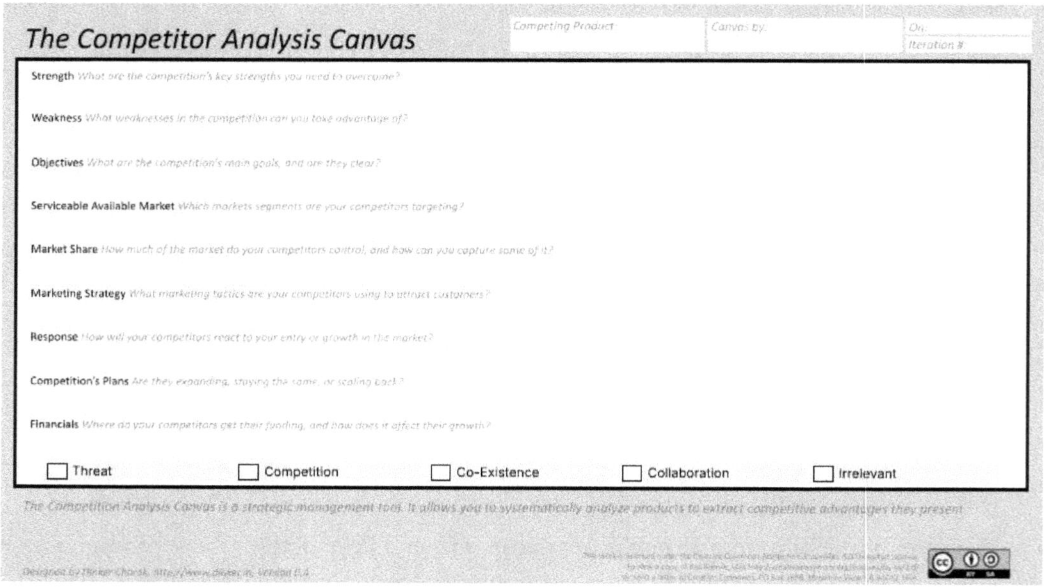

Figure 2.1: The Competitor Analysis Canvas

Here is a breakdown of the key sections of this canvas:

- **Strengths**: Competitors often have strong points, whether it is a well-known brand, superior technology, or excellent customer service. Entrepreneurs need to identify these areas and develop strategies to either counteract or surpass them.

- **Weaknesses**: No competitor is flawless. Finding and exploiting gaps in their offerings can give entrepreneurs a distinct advantage of learning from others' mistakes.

- **Objectives**: Understanding the long-term goals of competitors allows entrepreneurs to anticipate their next strategic moves. Whether a competitor is aiming for international expansion or focusing on niche markets, this insight supports better decision-making.

- **Serviceable available market**: It is important to know which markets competitors are targeting, whether it is specific industries, demographics, or regions. Identifying these focus areas helps guide decisions on market entry or expansion strategies.

- **Market share**: Evaluating a competitor's market share provides insight into their influence and reach. This gives entrepreneurs a clear idea of how big the market is and whether it is worth playing in the same market segment.

- **Marketing strategy**: Look at how competitors market their products, whether through digital ads, influencer campaigns, or other channels. Understanding their strategy can offer clues about their target audience and engagement methods.

- **Response**: When launching or scaling a product, predicting competitors' reactions, like price cuts, marketing efforts, or new partnerships, prepares entrepreneurs to respond strategically.

- **Competitors' plans**: Understanding whether competitors are expanding or pulling back offers valuable insight into their direction. This can be discovered through public statements, strategic reports, or financial filings.

- **Financials**: A competitor's funding sources and financial health are important indicators of their stability, growth potential, and ability to invest in new developments.

After completing the analysis, entrepreneurs can categorize competitors into five groups:

- **Threat**: Those with the potential to seriously disrupt your market position.

- **Competition**: Direct competitors offering similar products to the same audience.

- **Co-existence**: Businesses in the same space that do not impact each other's operations.

- **Collaboration**: Potential partners who may offer opportunities for resource sharing.

- **Irrelevance**: Competitors who do not significantly affect your strategy or market position.

This canvas is best used for top competitors when entering a new market. It helps identify threats and opportunities to inform key strategic decisions for an entrepreneur's MVP plans.

In order to differentiate her product in a competitive market, Tara conducted a comprehensive analysis of her main competitor, *Amazon India*.

The Competitor Analysis Canvas provided her with a structured approach to break down Amazon India's strategies, strengths, and market position. Here is a summary of Tara's analysis:

- **Strength**: Amazon India has an unmatched reach with millions of customers across the country, providing a vast selection of products, strong logistics, and fast delivery services. They are known for trustworthiness, user-friendly experiences, and competitive pricing. We would need to overcome this trust and scale advantage.

- **Weakness**: While Amazon is dominant, it often focuses on mass-produced goods. There is a lack of emphasis on promoting handmade, local artisan goods in a unique or storytelling manner. Our platform can focus on authenticity, direct support to artisans, and offer a niche market that values handcrafted products.

- **Objectives**: Amazon India aims to be the one-stop shop for everything under the sun. Their focus is on expanding their market share across product categories, including groceries, electronics, and apparel. However, they may not prioritize the niche artisan market that we are targeting.

- **Serviceable available market**: Amazon India targets a wide range of customers, from budget-conscious consumers to premium buyers across various sectors. We can focus on urban shoppers interested in sustainable, unique artisan products, creating a niche within Amazon's broader customer base.

- **Market share**: Amazon India controls a significant portion of the Indian e-commerce market. However, we can tap into the niche market of conscious consumers and art lovers, aiming to capture the segment that seeks exclusive, handmade goods.

- **Marketing strategy**: Amazon uses aggressive digital marketing, flash sales, discounts, and influencer campaigns to attract buyers. Our marketing strategy can focus on storytelling, social impact, and building communities around local craftsmanship, something that Amazon does not emphasize for artisan products.

- **Response**: Amazon India might not aggressively react to a niche platform like Tara's in the short term, as their focus remains on scaling their core offerings. However, if we gain traction, Amazon could ramp up its focus on local artisans through partnerships or launching competing initiatives like *Amazon Karigar*.

- **Competition's plans**: Amazon is continuously expanding, with a focus on increasing its seller base, logistics capabilities, and diversifying product categories. While their plans do not solely focus on local artisans, they may expand into this space if they notice the potential for growth.

- **Financials**: Amazon India is backed by massive international funding, which gives it a strong financial base for continuous growth, investments, and rapid market response. We must remain Agile and capitalize on her niche to compete against Amazon's financial power.

Through this structured approach, Tara is able to better understand Amazon India's position and identify opportunities where she can stand out, primarily by offering a specialized marketplace that connects local artisans with consumers seeking unique, handmade products.

Understanding legal, regulatory, and compliance

Entrepreneurs can discover their legal, regulatory, and compliance obligations through various steps and resources.

We will cover a structured approach, shown as follows:

- **Consult experts**: Entrepreneurs should hire a lawyer who specializes in Indian business law, startup regulations, or their specific industry. This legal expert can provide guidance on corporate setup, intellectual property, employment law, and various regulatory requirements. Additionally, bringing on a compliance consultant offers tailored advice on taxation, labor laws, and environmental regulations to help meet specific legal obligations. It is also important to hire a chartered accountant to manage financial compliance and ensure proper tax filings. Lastly, entrepreneurs should seek legal advice on labor law to navigate employee-related regulations effectively and avoid any potential issues.

- **Obtain necessary licenses and permits**: Depending on the state of operation, entrepreneurs should check the *Shop and Establishment Act* rules for working hours, holidays, and wage regulations.

  Research required *trade licenses* from local municipal corporations, including sector-specific licenses like FSSAI for food businesses or pollution control board clearances for manufacturing units.

  Businesses with a turnover above a certain threshold must register for **Goods and Services Tax** (**GST**). Entrepreneurs can visit the GST portal for registration and compliance information.

  For businesses engaged in international trade, applying for an **Import-Export Code** (**IEC**) through the **Directorate General of Foreign Trade** (**DGFT**) is mandatory.

- **Use compliance management tools**: Tools like *Zoho Compliance* or *Legasis* help entrepreneurs track and manage compliance deadlines, such as tax filings, labor law requirements, and regulatory updates.

- **Leverage online legal resources**: Online platforms like *Vakilsearch* and *IndiaFilings* provide comprehensive services, including company registration, trademark filing, tax compliance, and regulatory updates, allowing entrepreneurs to streamline legal processes.

  Entrepreneurs can use platforms like *ClearTax* for GST, income tax filing, and compliance management, with detailed guides and filing services available online.

- **Explore government portals and resources**: The Startup India initiative provides extensive resources for startups, including information on government schemes, compliance requirements, tax exemptions, and more. Entrepreneurs can visit the Startup India website (**https://www.startupindia.gov.in/**) for detailed guides on legal and regulatory matters.

Entrepreneurs should check the **Ministry of Corporate Affairs (MCA)** portal for information on company registration, compliance filings, corporate governance rules, and more. The MCA portal also provides access to the *Companies Act* and other legal frameworks.

For GST registration and compliance, visit the **Central Board of Indirect Taxes and Customs (CBIC)** website to understand the tax obligations and filing requirements.

If operating in a Special Economic Zone, SEZ India provides regulatory and compliance details specific to businesses in these areas.

- **Join industry associations and Chambers of Commerce: Federation of Indian Chambers of Commerce and Industry (FICCI)** and **Confederation of Indian Industry (CII)** offer resources and insights into sector-specific regulatory issues, legal updates, and compliance best practices.

  Tech entrepreneurs can follow the **National Association of Software and Service Companies (NASSCOM)** for regulatory insights in the software and IT services industry.

- **Network with entrepreneurs and mentors**: Programs like iSPIRT and NASSCOM's 10,000 startups offer guidance on navigating the regulatory landscape for Indian startups. Networking with other entrepreneurs and industry veterans provides real-world insights into managing legal compliance.

- **Follow industry-specific regulations**: Many industries in India are governed by specific regulators. For example:

  - *FSSAI* for the food industry.
  - *IRDA* for insurance companies.
  - *SEBI* for businesses in capital markets or securities.
  - **Telecom Regulatory Authority of India (TRAI)** for telecommunications.
  - **Drugs Controller General of India (DCGI)** for the pharmaceutical industry.

Each regulator provides guidelines, licenses, and compliance requirements that entrepreneurs must follow, such as:

- **Understand taxation and financial compliance**: For direct tax-related obligations such as filing returns and understanding tax exemptions, the Income Tax Department website is the go-to resource.

For businesses with employees, entrepreneurs need to comply with **Tax Deducted at Source (TDS)**, **Employees' Provident Fund (EPF)**, and **Employees' State Insurance (ESI)** requirements. The respective websites provide guides on registration, payment, and filing processes.

Entrepreneurs dealing with foreign exchange or seeking external funding (FDI, FPI) should consult **Reserve Bank of India (RBI)** guidelines on permissible transactions, foreign investment routes, and repatriation rules.

- **Monitor changes in legislation**: Keep an eye on changes in business laws and compliance requirements by regularly checking government notifications issued by the MCA, CBIC, and the **Department for Promotion of Industry and Internal Trade (DPIIT)**.

Websites like *LiveLaw* and *Bar & Bench* provide updates on legal developments in India, including new regulations affecting startups and businesses.

Entrepreneurs must stay informed and ensure their business complies with the complex legal and regulatory framework by seeking competent legal and financial advice. Relying solely on sources like Google or ChatGPT is not sufficient when navigating these critical areas.

- **Validating market demand**: A product is more valuable for both the manufacturer and consumer after it is exchanged in the market. For the manufacturer, this value may come from profit, while for the consumer, it is the benefit gained from using the product. Identifying this benefit is the core goal for an entrepreneur.

Once the pain point is clear, a serviceable market is identified, and the target customer segment is narrowed down, the entrepreneur can move forward by selecting personas, analyzing trends, and finally, establishing a hypothesis of value. This hypothesis becomes the foundation upon which the entrepreneur can run experiments and methods to validate whether the product truly delivers the expected value.

This validation step acts as the culmination of all the efforts thus far, understanding customer needs, maintaining a customer-centric focus, conducting thorough user research, prioritizing features, identifying stakeholders, mapping the support ecosystem, empathizing with customers, and conducting Value Stream Mapping to pinpoint their problems. The entrepreneur has also performed market opportunity analysis, calculated the TAM, identified the right market segment, arrived at the **serviceable available market (SAM)**, and conducted trend analysis of that SAM using both primary and secondary research. Additionally, they have identified competitors, performed in-depth competition analysis, and ensured compliance with legal and regulatory standards.

At this stage, the key question becomes: *Will the problem statement we identified, using the right methods, for the right set of customers, deliver real value?* This process is known as **validating market demand**.

- **Establishing a value hypothesis**: A value hypothesis is a clear, testable statement that defines the key ability the product will offer to the customer and explains how it will alleviate their pain point to solve the identified problem. This hypothesis is informed by the entrepreneur's intuition, user feedback, and market research. It sets the stage for testing whether the proposed solution truly delivers value to the target audience.

To ensure the value hypothesis is validated, entrepreneurs establish specific checks and criteria. A common tool used for this purpose is the Experiment Canvas. **The Experiment Canvas**, as shown in *Figure 2.2*, provides a structured framework for entrepreneurs to articulate their value hypothesis, along with the success and failure criteria for validation:

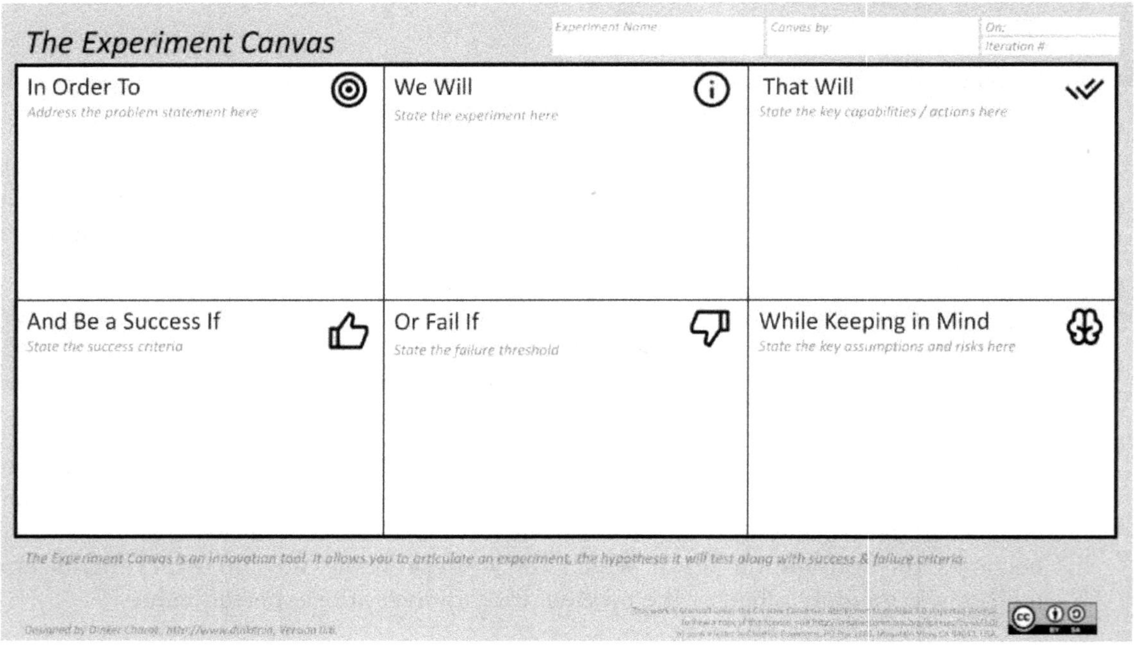

Figure 2.2: *The Experiment Canvas*

The various sections of the Experiment Canvas are outlined as follows. The first three focus on describing the value hypothesis, while the remaining three detail how to validate it:

- **In order to:** This section addresses the pain point or problem being solved. The entrepreneur describes the problem in a way that highlights the current challenges or inefficiencies.

- **Hints on how to frame:**
  - *In order to make it simple to <describe the complexity of the current process>.*
  - *In order to avoid <explain the convoluted path that exists today>.*
  - *In order to reduce the cost of <highlight the expense involved in the current approach>.*

- **We will**: Here, the entrepreneur explains the approach to solving the pain point without getting into technical jargon or specific solutions. The focus is on how the approach will improve the current scenario.

- **Hints on how to frame**:
  - *We will simplify by <describe how simplicity will be achieved>.*
  - *We will build a better alternative by <describe how the alternative will work>.*
  - *We will make it cheaper by <explain how costs will be reduced>.*

It is essential to frame this from the customer's perspective, avoiding overly technical or solution-specific language like, *We will build an app.*

- **That will**: This section defines the value the product will deliver. If the hypothesis holds, this becomes the key value proposition or core feature of the final product.

- **And be a success if**: Here, the entrepreneur defines the success criteria that will validate the hypothesis. Success metrics should be based on research and represent meaningful improvements. The criteria should be realistic and set at a level that demonstrates the product is addressing the problem effectively.

Some of the common success criteria include:

  - The rate of product adoption among target users
  - User engagement and retention
  - Customer satisfaction with the product's value
  - Willingness to pay for the product and how much
  - Market share within the target segment
  - Likelihood of users recommending the product to others
  - Differentiation from competitors through unique value

Unachievable criteria should be avoided, as they may set the product up for failure or lead to misleading validation efforts.

- **Or fail if**: This section outlines the failure criteria. Not meeting success criteria does not automatically indicate failure. Failure criteria are minimum thresholds, signaling that if these are not met, the value hypothesis has likely not been validated.

- **While keeping in mind**: Here, the entrepreneur lists the assumptions that could affect the value hypothesis. These assumptions help set the boundaries for the experiment.

Some of the common assumptions include:

  - The hypothesis is valid for a specific SAM
  - The value is meaningful for the defined customer segment(s)
  - Legal, regulatory, and compliance factors have been considered and accounted for

For better understanding, let us consider Tara's example. Tara has completed her research and is ready to move on to the next phase of iterating on a solution. To ensure clarity about the problem she is addressing and the value it will bring to her customers, she fills out The Experiment Canvas. This will serve as a valuable reference for herself and a tool for sharing her vision with others.

Although she included some metrics based on her initial research, it is clear that as the journey progresses, these metrics may evolve, either being replaced with more appropriate ones or adjusted to reflect new insights and objectives.

Here is her Experiment Canvas for the *Marketplaces for Local Artisans* with the online shopper persona as the customer:

- *In order to* simplify the process of finding authentic, handmade artisan products, which currently requires browsing multiple unreliable platforms or local markets.

- *We will* create a unified, trustworthy platform that directly connects online shoppers with local artisans.

- *That will* allow online shoppers to easily discover unique, handmade products from local artisans with the confidence that the items are authentic and will be delivered reliably and on time.

- *And be a success if* at least 20% of online shoppers visiting the platform make a purchase within the first three months, shoppers are willing to pay a price premium of at least 10% for the assurance of authentic handmade products.

- *Or fail if* the platform fails to differentiate itself from existing competitors like Amazon Karigar.

- *While keeping in mind* the assumption that online shoppers highly value product authenticity and are willing to pay a premium for it.

Validating the value hypothesis

Validating the value hypothesis requires reaching out to individuals within the SAM who belong to the identified customer segment. To ensure meaningful results, entrepreneurs should apply the appropriate sampling methods, as discussed earlier, to obtain a representative cross-section of responses. While some methods for reaching out have already been covered, we will explore additional approaches as well.

Since the goal is to gather a clear, albeit probabilistic, picture, it is essential to follow best practices to avoid bias, personal beliefs, tunnel vision, or assumptions that could lead to inaccurate conclusions. This ensures a more objective validation of the value hypothesis, guiding the entrepreneur toward informed decision-making.

Here are a few effective techniques for validating a value hypothesis that entrepreneurs can use during the vision stage.

Landing page

A landing page is a simple website designed to explain the product concept and encourage visitors to take action, such as signing up for a waitlist. As entrepreneurs engage with potential customers within the SAM while discussing the prioritized problem statement, sharing the landing page web address serves as a memorable takeaway. Tracking visitor sign-ups and expressions of interest provides valuable insights, helping entrepreneurs gauge demand. This approach is a cost-effective, scalable method to test market interest without needing to fully develop the product.

Zoho LandingPage, Wix, Instapage, Squarespace, and Google Sites are a few common services that enable an entrepreneur to build one in a matter of hours.

Pre-booking

Pre-bookings allow potential customers to reserve a product before its official launch, offering a valuable gauge of market demand and validating interest in the solution. A strong volume of pre-bookings indicates that the product addresses a real need and that customers are eager to buy it. If an upfront payment option is offered instead of paying later, it can also help generate early revenue that can be reinvested into further development. However, since buyers are expressing a commitment, entrepreneurs should reciprocate by providing clear, transparent timelines to manage expectations and build trust.

Shopify, Squarespace, and WordPress are a few common services that offer services that enable entrepreneurs to set up in a matter of hours.

Surveys

Surveys are one of the most effective ways to directly validate customer needs and preferences. By asking targeted questions about pain points, pricing expectations, and willingness to use or pay for a product, entrepreneurs can gather valuable insights. To ensure the data is reliable, it is essential to apply the appropriate sampling methods, as discussed in this section to capture responses that accurately reflect the target market.

SurveyMonkey, Mentimeter, Zoho, Google Forms, and Microsoft Forms are few common services that offer services that enable entrepreneurs to set one up in a matter of hours.

Actions for the entrepreneur

1. Calculate the TAM, market segmentation, and SAM for the prioritized problem statement.
2. Conduct primary research related to the prioritized problem statement.
3. Analyze existing products that partially or closely address the prioritized problem statement.

Validate market demand for a solution by using the Experiment Canvas to establish a value hypothesis and test it through primary research.

Conclusion

Entrepreneurs should avoid relying solely on instinctual analysis based on personal experience or anecdotal input from peers. Instead, they must equip themselves with robust tools and techniques to thoroughly assess the viability of their business idea. By understanding the TAM, identifying trends, analyzing competitors, and addressing entry barriers, they can confidently evaluate the potential of their opportunity. Furthermore, through primary and secondary research and the validation of market demand using value hypotheses and practical strategies, entrepreneurs now have a clear roadmap for informed decision-making. This comprehensive understanding of market dynamics, customer needs, and competitive positioning sets the foundation for crafting effective business strategies and building a successful MVP.

In the next chapter, the entrepreneur will learn the importance and techniques for prioritization.

Join our Discord space

Join our Discord workspace for latest updates, offers, tech happenings around the world, new releases, and sessions with the authors:

https://discord.bpbonline.com

CHAPTER 3

Opportunity Prioritization

Introduction

Once the customer pain points to be solved have been identified and the business opportunities around it measured, the next step is to prioritize the right business opportunity in the form of a problem statement for the audience to ensure that the entrepreneur has hit the right fitment.

Effective prioritization of problems involves utilizing frameworks like the value-complexity matrix to identify and rank issues based on their significance. Establishing a prioritization framework with rubrics helps evaluate problems based on multiple parameters such as impact, urgency, and feasibility.

Internal fitment of prioritized problems is crucial, ensuring alignment with the startup's goals and schedule for addressing each opportunity. By strategically aligning problem-solving efforts with business objectives and market needs, startups can optimize resource allocation and focus on tackling high-impact challenges to drive sustainable growth and success.

Structure

In this chapter, we will cover the following topics:

- Prioritization techniques
- Business opportunity definition

Objectives

By the end of this chapter, the entrepreneur will have a toolkit for identifying, prioritizing, and validating the most impactful business opportunity to address. They will be able to apply multiple prioritization techniques to focus on high-impact opportunities and will learn how to ensure that their chosen problems align with both their startup's goals and broader market needs. Additionally, the entrepreneur will gain insights into validating opportunity and customer fit, confirming they are addressing the right pain points for the correct audience, with a clear pathway to the goals of the MVP.

Prioritization techniques

Prioritization is one of the most essential skills that an entrepreneur needs to develop. In a startup environment, possibilities are endless, resources are limited, timelines are tight, and the need for traction is immediate. Without careful prioritization, it is easy to get pulled in multiple directions.

Effective prioritization is not only about deciding what to do but also deciding what not to do. By honing this skill, entrepreneurs can channel their time, budget, and energy into the right areas, building solutions that truly address the identified pressing problems.

In many ways, prioritization is a mindset: it is about staying attuned to the big picture while navigating day-to-day decisions with purpose. Entrepreneurs who embrace this approach find themselves saying *No* far too often and yet remain adaptable as they move toward their vision.

To learn various techniques for prioritization, we need to familiarize ourselves with the term **backlog**. A backlog refers to an accumulation of uncompleted tasks, items, requests, or ideas that need to be addressed. It represents work that is not completed, has been delayed or postponed, often due to limited resources, prioritization, or time constraints.

Prioritization, thus, is managing a backlog effectively to ensure that high-priority items are addressed in a timely manner and that work is systematically completed to make progress.

Eisenhower Matrix

The Eisenhower Matrix, attributed to former U.S. President *Dwight D. Eisenhower*, is a straightforward yet powerful tool for prioritizing tasks based on urgency and importance. It helps entrepreneurs focus on what truly matters and manage their time more effectively.

The Eisenhower Matrix is a 2x2 grid that categorizes backlog items according to two key criteria: urgency and importance.

The following figure shows how the 2x2 grid represents the two criteria:

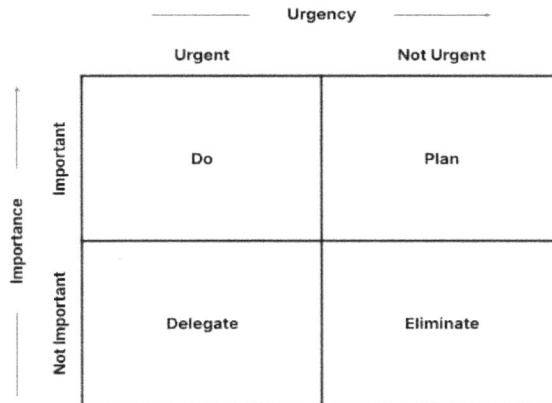

Figure 3.1: *Eisenhower Matrix*

By evaluating backlog items this way, entrepreneurs can prioritize their workload strategically.

This approach divides tasks into four distinct quadrants, namely:

- **Urgent and important**: Tasks requiring immediate attention that also contribute to long-term goals or values. These should be tackled right away.

- **Important, but not urgent**: Tasks that are significant but do not need to be completed immediately. These are best scheduled for later, ensuring they receive the attention they deserve without interrupting other priorities.

- **Urgent, but not important**: Tasks that need immediate action but have little impact on long-term goals. Delegating these, when possible, can help maintain focus on higher-impact work.

- **Neither urgent nor important**: Tasks that are neither time-sensitive nor impactful on long-term goals. These are usually distractions and should be minimized or eliminated where possible.

On delegation

This approach introduces another essential skill for an entrepreneur: the ability to delegate. Many entrepreneurs struggle with delegation for various reasons, and addressing these challenges can be transformative. Some of the reasons are:

- **Lack of a team**: Some entrepreneurs simply do not have a team yet, leading them to handle every task on their own. This approach can quickly become exhausting and increase the risk of burnout. If that is the case, it is crucial to focus on building a team. Delegating urgent tasks that others can handle effectively frees up the entrepreneur to focus on higher-level priorities.

- **Perfectionism**: Entrepreneurs may believe that only they can perform tasks to the required standard, doubting their team's capability. In such cases, investing in the team's learning and development is key. Hiring people with the right skill sets in the first place is always the right approach. Building a competent team ensures that they do not have to micromanage or step in constantly, which can drain time and energy. Entrepreneurs should also recognize that not every task needs perfection—often, completing a task to a good enough standard is more than sufficient. Defining outcomes objectively can guide the team to accomplish exactly what is needed.

- **Fear of losing control**: Some entrepreneurs feel insecure or worry about losing control if they delegate. However, a well-functioning team reflects strong leadership. By shifting focus from control to growth, entrepreneurs can achieve far more, often amplifying productivity tenfold, than they could alone. Embracing delegation allows the business to scale and succeed at a pace that one person could never achieve on their own.

Value vs. complexity

The value-complexity map is a 2x2 grid that helps entrepreneurs categorize backlog items based on two crucial criteria: value and complexity. The following figure shows how the 2x2 grid represents the two criteria:

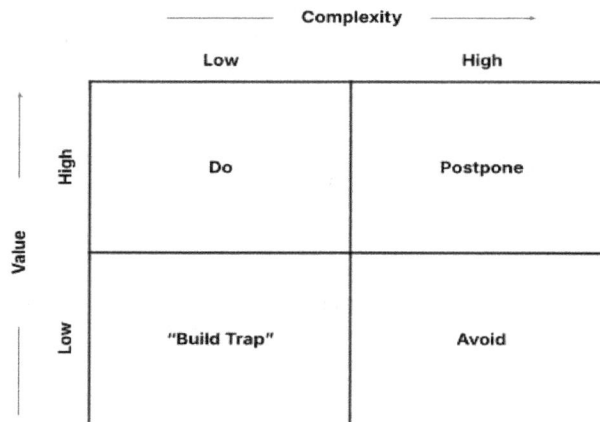

Figure 3.2: Value-complexity map

Let us understand it:

- Value (Y-axis) can be either low or high. This refers to the impact or benefit the task provides, whether that is in terms of business growth, user satisfaction, or another meaningful gain.

- Complexity (X-axis) can also be low or high. Complexity factors include cost, available talent within the team, required effort, or how far a task pushes the entrepreneur beyond their existing capabilities or comfort zone.

This mapping allows entrepreneurs to prioritize their workload strategically, ensuring that resources and time are invested wisely. Here is how backlog items break down across the four quadrants:

- **High value, low complexity**: These tasks offer a lot of impact without heavy lifting. Entrepreneurs should prioritize these tasks, as they provide immediate value with lower effort or cost. This quadrant should be the focus for any MVP development.

- **High value, high complexity**: These tasks are impactful but come with a significant cost, whether financial, technical, or time-based. While valuable, they can be postponed until after the MVP phase, allowing resources to be conserved for more immediate needs.

- **Low value, low complexity**: Tasks in this category, often referred to as *low-hanging fruit,* are tempting because they are easy to complete, increase output, and keep the team busy. However, focusing too much on these can lead to a *build trap*, where effort is spent on low-impact work that clutters the MVP with unnecessary features. Over time, this can lead to deadweight features that are quickly outdated and harder to manage.

- **Low value, high complexity**: These tasks are the ones to avoid, as they offer little benefit for the effort required. Entrepreneurs should say no to these tasks and instead explore ways to achieve similar results at a lower cost, if they need to be revisited at all.

MoSCoW method

The MoSCoW method provides entrepreneurs with a practical framework for prioritizing features and tasks when developing an MVP. Each item in the backlog is assigned one of the following priorities:

- **Must have**: Essential items that are non-negotiable and critical to the MVP's core functionality and purpose.

- **Should have**: Important features that enhance the MVP but can be postponed if necessary for the initial release.

- **Could have**: Nice-to-have elements that add value but do not impact the MVP's main objectives.

- **Would not have**: Features that are acknowledged but intentionally excluded from the MVP, potentially reserved for future versions.

After prioritizing backlog items, the next step is to find a strategic balance between *must have,* *should have,* and *could have* items. Focusing exclusively on *must have* features will certainly ensure critical outcomes. However, it is essential for the entrepreneur to remember that *should have* and *could have* items are included for a reason; they often bring excitement and showcase the MVP's future potential. Additionally, *should have* items may represent valuable features that, while not essential now, will enhance the product over time.

A practical approach is to allocate about 70% of effort to *must have* items, with the remaining 30% split between *should have* (20%) and *could have* (10%). This allocation ensures that essential features are prioritized without losing sight of longer-term goals. It also helps the entrepreneur maintain a balanced perspective—addressing immediate needs while gradually chipping away at future tasks. This proactive approach means that when a *should have* item becomes a *must have* later, it feels more manageable and less overwhelming.

Kano Model

The Kano Model, developed by professor *Noriaki Kano* in the 1980s, offers a structured approach for prioritizing product features based on their impact on customer satisfaction.

This model helps entrepreneurs identify which features will make the most meaningful impression on users, guiding effective prioritization during the MVP phase. The model classifies features into five categories:

- **Basic needs**: These are essential features that users expect as a minimum requirement. While their absence leads to dissatisfaction, their presence is usually taken for granted and does not increase satisfaction. During the MVP phase, entrepreneurs should focus on a targeted few of these basics, aiming to meet only the essentials for the targeted customer segment rather than covering all potential basic needs.

- **Performance needs**: These features drive satisfaction if implemented well and dissatisfaction if they are lacking. For the MVP, entrepreneurs should focus on a few performance needs that highlight the unique approach to solving the problem, reinforcing the product's core value.

- **Exciters/delighters**: These are unexpected features that bring extra delight to users if included, but their absence does not cause dissatisfaction. For an MVP, entrepreneurs should identify a few selective delighters that showcase the product's unique qualities and differentiate it in the market.

- **Indifferent needs**: These features have little impact on user satisfaction and are generally not noticed by users. Entrepreneurs should avoid prioritizing these during the MVP phase, as they do not contribute meaningfully to the product's value or user experience.

- **Reverse needs**: These features may appeal to one group of users but potentially alienate another. For the MVP phase, entrepreneurs should carefully evaluate and selectively target any reverse needs if they align with the product's position and the specific audience in the TAM. It is better not to include such features unless there are identified users for whom such features are non-negotiable.

RICE

Every entrepreneur faces the challenge of deciding where to focus their limited time, resources, and energy. When multiple opportunities or tasks are vying for attention, it is crucial to have a reliable and objective method for prioritization.

The RICE framework quantifies each initiative using four criteria: reach, impact, confidence, and effort. These criteria are then combined into a single score that ranks tasks or opportunities, making it easier to focus on those that promise the greatest value for the least cost.

Let us look at each component in the coming sections.

Reach

The number of people or events that will be affected by the initiative over a specific period.

This number is always an estimate. To estimate the reach, the entrepreneur should first be clear on the unit to be used to measure the reach. This can be in terms of, say, customers, transactions, or page views. To estimate this, an entrepreneur can use data-driven projections based on market research, customer surveys, or historical trends.

The questions the entrepreneur needs to answer are:

- *Who will be impacted by this initiative?*
- *How many people or events are expected to benefit over a defined time frame?*

Example: If an initiative is expected to reach 1,000 customers in a month, the reach value would be 1,000.

Impact

The potential benefit or change the initiative will bring to those affected, usually rated on a scale.

If there is a way to measure the impact, the entrepreneur should do that. Else, the entrepreneur can use variation of Likert scale we discussed in secondary research of *Chapter 2, Market Analysis and Validation*, like:

- 5 = Massive impact
- 4 = High impact
- 3 = Medium impact
- 2 = Low impact
- 1 = Minimal impact

The questions the entrepreneur needs to answer are:

- *How will this initiative improve customer satisfaction or business outcomes?*
- *Will it significantly address customer pain points or drive conversions?*

Example: If implementing a feature improves customer retention by 30%, it might score a 3 / medium for impact.

Confidence

The level of certainty about the estimates for reach and impact is expressed as a percentage. This is again a very subjective number. Thus, it is important to establish a scale and use it consistently. A suggestion for using this scale is given as follows:

- 100% = Very high confidence as based on solid data, historic trends, or primary research
- 75% = High confidence based on industry references and secondary research
- 50% = Medium confidence as based on prelim or limited research
- 25% = Low confidence based on personal experience and anecdotal information
- 5% = Very low confidence as based on limited or unclear data

The questions the entrepreneur needs to answer are:

- *How reliable is the data supporting reach and impact estimates?*
- *Are there gaps in information that could lower confidence?*

Example: If reach and impact estimates are backed by strong customer surveys and past performance, assign 100%. If based on assumptions or limited data, lower the confidence score.

Effort

The time, resources, or person-hours required to complete the initiative.

A typical way to measure effort is in weeks or person-months (e.g., *5 people for 2 weeks = 2.5 person-weeks*). As this directly translates into the cost of hiring additional help, this is a go-to method for estimating effort. This is commonly used by any vendor offering professional help, like helping to do research or building tech products.

An entrepreneur should include all associated costs, such as external resources or dependencies.

The questions the entrepreneur needs to answer are:

- *What resources will be required to implement this initiative?*
- *Are there any hidden costs or dependencies that might increase the effort score?*

Example: If a task requires a team of 3 people for 2 weeks, effort = 6 person-weeks.

Quantifying using a formula

Any initiative that has higher reach, impact, and confidence should be definitively prioritized higher. This higher reach, impact, and confidence multiply the value of an initiative.

On the other hand, the higher the effort, the higher the cost, and thus, all else being equal, the lower effort initiative should be prioritized.

This leads to a formula for calculating the RICE score, making it easier to focus on those initiatives that promise the greatest value for the least cost:

RICE score= (Reach × Impact × Confidence) / Effort

Meanwhile, Tara is considering three initiatives for her MVP marketplace for local artisans:

- Adding a product recommendation engine.
- Partnering with social media influencers.
- Creating an artisan storytelling feature.

She does a quick RICE analysis, as shown in the following table:

Initiative	Reach	Impact	Confidence	Effort	RICE score
Recommendation engine	500	2	90%	6	150
Social media influencer campaign	1,000	3	80%	10	240
Artisan storytelling feature	300	3	70%	4	157.5

Table 3.1: *Example RICE score calculation*

The social media influencer campaign scores the highest and should be prioritized first, followed by the artisan storytelling feature.

Weighted scoring model

The weighted scoring model (or rubric-based prioritization) helps entrepreneurs evaluate and prioritize items using a set of predefined criteria.

Each criterion reflects the current priorities and focus areas, making it easier to rank tasks or features based on which criteria they align with. In this model, each criterion is assigned a score based on its significance.

For example, consider the criteria, shown in the following table, that an entrepreneur wants to use to prioritize backlog items:

Criteria	Score
Pricing differentiating	2
Product adoption	5
Cost reduction	2
Basic needs /hygiene	3

Table 3.2: *Sample criteria and their scores*

Then, each backlog item is scored on how well it meets those criteria. It is a good practice to keep this list small and ensure the criteria are mutually exclusive. This ensures that assigning the right criteria to each item does not become a time-consuming or hunch-based exercise.

For example, consider the following weightage that an entrepreneur wants to assign to measure how well a backlog item addresses the criteria:

Alignment	Weightage
High	5
Medium	3
Low	1

Table 3.3: Sample weightage

The score is multiplied by the weight, and the resulting value represents the importance rank of the backlog item, as shown in the following table:

Backlog item	Category	Weightage	Rank
Item A	Product adoption (5)	High (5)	*20 (5 * 5)*
Item B	Pricing differentiating (2)	Medium (3)	*6 (2 * 3)*
Item C	Product adoption (5)	Low (1)	*5 (1 * 5)*

Table 3.4: Prioritization using weighted scoring model

Items with higher ranks move up in priority, making it easier for entrepreneurs to focus on the tasks that will have the most significant impact.

This allows for systematic prioritization where there are multiple factors in play and a one-dimensional ranking is not possible. In the example given above, the method makes it possible to prioritize based on two factors, allowing for multi-dimensional ranking.

If priorities shift in the future, a weighted scoring model adapts easily. By assigning new scores to criteria or adjusting the weight of a backlog item, the model recalculates each item's value, automatically readjusting the prioritized backlog to reflect the latest priorities. This flexibility ensures that the backlog remains aligned with changing goals, allowing entrepreneurs to stay responsive to new insights or market conditions.

Buy-a-feature

Entrepreneurs often grapple with the challenge of deciding which features or initiatives to prioritize, especially when there are multiple influential stakeholders with different opinions. The **buy-a-feature** method offers a collaborative and customer-centric approach to prioritization by directly involving stakeholders, such as customers, team members, or investors, in the decision-making process. This method combines insights into customer preferences with a gamified experience to make prioritization both engaging and effective.

The buy-a-feature method asks participants to purchase features or initiatives from a pre-defined list using a limited budget. Each feature is assigned a cost based on its complexity, effort, or estimated value. Participants then allocate their budget to the features they value the most. The results reflect collective preferences, providing clear insights into which features stakeholders prioritize.

Tara wants to decide which features to prioritize for her MVP marketplace for local artisans. She brings back the following advisors:

- *Elisa,* a friend who works for an e-commerce platform, bringing her expertise in online marketplaces and product listings.

- *Lalu,* a logistics/shipping expert she connected with on LinkedIn, who can offer insights into the challenges and opportunities in product delivery.

- *Chandan,* Elisa's colleague, who has experience as a customer support specialist and is currently on a break, providing a perspective on customer interactions and issue resolution.

- *Danish,* a digital marketing specialist, she met at an industry event, who can discuss strategies for promoting artisan products and attracting customers.

- *Pascal,* a student at a leading design school with an interest in packaging and branding, can contribute ideas on how to enhance product presentation and protection during transit.

Tara then prepares the list of initiatives she wants to prioritize, as shown in the following table:

Feature	Cost (in credits)	Description
Product reviews	30	Allow customers to leave and read reviews.
Artisan profiles	50	Showcase artisans' stories and products.
Social media sharing	20	Enable sharing products on social platforms.
Advanced search filters	40	Allow filtering by price, category, or region.
Gift wrapping option	10	Add an option for gift wrapping at checkout.

Table 3.5: Prioritization using buy-a-feature

Each participant gets 100 credits. These were the results of the collaborative exercise:

- **Artisan profiles**: Purchased by two participants by pooling credits.
- **Product reviews**: Purchased by one participant.
- **Social media sharing**: Purchased by two participants.
- **Advanced search filters**: Partially funded but not fully purchased.
- **Gift wrapping option**: Not purchased.

Tara decides to prioritize artisan profiles, product reviews, and social media sharing for the deeper dive, while shelving the other features for future consideration.

Dot voting

Assigning accurate costs to initiatives can be challenging. The **dot voting method** is a simpler alternative to buy-a-feature that helps entrepreneurs and stakeholders to collectively determine the most valuable options to pursue.

Dot voting, sometimes referred to as **sticker voting** or **multi-voting**, is a collaborative decision-making tool. Participants are given a fixed number of dots (votes) to allocate to a list of options, such as features, initiatives, or problem statements. They can distribute their votes across multiple options or concentrate them on a single choice. The options with the most votes are considered the highest priority.

This method is often plagued with popularity bias; participants might be influenced by others' votes. In such scenarios, consider anonymous voting methods if possible. Online collaboration tools like mural offer such capabilities.

Weighted shortest job first

The **weighted shortest job first** (**WSJF**) method offers an entrepreneur a structured way to decide what to work on next. By balancing the potential value of a task against the effort required to complete it, WSJF helps teams make economically sound decisions, ensuring they focus on high-impact work.

WSJF is a prioritization model that evaluates items in a product backlog based on the following two factors:

- **Cost of Delay (CoD)**: The economic impact of delaying a job or feature.
- **Duration**: The time required to complete the job.

Let us look at each component.

CoD

CoD represents the potential loss or missed opportunity if a task or feature is delayed. It considers how important the feature is to the end-user, how urgent it is to deliver the feature or task (for example, is it tied to a specific event or deadline?), and how much the job mitigates risk or creates new opportunities.

The total CoD is typically calculated as:

$$CoD = User\ value + Time\ sensitivity + Risk\ reduction$$

Each component can be rated on a relative scale (e.g., 1-5) to provide a composite score. While this is a subjective point-of-view, it is important to keep this scale consistent across the whole analysis.

Duration

Duration is the estimated time or effort required to complete the job. It is often expressed in story points, person-hours, or any unit that reflects the size or complexity of the work.

Quantifying using a formula

The WSJF score is calculated by dividing the CoD by the duration:

$$WSJF = CoD / Duration$$

Jobs with the highest WSJF score are prioritized, as they provide the greatest value in the shortest time.

Tara's marketplace for local artisans is planning the next set of features to include in its MVP. She is considering deeper dives on:

- **Artisan profiles**: Allows artisans to showcase their work and story.
- **Advanced search filters**: Helps shoppers find products quickly.
- **Customer reviews**: Builds trust by displaying feedback from past buyers.

She arrives at the following WSJF score:

Feature	User value	Time sensitivity	RR/OE	Total CoD	Duration (days)	WSJF score
Artisan profiles	5	4	4	13	5	2.6
Advanced search filters	4	3	2	9	3	3
Customer reviews	3	5	4	12	4	3

Table 3.6: *Prioritization using WSJF*

Based on the WSJF scores, Tara decides to work on advanced search filters and customer reviews first, as they provide the most value relative to the effort required.

Summary of prioritization techniques

Let us compare and contrast the various techniques we have learnt till now:

	Eisenhower Matrix	**Value v/s complexity**	**MosCoW**
Summary	Categorizes in a 2x2 matrix across importance and urgency	Categorizes in a 2x2 matrix across high value and low cost	Categorizes as must have, should have, could have and would not have
Use when	<ul><li>When goal is clear</li><li>When managing workload is the key</li><li>When looking for a simple approach</li></ul>	<ul><li>When goal is clear</li><li>Strategy level decision making</li><li>Visual and easy to understand m ethod</li><li>Stakeholders with varied priorities on few options</li></ul>	<ul><li>When the goal is clear</li><li>Fixed deadline / resources</li><li>MVP or hypothesis testing</li><li>Complex dependencies</li></ul>

Table 3.7: *Comparing Eisenhower Matrix, value v/s complexity, and MoSCoW*

Let us continue to compare and contrast other techniques we have learnt till now, as shown in the following table:

	Kano	RICE	Weighted score model
Summary	Categorizes as basic, performance, exciters, indifferent or reverse	Categorizes as reach, impact, confidence, and effort	Rubrics-based approach
Use when	• Customer-centric • Focus on new features • Balance BAU and new • Competitive market	• Features with varied benefits • Large and scaling user base • Stakeholders with varied priorities • Availability of accurate data	• When goal is clear • Features with varied benefits • Stakeholders with varied priorities • Complex dependencies • Customer-centric • Focus on new features • Balance BAU and new • Competitive but well-known market

Table 3.8: Comparing Kano, RICE, and weighted score model

Continuing to compare and contrast other techniques:

	Buy-a-feature	Dot voting	WSJF
Summary	Limited budget and they buy features using it	Everyone has a vote or few and they vote features	Divide the CoD by the duration (or job size)
Use when	• The key stakeholder has mental image of value, unable to articulate or quantify it and feels they know the value instinctively	• Large group of near-similar customers and lot of near-similar features to choose from	• Prioritizing the backlog based on the economic value and effort required • Availability of accurate data

Table 3.9: Comparing buy-a-feature, dot voting and WSJF

Business opportunity definition

Let us recap the journey the entrepreneur has taken so far:

- **Generated a backlog**: Compiled a backlog of customer needs based on the entrepreneur's vision, insight into the market, and other aspects discussed in *Chapter 2, Market Analysis and Validation*.

- **Prioritized problem statements**: Refined and prioritized a list of problem statements to address, drawing on factors such as passion, industry awareness, network access, and potential impact.

- **Stakeholder identification**: Listed all stakeholders affected by each problem statement, including customers, users, partners, suppliers, and others relevant to the business ecosystem.

- **Developed empathy for stakeholders**: Built empathy for each stakeholder group by understanding their pains, potential gains, thoughts, and feelings related to each problem statement.

- **Mapped the current value stream**: Created a Value Stream Map to capture the current (as-is) process, revealing opportunities for improvement and gaps to address.

- **Defined the TAM**: Estimated the TAM for each problem statement, giving a sense of the total revenue opportunity if every potential customer were served.

- **Segmented the market**: Identified and analyzed various customer segments within the TAM, refining the focus for more targeted solutions.

- **Established the SAM**: Narrowed down from the TAM to the SAM by homing in on the segments that are realistically reachable based on resources, positioning, and relevance.

- **Analyzed market trends**: Studied trends at the intersection of the SAM and the problem statement, identifying patterns, shifts, and emerging opportunities that could impact strategy.

- **Assessed the competitive landscape**: Examined the competitive environment to understand how other players are addressing the problem for the SAM, pinpointing strengths to avoid challenging head-on and gaps that offer opportunities.

- **Reviewed legal, regulatory, and compliance factors**: Identified relevant legal, regulatory, and compliance requirements specific to the SAM and the problem statement, ensuring the venture aligns with industry standards.

- **Validated demand**: Tested demand for a solution addressing the problem statement within the SAM, using feedback and data to confirm the viability of the market and customer interest.

At this stage, the entrepreneur has gathered a set of opportunities, each with its own potential to transform into a successful venture. However, to move forward effectively, it is essential to narrow this focus to a single, well-defined business opportunity that will form the foundation for the MVP. This convergence process ensures that the entrepreneur is concentrating resources and energy on the opportunity with the strongest fit, highest impact, and clearest path to market.

By focusing on one core opportunity, the entrepreneur maximizes the chances of creating a product that resonates deeply with the target audience, addresses a significant pain point, and stands out in the competitive landscape. This clarity will guide the MVP's development, helping to validate assumptions and build a product with strong market alignment.

Defining the opportunity

A business opportunity is a set of circumstances that enables an entrepreneur to introduce a product or service to the market with the potential to solve a problem, fulfill a need, or meet a demand. Identifying and clearly articulating this opportunity reflects the entrepreneur's vision for creating value for a specific audience in a way that aligns with market demands and generates profit.

By defining a business opportunity thoughtfully, an entrepreneur shows readiness for the journey of building a successful business, not just launching a website or an app.

Here are the key aspects to understand and evaluate:

- **Problem statement**: The foundation of any business opportunity is a clear, well-defined problem statement. This outlines the primary challenge or pain point the target audience is facing. By articulating the problem accurately, the entrepreneur sets a focused direction for product development and ensures alignment with real customer needs.

- **Key stakeholders**: Identifying the stakeholders involved is crucial, as they play different roles in the ecosystem surrounding the opportunity. Stakeholders may include customers, users, partners, suppliers, investors, and even regulatory bodies. Understanding their interests, pain points, and motivations can inform product design, marketing, and partnership strategies.

- **As-is key Value Stream Map**: A Value Stream Map of the current process helps visualize how value flows from one stage to another and where inefficiencies or bottlenecks occur. By mapping the existing flow, the entrepreneur can pinpoint areas where their solution can add significant value, streamline operations, or address unmet needs.

- **SAM**: Understanding the SAM means evaluating the subset of the TAM that is actually accessible to the entrepreneur, considering current limitations such as geography, resources, and business model constraints. This ensures that the opportunity being pursued has a feasible and reachable market with realistic potential for adoption.

- **Gaps in competitive landscape**: Examining the competitive landscape and identifying gaps allows the entrepreneur to find areas where their solution can offer a unique advantage. Whether these gaps stem from underserved segments, unmet customer needs, or weaknesses in competitors' offerings, this insight helps craft a differentiated product with a strong value proposition.

- **Legal and regulatory considerations**: Every business opportunity operates within certain legal and regulatory boundaries. It is essential to assess these early to avoid compliance issues that could hinder product development or market entry. Understanding relevant regulations also ensures the entrepreneur is prepared for industry-specific requirements that could affect product design or delivery.

- **Hypothesis of value to customers**: Formulating a clear hypothesis about the value the product will deliver helps align the entire team around a shared understanding of the product's purpose. This hypothesis should capture how the solution alleviates the identified pain point, improves customers' experiences, or brings added benefits. This initial hypothesis serves as a guiding beacon to be validated through customer feedback and testing.

Ensuring optimal timing

In Silicon Valley, they often say there is a massive graveyard of startups that were simply ahead of their time. While prioritizing the right problem statement is essential, choosing the right timing to address it can be just as critical to an entrepreneur's success.

Tackling a problem too early—before the market or supporting infrastructure is ready will require significant resources, as new market development requires huge marketing budget and investment to set up distribution. On the other hand, waiting too long risks losing customers to competitors or missing the peak of market demand entirely. Finding the right moment is key to maximizing impact and ensuring a lasting foothold in the market.

To ensure the optimal timing for each prioritized problem, entrepreneurs can consider several factors:

- **Market readiness**: Gauge whether the market is prepared for the solution. If a market or segment shows growing demand or urgent need for a solution, addressing it early can be advantageous. Market trends, customer adoption rates, and competitor activity can offer cues on whether to act now or wait for further demand.

- **Customer urgency**: Problems that represent immediate pain points for customers should take precedence. If a solution could quickly alleviate a high-priority need or significantly improve customer experience, then timing it right to capture customer interest can be highly rewarding. Customer interviews, surveys, and feedback loops can provide insight into urgency.

- **Strategic fit and growth**: Align problem-solving efforts with the startup's growth opportunities. For example, during the early stages, the focus might be on foundational features (must haves), while subsequent releases can address enhancement features (should haves) and differentiators (delighters). As the startup grows, priorities may shift towards competitive differentiation and innovation, but early timing for these can disrupt focus if not aligned with the growth phase.

- **Competitive landscape**: Analyze competitor moves and market shifts to determine if immediate action is required. If a competitor is addressing a similar problem or making gains in the market, it may be wise to prioritize that problem to prevent losing market share. However, lack of competition should not be looked at as a good thing. It might be an indication that either the opportunity in this space is very less, the failure rate is very high, or the cost of solving the problem is high.

Validating internal fitment

In the entrepreneurial journey, there is often a strong emphasis on external factors—customers, market dynamics, and competition. However, an entrepreneur also needs to ensure an internal alignment to truly maximize their potential for success.

Internal fitment requires assessing the team's current capabilities, readiness to embrace feedback, and resilience in facing setbacks. As part of this continuous learning process, deeply held beliefs may be challenged, which can be particularly tough for those with prior successes. Established working and mental models may no longer apply, making the ability to unlearn and relearn a critical skill.

Some problems may also demand significant funding or an expanded workforce capacity, which means they may need to be deferred until the necessary resources are in place. Planning for phased investment and team scaling can help ensure that resources align with when each issue needs to be tackled.

By factoring in these internal considerations, an entrepreneur can make more strategic choices as they narrow down and commit to a business opportunity.

Opportunity scoring model

Opportunity prioritization involves multiple factors, making the weighted scoring model an effective framework to guide this process. Entrepreneurs should consider the following aspects when evaluating and scoring an opportunity.

When defining an opportunity, ensuring optimal timing, and validating internal fitment, entrepreneurs can use a set of considerations tailored to their specific situation. These considerations can be weighted according to their relative importance, as not all will carry the same impact. Each factor can be rated, with the best-case scenario receiving a higher score and the worst-case scenario the lowest. To calculate the final score, multiply each consideration's score by its weight, then sum the results. The following table is a template for opportunity scoring:

Consideration	Consideration weightage (sample values)	Criteria score (sample values)	Opportunity 1 Score	Opportunity 2 Score
Problem statement	High (5)	Very clear (5) Somewhat clear (3) Not clear (1)		
Key stakeholders	Medium (3)	Accessible (5) Need to network (3) Inaccessible (1)		

As-is key Value Stream Map	Medium (3)	Available with issues identified (5) Available with issues somewhat identified (3) High-level version available (1)		
SAM	Medium (3)	Very large (5) Large (3) Limited (1)		
Gaps in the competitive landscape	High (5)	Very large (5) Large (3) Limited (1)		
Legal and regulatory landscape	High (5)	Limited (5) Large (3) Very large (1)		
Value hypothesis	High (5)	Very clear (5) Somewhat clear (3) Not clear (1)		
Market readiness	High (5)	Ripe (5) Needs effort (3) Not ready (1)		
Customer urgency	High (5)	High (5) Medium (3) Low (1)		
Strategic fit and growth potential	Low (1)	High (5) Medium (3) Low (1)		
Team readiness	High (5)	High (5) Medium (3) Low (1)		
Funding	High (5)	Sufficient (5) Needs Boost (3) None (1)		
Rank (sample values)			*Sum of (score * weightage)*	*Sum of (score * weightage)*

Table 3.10: Rubric for opportunity scoring model

Opportunity scoring model helps an entrepreneur prioritize opportunities by picking the highest scoring opportunity first.

After careful consideration and informed by the weighted score model, Tara has identified the business opportunity she wants to pursue and build an MVP around, as shown in the following table:

Consideration	Consideration weightage	Criteria score	Lack of marketplaces for local artisans, focusing on online customers	Lack of marketplaces for local artisans, focusing on supporters
			Score	Score
Problem statement	High (5)	Very clear (5) Somewhat clear (3) Not clear (1)	5	5
Key stakeholders	Medium (3)	Accessible (5) Need to network (3) Inaccessible (1)	5	3
As-is key Value Stream Map	Medium (3)	Available with issues identified (5) Available with issues somewhat identified (3) High-level version available (1)	5	3
SAM	Medium (3)	Very large (5) Large (3) Limited (1)	5	5
Gaps in the competitive landscape	High (5)	Very large (5) Large (3) Limited (1)	1	1
Legal and regulatory landscape	High (5)	Limited (5) Large (3) Very large (1)	5	3
Value hypothesis	High (5)	Very clear (5) Somewhat clear (3) Not clear (1)	3	1
Market readiness	High (5)	Ripe (5) Needs Effort (3) Not Ready (1)	3	3
Customer urgency	High (5)	High (5) Medium (3) Low (1)	3	3

Strategic fit and growth potential	Low (1)	High (5) Medium (3) Low (1)	5	3
Team readiness	High (5)	High (5) Medium (3) Low (1)	5	5
Funding	High (5)	Sufficient (5) Needs Boost (3) None (1)	5	5
Rank			200	166

Table 3.11: Tara's rubric for opportunity scoring model

With an eye toward investor meetings and early team building, she has crafted a document that clearly outlines her vision. This document is designed not only to serve as her guide but also to attract a few potential recruits as early employees, helping them understand the business's core and mission.

- **Problem statement**: *Lack of marketplaces for local artisans.*

  Tara has identified a significant gap in the market where local artisans struggle to reach a broader audience. This opportunity is built around creating a platform that bridges this gap, enabling artisans to showcase their work and allowing customers to discover unique, handmade products.

- **Key stakeholders**: The following are the key stakeholders:

  o **Customers**: Online shoppers looking for distinctive, artisan-made products.

  o **Users**: Local artisans seeking better avenues to sell their work.

  o **Regulatory support**: **Chartered accountant (CA)** to ensure compliance with tax and regulatory standards.

  o **Suppliers**: Contacts in packaging and logistics, which are crucial for a seamless delivery experience.

  o **Partners**: Connections within e-commerce platforms to potentially extend reach.

  o **Influencers**: Social media influencers whom Tara knows personally, who could help generate awareness.

- **As-is key Value Stream Map**: With input from a working group, which she formed earlier, Tara has developed an initial Value Stream Map. This map captures the current processes, from artisan creation to product delivery, highlighting key pain points that her marketplace could resolve.

- **SAM**: Tara is targeting India's upper and middle-class demographics, specifically individuals aged 25-54 in metropolitan and urban areas. This group includes young professionals, parents, and retirees who are willing to try new things and appreciate quality craftsmanship. Based on an annual ARPU of *INR 3,174*, she estimates a SAM of *INR 25,435 crores* annually, demonstrating the sizeable potential for growth.

- **Gaps in the competitive landscape**: While most marketplaces focus on mass-produced goods, they often miss the appeal of unique, handmade products. Tara sees an opportunity for a specialized marketplace that not only features local artisan goods but also emphasizes storytelling, authenticity, and uniqueness—qualities that resonate with her target audience.

- **Legal and regulatory landscape**: Through discussions with her CA and a legal consultant, Tara has ensured that her venture will be compliant with all necessary regulations. This foresight allows her to confidently move forward, knowing that the business is built on a solid legal foundation.

- **Value hypothesis**: *Enable online shoppers to discover unique, handmade products from local artisans with confidence in authenticity, reliable delivery, and a high-quality experience.*

  Tara believes this platform will attract customers by providing an authentic, quality-driven shopping experience that connects them directly to artisans.

- **Market readiness**: Survey results indicate strong support for her hypothesis: *At least 20% of online shoppers visiting the platform will make a purchase within the first three months, with customers willing to pay a 10% premium for guaranteed authenticity, and handmade craftsmanship.* This data gives her confidence that there is real demand for her solution.

- **Customer urgency**: With the upcoming festival season and existing interest from potential buyers even before the platform launch, Tara sees a timely opportunity. The demand for authentic, artisan-made products is growing, and her marketplace is positioned to meet that need.

- **Strategic fit and growth potential**: The estimated SAM of *INR 25,435 crores* annually offers Tara ample room for growth and scalability, reinforcing her vision of a sustainable business that can expand over time.

- **Team readiness**: Tara is currently in discussions with experienced technologists who have a background in scaling startups, as well as young, motivated individuals ready to wear multiple hats in the early stages. She is confident that her network will provide access to early adopters and valuable industry insights, further strengthening her team.

- **Funding**: With sufficient seed funding, Tara is well-prepared to build an MVP that will validate the business model, generate early revenue, and establish a positive cash flow.

With thorough analysis and a clear plan, Tara is ready to dive into this opportunity and start building her MVP. Her well-rounded approach, combined with data-driven decisions, sets a strong foundation for success.

On a personal front, Tara continuously evaluates the urgency and importance of each task to decide whether she should tackle it immediately, schedule it for later, delegate it, or even remove it from her to-do list altogether.

Actions for the entrepreneur

The following actionable steps are recommended to help entrepreneurs apply the key concepts covered in this chapter:

1. Based on insights from the previous chapter, fully define the opportunity presented by the prioritized problem statement.

2. If the problem statement presents multiple opportunities, use the opportunity scoring model to determine the most viable one to pursue.

Conclusion

By leveraging structured frameworks like the Eisenhower Matrix, value-complexity matrix, MoSCoW method, and weighted scoring model, entrepreneurs now have a clear pathway to focus on high-impact initiatives that align with their goals and market needs. With these techniques, entrepreneurs should move beyond relying on gut instincts or being swayed by the loudest voices in the room. Moving forward, entrepreneurs should adopt the habit of regularly revisiting their prioritization frameworks as circumstances evolve. By embracing this disciplined approach, entrepreneurs will be better equipped to allocate their resources effectively, tackle high-priority challenges, and accelerate towards bringing MVP to the market.

In the next chapter, we will explore how, for a problem statement, one can ideate for a solution. We will also use the prioritization techniques used here to decide which solution idea to follow up on.

Join our Discord space

Join our Discord workspace for latest updates, offers, tech happenings around the world, new releases, and sessions with the authors:

https://discord.bpbonline.com

Section 2:
Solutions

CHAPTER 4
Ideation and Solution Generation

Introduction

Once the entrepreneur has prioritized the right problem and business opportunity, the next step is to generate innovative and practical solutions. Ideation is a critical phase that transforms opportunities into actionable plans, bridging the gap between identifying what needs to be solved and determining how to address it. Effective ideation involves structured brainstorming and problem-solving techniques, fostering creativity while ensuring that solutions are both feasible and impactful. For many entrepreneurs, ideation can be an intimidating step. It might seem like some people have a magical ability to conjure brilliant ideas out of thin air. On the other hand, many entrepreneurs start their journey with a preconceived solution in mind and often become overly attached to their initial idea. This attachment can lead to a reluctance to critically assess or evolve the idea in the light of new insights from discovery and prioritization efforts. Instead of adapting to what they have learned, they may unconsciously adjust their discovery and prioritization to fit their original concept. This inability to iterate, re-think, or modify their solution is frequently cited as one of the primary reasons startups fail.

This chapter equips entrepreneurs with the tools and methods needed to generate, refine, and evaluate solutions effectively. It emphasizes the importance of leveraging market insights, customer needs, and competition analysis to develop an effective solution.

Structure

In this chapter, we will cover the following topics:

- Ideation frameworks
- Double Diamond approach
- Design thinking
- Idea Canvas
- Ecosystem Mapping Canvas
- Ideation techniques
- Six Thinking Hats
- How Might We technique
- Mind Mapping
- Legal, compliance, and regulatory review
- Risk analysis
- SWOT analysis
- PESTEL analysis
- Actions for entrepreneurs

Objectives

By the end of this chapter, entrepreneurs will have gained the skills to generate innovative and practical solutions through structured ideation techniques such as the Double Diamond approach, Mind Mapping, SCAMPER, Six Thinking Hats, and the How Might We method. They will learn how to conduct effective brainstorming sessions and lean workshops, whether in-person, remote, or asynchronous, and utilize tools like the Idea Canvas to refine their concepts. Entrepreneurs will also develop the ability to draw insights from market trends, competition analysis, and customer feedback while considering the broader ecosystem to enhance their solutions. Finally, they will be equipped to assess and deal with risks associated with their ideas, including technical, market, legal, compliance, and execution risks, ensuring their solutions are both innovative and viable.

Ideation frameworks

Ideation is the creative process of generating, developing, and refining solutions to address a problem statement. It encompasses brainstorming, hypothesizing potential solutions, validating ideas, and problem-solving to explore viable strategies or innovations for an identified challenge or opportunity. This phase is crucial in disciplines like product development, design thinking, and business strategy. For entrepreneurs, ideation is a pivotal step in the journey toward building a MVP, bridging the gap between identifying customer pain points and crafting actionable, impactful solutions.

Ideation is not about finding the right idea immediately but about exploring possibilities and gradually refining them into effective and practical solutions.

There are multiple frameworks entrepreneurs can follow to organize brainstorming.

Double Diamond approach

The Double Diamond approach to ideation, developed by the *British Design Council*[1], is a structured framework for solving problems creatively and systematically.

It consists of four phases divided into two diamonds: discover, define, develop, and deliver. The process is visually represented as:

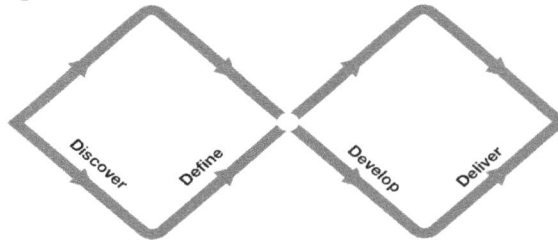

Figure 4.1: The Double Diamond by the Design Council (CC BY 4.0 license)

Here is how this approach can be applied to arrive at a solution to the identified opportunity or problem statement.

Discover

The goal of this phase is to explore and gather as much information as possible about the problem space. Entrepreneurs can use this phase to deeply understand the business problem, customer needs, and market dynamics. This phase is covered in *Chapter 1, Understanding Customer Pain Points* and *Chapter 2, Market Analysis and Validation.*

To recap, this phase requires the entrepreneur to conduct both primary and secondary research, such as interviews, surveys, and competitive analysis. By leveraging tools like Empathy Maps, Customer Journey Maps, and Value Stream Maps, they can gain a deeper understanding of customer pain points and workflows. Additionally, gathering insights from key stakeholders— including customers, partners, and internal teams- helps to paint a comprehensive picture of the problem space. Finally, identifying trends, behaviors, and barriers in the market provides valuable context for shaping solutions.

1 "Home." Design Council - Design for Planet, **www.designcouncil.org.uk/our-resources/the-double-diamond**. Accessed 03 Jan. 2025.

Define

This phase refines the focus by synthesizing the insights collected during the discovery phase into a well-defined and actionable problem statement. By analyzing data from customer research, stakeholder feedback, and market trends, the entrepreneur can distill complex findings into a single, prioritized challenge to address. This process ensures that the identified problem aligns with both customer needs and business goals, serving as a solid foundation for developing effective solutions. The methodologies involved in this phase are partially covered in *Chapter 3, Opportunity Prioritization*.

To recap, this phase requires the entrepreneur to analyze the collected information, identifying patterns or recurring themes that reveal underlying customer needs or challenges. From this analysis, a hypothesis problem statement is framed, capturing the essence of the issue to be addressed. The problem statement is then validated by cross-checking it against customer and market insights to ensure its relevance and alignment with real-world data. This structured approach helps ensure that the entrepreneur focuses on solving a problem that genuinely matters to their target audience.

Develop

The second diamond begins at this stage, shifting the focus to ideation and brainstorming potential solutions. This phase is characterized by creativity, exploration, and experimentation as entrepreneurs generate and refine ideas to address the defined problem statement. It encourages thinking beyond conventional boundaries, leveraging diverse perspectives and structured methodologies to uncover innovative possibilities. In this chapter, we will delve extensively into techniques and frameworks tailored for this phase, equipping entrepreneurs with the tools to approach solution generation systematically and effectively.

Deliver

This phase emphasizes refining and selecting the most viable solution(s) for testing and implementation. It involves critically evaluating the generated ideas to ensure they align with business objectives, address customer needs effectively, and are feasible within the given constraints of resources, time, and market conditions. The focus is on narrowing down options to those with the highest potential impact and likelihood of success. In the upcoming chapters, we will explore this process in detail, including techniques for solution validation, prioritization, and planning for implementation, enabling entrepreneurs to move forward with confidence and clarity.

To understand the phases, we will discuss a report prepared by Tara to summarize the insights and progress achieved so far, as requested by a potential investor. It provided a comprehensive overview of the research, analysis, and strategic decisions undertaken, highlighting the learning and direction of the venture to date.

Here is the report:

To provide a clear overview of Tara's entrepreneurial journey, this report uses the Double Diamond approach—a widely adopted framework for problem-solving and innovation. This approach is divided into four phases: discover, define, develop, and deliver. So far, her work has focused on the discover and define phases, ensuring a strong foundation for building an MVP that addresses a validated market need:

- **Phase 1: Discover**: The discover phase is about exploring the problem space, gaining a deep understanding of the stakeholders, and identifying the pain points. Tara's efforts in this phase involved extensive research and stakeholder engagement, summarized as follows:

  o **Problem exploration**: **Problem statement identified**: *Lack of marketplaces for local artisans.*

    - Artisans face significant challenges in reaching a broad customer base.

    - Online shoppers struggle to find authentic, handmade products from local artisans.

  o **Stakeholder identification**: Tara categorized stakeholders into five key groups to ensure a comprehensive understanding of the ecosystem:

    - **Customers**: Online shoppers looking for unique, handmade products.

    - **Users**: Local artisans seeking access to broader markets.

    - **Regulatory support**: CAs to ensure compliance.

    - **Suppliers**: Packaging and logistics providers critical for reliable delivery.

    - **Partners and influencers**: E-commerce platforms and social media influencers to amplify reach.

  o **Primary research**:

    - Conducted interviews and surveys with online shoppers and local artisans.

    - Created Empathy Maps for both online shoppers and artisans to understand their emotions, thoughts, actions, and pain points.

  o **Secondary research**:

    - Analyzed market trends, existing marketplaces (e.g., Amazon Karigar), and competitive gaps.

    - Studied the legal and regulatory landscape to ensure compliance.

  o **Key insights from the discovery phase**:

    - Online shoppers seek authenticity, quality, and convenience when purchasing handmade goods but face challenges such as trust and reliability in existing marketplaces.

- Local artisans struggle with visibility, logistics, and sustainable income streams due to the lack of a dedicated platform for showcasing their work.

- The competitive landscape lacks platforms emphasizing unique, handmade products with a focus on storytelling and quality assurance.

- **Phase 2: Define**: The define phase focuses on synthesizing the insights gained during the discover phase into clear, actionable problem statements and priorities.

  o **Synthesizing insights**: Using tools like Empathy Maps and Customer Journey Maps, Tara distilled recurring patterns:

    - Customers value authenticity, storytelling, and quality.

    - Artisans need accessible tools and reliable support to scale their sales online.

  o **Problem statement defined**: *Create a marketplace that enables local artisans to connect directly with online shoppers, addressing issues of authenticity, quality assurance, and logistical support.*

  o **SAM**:

    - Targeting India's urban and upper-middle-class demographic aged 25-54.

    - Estimated SAM is INR 25,435 crores annually, based on an ARPU of INR 3,174.

  o **Competitive gaps**:

    - Most marketplaces focus on mass-produced goods.

    - Lack of platforms that emphasize storytelling, authenticity, and the unique appeal of handmade goods.

  o **Validation of the opportunity**:

    - **Hypothesis of value defined**: *At least 20% of online shoppers visiting the platform will make a purchase within three months, with customers willing to pay a 10% premium for guaranteed authenticity.*

      Initial survey results align with this hypothesis, confirming both demand and customer willingness to pay a premium.

- **Next steps**: **Develop and deliver**: While the discover and define phases have laid a strong foundation, the next steps will focus on generating innovative solutions (develop) and building and testing the MVP (deliver).

- **Conclusion**: The Double Diamond approach has ensured a systematic, thorough exploration and definition of the business opportunity. By focusing on real customer pain points and leveraging data-driven insights, Tara has identified a significant gap in the market with a clear path forward.

Design thinking

Design thinking is a human-centered, iterative, often non-linear approach to problem-solving and innovation that emphasizes understanding user needs, generating creative solutions, and testing them in a real-world context.

The term itself gained prominence through the work of *Herbert A. Simon*, who introduced the concept of design as a way of thinking in his 1969 book, *The Sciences of the Artificial*. *Simon* proposed that design is a creative process focused on improving existing conditions toward desired outcomes[2].

In the 1980s and 1990s, *IDEO*, a global design and innovation firm, popularized the framework as a formalized approach to innovation. *IDEO's* co-founder, *David Kelley*, and other practitioners advocated for a design-driven methodology that prioritized empathy, creativity, and rapid iteration. This approach resonated with both businesses and academia, laying the groundwork for design thinking's widespread adoption.

Design thinking provides a structured framework that entrepreneurs can follow to move from a vague idea to a fully realized, user-centered product. This journey starts with the simplest tools and gradually evolves into high-fidelity prototypes and, ultimately, a working product.

In the early stages, entrepreneurs often rely on basic, low-fidelity methods like pen and paper sketches or hand-drawn wireframes. These lo-fi approaches allow for quick exploration and testing of ideas without committing significant resources. Over time, these sketches evolve into clickable PDFs or static wireframes, allowing for basic navigation and flow testing. As ideas become clearer and feedback is incorporated, these designs progress to clickable pages with layouts and rudimentary interactions, eventually leading to high-fidelity prototypes. These prototypes offer near-realistic experiences, bridging the gap between conceptualization and implementation. Finally, the iterative process culminates in a fully functional MVP, validated through real-world inputs.

Let us understand the five phases of design thinking, which are also shown in the following figure:

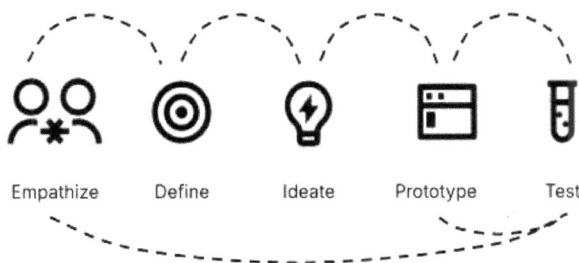

Figure 4.2: *Design thinking*

---

2 Dam, Rikke Friis, and Teo Yu Siang. "The history of design thinking." The Interaction Design Foundation, 3 Jan. 2025, **www.interaction-design.org/literature/article/design-thinking-get-a-quick-overview-of-the-history**.

Empathize

The empathize phase is the cornerstone of design thinking. It centers on gaining a deep understanding of users by engaging directly with them to uncover their needs, experiences, and challenges. This phase is rooted in a human-centered approach, ensuring that solutions are not only innovative but also deeply aligned with real-world problems.

Empathy allows entrepreneurs to step into their users' shoes, moving beyond assumptions and preconceived notions to uncover genuine pain points. By prioritizing user experiences, entrepreneurs can design solutions that resonate on a practical and emotional level, building trust and relevance.

Key tools like Empathy Maps and Value Stream Maps play a critical role in organizing insights. These visual representations help entrepreneurs capture the user's emotions, actions, and pain points at each stage of their journey, creating a comprehensive understanding of the problem space.

This phase is extensively covered in *Chapter 1, Understanding Customer Pain Points,* and *Chapter 2, Market Analysis and Validation.* Together, these chapters equip entrepreneurs with the tools and techniques to conduct meaningful research and lay the groundwork for informed decision-making.

Define

The define phase narrows the focus by synthesizing insights from the empathize phase into a clear, actionable problem statement. This is a critical step where observations are distilled in meaningful direction, often articulated through How Might We questions.

Defining the problem correctly ensures that the team is solving the right challenge. Without a clear problem statement, efforts risk being misaligned, wasting time and resources on solutions that fail to address the core issue. Additionally, this phase fosters collaboration, integrating diverse perspectives from cross-functional teams to enrich understanding and refine the problem scope.

For example, a problem statement for Tara's marketplace might be:

How Might We enable local artisans to sell their handmade goods online while ensuring a seamless experience for buyers?

Methodologies for this phase are partially addressed in *Chapter 2, Market Analysis and Validation,* and *Chapter 3, Opportunity Prioritization,* and will be further explored in this chapter, ensuring that entrepreneurs can define problems with clarity and precision.

Ideate

The ideate phase is where creativity flourishes. Entrepreneurs brainstorm, explore, and develop a wide range of potential solutions to the defined problem statement. Ideation fosters exploration and innovation. By generating a diverse range of ideas, entrepreneurs increase the likelihood of uncovering breakthrough solutions that address user needs effectively.

Prototype

Prototyping is the process of transforming abstract ideas into tangible, testable representations, enabling entrepreneurs to explore and refine how potential solutions might work in practice.

This phase serves as a critical bridge between ideation and implementation, providing a practical medium for testing concepts, gathering user feedback, and iterating quickly, all without committing substantial resources upfront.

The process typically begins with low-fidelity methods, such as hand-drawn sketches or rough outlines on paper. These lo-fi prototypes are invaluable for capturing initial feedback and making swift adjustments. As the concept matures, it transitions to digital tools, such as clickable PDFs, which allow for basic flow and navigation testing. Over time, these prototypes evolve into more detailed designs with layouts and interactivity, eventually culminating in high-fidelity prototypes that mimic the functionality and experience of a fully developed tech product.

This iterative approach ensures continuous learning and refinement, helping entrepreneurs align their solutions with user needs while minimizing risks and resource waste.

Test

The test phase focuses on sharing prototypes with users to gather actionable feedback and iteratively refine solutions. This critical step ensures that the proposed solution aligns with user needs, expectations, and pain points.

Testing provides invaluable insights that guide refinements, improving the solution's usability and effectiveness while increasing its likelihood of success. The feedback collected during this phase informs adjustments to prototypes and can even prompt a reevaluation of earlier phases, such as ideation or definition, creating a continuous improvement cycle. This iterative process allows entrepreneurs to validate changes, address shortcomings, and align their solutions more closely with market and user demands.

Idea Canvas

Many promising ideas fail to evolve into viable solutions—not due to a lack of potential, but because they are inadequately expressed, insufficiently analyzed, or poorly articulated. To address these challenges, the Idea Canvas[3] provides entrepreneurs with a structured and comprehensive framework for idea development. This structured approach helps entrepreneurs transform initial sparks of inspiration into robust, well-validated concepts, ready for presentation, collaboration, and execution. By ensuring that every facet of an idea is

---

3 Product Life Cycle Untangled: The Art and Science of Building Products. N.p., Notion Press, 2024.

thoughtfully addressed, the Idea Canvas increases the likelihood of success in turning ideas into impactful solutions.

The Idea Canvas serves as a step-by-step guide, enabling entrepreneurs to systematically refine their ideas, as shown in the following figure:

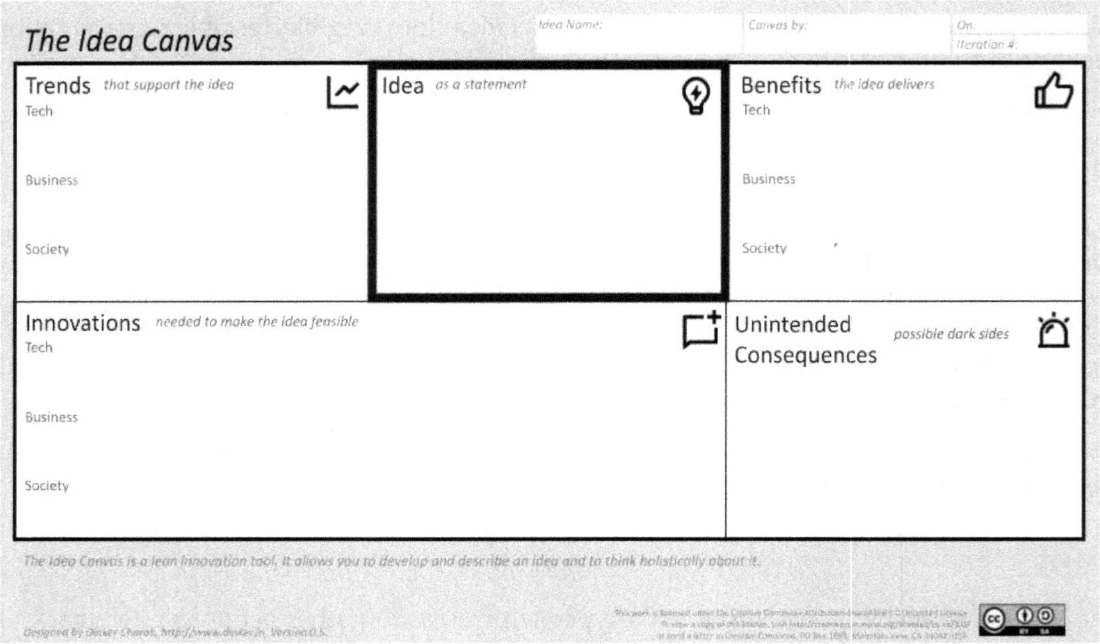

Figure 4.3: *Idea Canvas*

The various sections of the Idea Canvas are outlined in the upcoming section.

Idea as a statement

This section captures the essence of the idea in a succinct, one-line description. It forms the foundation for the subsequent exploration and is a critical starting point for building clarity and focus.

Example: `A platform connecting local artisans with urban buyers to promote handmade goods.`

Trends supporting the idea

Ideas do not exist in isolation—they thrive in the context of trends. This section identifies external factors across three key areas that validate the idea's relevance and feasibility:

- **Tech trends**: Recent technological advancements or innovations that make the idea viable.

Example: The proliferation of e-commerce platforms and digital payment systems supports online marketplaces.

- **Business trends**: Market dynamics, emerging startups, or innovative business models that align with the idea.

  Example: Growing consumer demand for sustainable, locally sourced products.

- **Social trends**: Changes in societal behaviors or values that resonate with the idea.

  Example: A rising preference for supporting local communities and artisanal craftsmanship.

Benefits the idea delivers

This section analyzes the tangible and intangible values the idea can generate across three dimensions:

- **Benefits to tech**: How the idea advances technology or supports technical teams.

  Example: Introducing advanced logistics algorithms to optimize artisan product delivery.

- **Benefits to business**: How the idea impacts revenue, cost efficiency, or operational processes.

  Example: Providing artisans with direct market access, reducing intermediary costs, and boosting sales.

- **Benefits to society**: Broader societal implications and value.

  Example: Promoting cultural heritage and improving the livelihoods of local artisans.

Some ideas require new developments or innovations to become reality. This section explores:

- **Innovations in tech**: Technological breakthroughs or improvements necessary for implementation.

  Example: Developing AI-driven authentication systems to verify the authenticity of handmade goods.

- **Innovations in business**: Strategic models or operational changes needed for execution.

  Example: Creating monetization model such as subscription models for regular buyers to ensure steady artisan income.

- **Innovations in society**: Shifts in societal acceptance or practices required for the idea's success.

  Example: Encouraging consumers to prioritize handmade products over mass-produced alternatives.

Unintended consequences

No innovation is without risks. This section anticipates potential negative outcomes or challenges to mitigate.

Example: `Could the platform unintentionally drive up artisan product prices, making them inaccessible to geographically local buyers? Could demand exceed supply, leading to scalability issues?`

The following Idea Canvas provides a structured, multi-dimensional view of Tara's concept, offering a well-rounded basis for discussions with investors, potential collaborators, and early team members:

Section	Details
Idea as a statement	Build a specialized online marketplace connecting local artisans with customers seeking unique, handmade products, focusing on authenticity and storytelling.
Trends supporting the idea	
Tech trends	Growth of e-commerce and digital payment solutions; increased adoption of AI for personalized recommendations and fraud detection.
Business trends	Rising demand for niche, curated marketplaces; shift toward sustainability and locally sourced products.
Social trends	Consumers increasingly value supporting small businesses and preserving cultural heritage through traditional crafts.
Benefits the idea delivers	
Benefits to tech	Opportunity to innovate with features like AI-based product authenticity verification and seamless logistics integration.
Benefits to business	Creation of a differentiated marketplace that targets an underserved niche, driving customer loyalty and enhancing revenue potential.
Benefits to society	Economic empowerment of local artisans, preservation of traditional craftsmanship, and encouragement of sustainable consumer behaviors.
Innovations needed for feasibility	
Innovations in tech	Development of an authenticity verification system; building a user-friendly platform with optimized search and discovery features.
Innovations in business	Formulation of a fair pricing model that ensures equitable artisan compensation while remaining competitive for customers.
Innovations in society	Campaigns to educate consumers about the cultural and economic importance of artisan-made goods; partnerships to enhance artisan digital literacy.

Section	Details
Unintended consequences	
Tech consequences	Over-reliance on technology may exclude artisans with limited digital access; potential cybersecurity and data privacy concerns.
Business consequences	High operational costs for logistics and quality assurance if not managed efficiently; risk of diluting the uniqueness of artisan products through scaling.
Social consequences	Over-commercialization could erode the cultural significance of artisan products; potential exploitation if fair trade practices are not enforced.

Table 4.1: *Tara's Idea Canvas*

Ecosystem Mapping Canvas

An ecosystem encompasses the interconnected network of products, services, technologies, and stakeholders that currently address or influence a specific problem statement. It includes not only direct competitors but also complementary offerings, substitute solutions, and adjacent innovations that collectively define the market dynamics around the identified challenge.

The ecosystem provides critical insights into customer preferences, technological advancements, competitive landscapes, and potential barriers to entry. For entrepreneurs, understanding this ecosystem is pivotal in gaining a comprehensive view of the environment in which their MVP must thrive.

By thoroughly analyzing the ecosystem, entrepreneurs can uncover gaps, identify opportunities to leverage existing strengths, and design solutions that not only address the core problem but also align with existing market structures. This reduces friction, ensuring their solution integrates seamlessly into the broader landscape and delivers meaningful value to stakeholders.

Here is how understanding the ecosystem specifically helps entrepreneurs with solutioning:

- **Unmet needs**: By analyzing existing products, entrepreneurs can identify gaps where current solutions fall short or fail to address specific customer needs. These gaps represent opportunities to innovate and offer better alternatives.

- **Overlooked features**: Understanding the ecosystem helps pinpoint features or use cases that competitors may have overlooked, allowing entrepreneurs to differentiate their offerings.

- **Preventing reinvention**: By studying the ecosystem, entrepreneurs can avoid duplicating features or services already offered by competitors, focusing instead on unique value propositions.

- **Leveraging existing solutions**: Entrepreneurs can identify areas where collaboration or integration with existing products may be more effective than building from scratch.

- **Compatibility and integration**: Knowledge of the ecosystem helps ensure that new solutions can integrate seamlessly with existing products, providing added value to users.

- **Crafting unique selling points (USPs)**: Understanding the strengths and weaknesses of competitors helps entrepreneurs emphasize the unique aspects of their solution, setting it apart in the market.

- **Partnership opportunities**: Identifying complementary products or services within the ecosystem opens doors for strategic partnerships, cross-promotions, or integrations.

- **Industry standards**: Existing products often comply with regulatory requirements and standards. Understanding these helps entrepreneurs ensure that their solution meets the necessary legal and compliance benchmarks.

- **Avoiding IP conflicts**: Researching existing products helps identify potential intellectual property issues, reducing the risk of legal disputes.

- **Entry barriers**: Entrepreneurs can identify potential barriers to adoption, such as user loyalty to existing products, and strategize ways to overcome these challenges.

- **Ecosystem fit**: By considering how the solution will interact with other products, entrepreneurs can design offerings that integrate smoothly into the broader ecosystem, enhancing usability and customer satisfaction.

- **Future-proofing**: A deep understanding of the ecosystem helps entrepreneurs anticipate how their solution will evolve as the ecosystem changes, ensuring long-term relevance.

The Ecosystem Mapping Canvas is a tool that enables entrepreneurs to systematically identify and analyze the network of systems, stakeholders, and processes that influence their solution. By mapping how the solution interacts with the existing ecosystem—whether through systems, products, processes, or services it depends on (**Value In**) or those it enhances or contributes to (**Value Out**)—the canvas provides a detailed and comprehensive view of the ecosystem dynamics.

This tool highlights the importance of understanding dependencies, both internal and external, that can shape the development and delivery of the solution. It also prompts teams to address critical controls, such as security, regulatory compliance, and data management, ensuring the solution is built on a solid, scalable, and secure foundation.

Using **The Ecosystem Mapping Canvas**, entrepreneurs can uncover integration opportunities, identify potential risks, and discover how their solution can seamlessly align within the ecosystem. This approach transforms their solution from a standalone offering into one that fits naturally into a larger network, adding value and enhancing adaptability in the market.

The canvas is presented is the following figure:

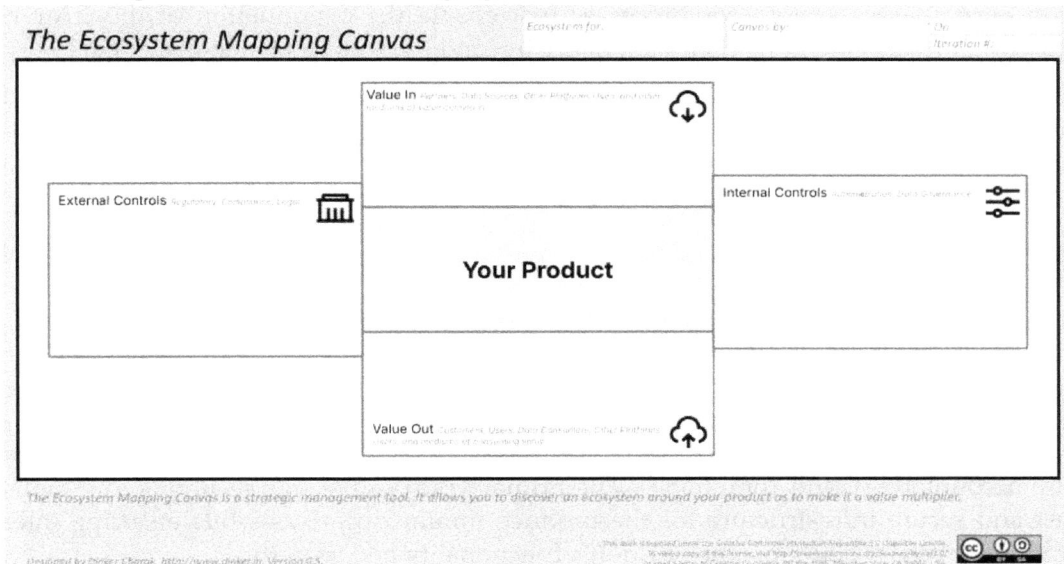

Figure 4.4: *Ecosystem Mapping Canvas*

The various sections of the Ecosystem Mapping Canvas are outlined in the following section.

Value In

This section is dedicated to identifying all the external systems, data sources, platforms, products, processes, and services that the solution relies on to function effectively. Data sources refer to systems or platforms that provide essential data for the product (e.g., APIs, databases). Platforms are those where the solution consumes value or builds upon existing offerings (e.g., cloud services, payment gateways). Additionally, this section encompasses systems or processes that enable the flow of the customer's journey, seamlessly integrating their experience into the solution being designed.

By mapping these components, entrepreneurs can gain a clear understanding of the dependencies that these systems bring to their solution and pinpoint the solution's role within the overall value stream. This insight helps ensure the solution is well-integrated, efficient, and aligned with the broader ecosystem.

Value Out

This section is dedicated to identifying all the external systems, platforms, products, processes, and services that the solution contributes to or interacts with, to deliver value. Data sinks refer to systems or platforms where the solution outputs data or information (e.g., reporting tools, analytics platforms). Platforms include those where the solution adds value or integrates as part of a larger offering (e.g., e-commerce platforms, logistics networks). Additionally, this section encompasses systems or processes that enable the continuation of the customer's journey, seamlessly extending their experience beyond the solution being designed.

By mapping these components, entrepreneurs can gain a clear understanding of how their solution delivers value to the ecosystem, identify opportunities for enhancing integration, and ensure their product contributes effectively to the broader value stream. This insight helps position the solution as a cohesive and valuable part of the ecosystem rather than an isolated entity.

Internal Controls

This section focuses on the mechanisms that ensure a solution operates securely and aligns with organizational policies. It encompasses key components such as security systems, which safeguard data in motion or at rest through tools like tokenization and encryption; access controls, which manage permissions and restrict data access using internal tools like admin portals and role-based workflows; and audit processes, which log and monitor activities to ensure accountability and compliance. The primary purpose of this section is to establish a robust and secure infrastructure for the product, minimizing risks while ensuring internal operations effectively support the solution's functionality and growth.

External Controls

This section focuses on ensuring the solution complies with applicable regulations and industry standards while meeting external requirements for security and data management. This includes adherence to general regulations such as PCI-DSS, GDPR, or CCPA, as well as any product-specific legal requirements. Key components may involve generating regulatory reports, maintaining detailed audit logs, and aligning with standards relevant to the industry or geography. This section ensures that the solution not only meets external compliance obligations but also proactively addresses potential risks related to audits, inspections, or legal scrutiny, providing a strong foundation for sustainable and lawful operations.

Using Ecosystem Mapping Canvas helped Tara proactively address dependencies, streamline operations, and position the MVP as a reliable, innovative solution within the artisan marketplace ecosystem. Here is the ecosystem map she built:

Section	Details
Value In	• **Data sources**: Social media platforms, online shopping behavior analytics, and artisan cooperatives providing product catalogs and inventory. • **Platforms**: Logistics providers, payment gateways, and e-commerce infrastructure for marketplace operations. • **Processes**: Onboarding artisans and their products, storytelling to enhance product value, and educating artisans on pricing and market trends. • **Value brought in**: Enables Tara's marketplace to curate authentic, unique products and ensures smooth integration with delivery and payment systems for a seamless customer experience.

Section	Details
Value Out	• **Systems**: API integrations with delivery services and tracking systems for customer convenience. • **Platforms**: Collaboration with influencers and social media for marketing and storytelling. • **Processes**: Streamlined order processing and real-time updates to customers. • **Value delivered**: Provides visibility for artisans' products, ensures reliable delivery for customers, and builds trust through transparency and storytelling.
Internal Controls	• **Security systems**: Encryption for payment data, tokenization of **personal identifiable information** (**PII**). • **Access controls**: Admin tools for role-based access permissions for staff, ensuring data security. • **Audit processes**: Regular monitoring of transactions, customer interactions, and system logs to ensure compliance and detect anomalies.
External Controls	• **Regulatory compliance**: Adherence to Indian e-commerce regulations, tax laws, and labor laws. • **Standards**: DPDP compliance for data protection. • **Reporting**: Systematic tracking for regulatory reporting and auditing, ensuring adherence to legal requirements.

Table 4.2: Tara's Ecosystem Mapping Canvas

Ideation techniques

Generating innovative and practical solutions requires a structured approach to unlock creativity while maintaining focus on solving the identified problem. Ideation techniques serve as tools to facilitate this process, guiding entrepreneurs through brainstorming sessions and solution-generation workshops. By leveraging these techniques, entrepreneurs can explore a wide range of possibilities, challenge assumptions, and foster collaborative thinking.

Let us look at the variety of proven methods. Each technique brings unique strengths to the table, whether it is structuring the creative process, encouraging divergent thinking, or narrowing ideas into actionable solutions.

SCAMPER

The **substitute, combine, adapt, modify (also magnify or minify), put to another use, eliminate, and reverse (also rearrange)** (**SCAMPER**) technique is a creative problem-solving and ideation tool designed to help individuals generate innovative ideas by systematically exploring different ways to modify, improve, or adapt an existing concept. This method encourages lateral thinking by prompting individuals to challenge assumptions and think beyond conventional boundaries.

Developed by *Alex Osborn*[4], co-founder of advertising agency *BBDO* and a pioneer in brainstorming methods, SCAMPER was later refined and popularized by *Bob Eberle* in his book *SCAMPER: Games for Imagination Development*[5]. Since its inception, the SCAMPER technique has been widely adopted across industries for product development, service design, and business strategy. Its simplicity and versatility make it a valuable tool for entrepreneurs seeking to unlock creative solutions and refine their ideas.

Substitute

Entrepreneurs explore whether any part of the product, process, or idea can be replaced with an alternative to achieve better results. This could involve swapping out materials, technologies, methods, or even team roles to improve performance, reduce costs, or enhance sustainability.

Example: Tara, while developing a marketplace for local artisans, could explore substituting costly packaging materials with eco-friendly, biodegradable options, appealing to environmentally conscious customers.

Combine

This step encourages the entrepreneur to merge two or more elements to create something entirely new or enhance the functionality of existing features. Combining different ideas, features, or processes can result in innovative offerings that add significant value to customers.

Example: Tara could combine the storytelling features of a blog with the product display of an e-commerce platform, creating a marketplace where artisans share the story behind their crafts alongside their products.

Adapt

The entrepreneur assesses how existing elements or ideas can be modified to fit new contexts, markets, or problems. Inspiration from other industries, competitors, or unrelated fields is often key in this step.

Example: An entrepreneur could adapt the gamification features used in fitness apps (like achievement badges) to encourage repeat purchases or artisan support on their marketplace.

Modify

In this step, the entrepreneur considers how to alter attributes such as size, shape, design, functionality, or scale to make the product more appealing, practical, or efficient.

Example: For a local artisan marketplace, modifying the checkout process to make it more intuitive and seamless can enhance user satisfaction and reduce cart abandonment rates.

4 Regent University. "Alex Osborn and the Journey of Brainstorming." Regent University, 6 July 2022, **www.regent.edu/journal/journal-of-transformative-innovation/the-history-of-brainstorming-alex-osborn**.
5 Eberle, Bob. Scamper: Games for Imagination Development. United Kingdom, Prufrock Press, 1996.

This step also includes **magnifying** (enhancing or enlarging aspects) and **minifying** (reducing or simplifying elements) to improve the product's value proposition.

While **magnifying,** the entrepreneur explores ways to expand, exaggerate, or amplify certain aspects of the product or service. This could mean enhancing features, increasing capacity, or adding layers of functionality to meet customer needs better.

Example: For a marketplace, magnifying could involve adding detailed artisan profiles with high-quality videos, elaborate product descriptions, and extensive customer reviews to enhance buyer trust and engagement.

While **minifying,** the entrepreneur focuses on simplifying, reducing, or streamlining elements of the product or service. This might involve removing complexities, making components smaller or lighter, or reducing the number of steps required for a process.

Example: For the same marketplace, minifying could mean simplifying the product upload process for artisans, such as by pre-filling details or offering easy templates, reducing the time and effort needed to list their products.

Put to another use

Entrepreneurs explore how a product, service, or process could serve an entirely different purpose, audience, or market. This step encourages thinking beyond the original intent of the product.

Example: A marketplace designed for local artisans could also serve as a platform for corporate gifting, providing curated, handmade products for businesses looking to purchase unique employee gifts.

Eliminate

Here, the entrepreneur identifies components or features that can be removed to simplify the product, reduce costs, or enhance usability. Often, eliminating unnecessary elements can increase focus on the product's core value.

Example: Removing rarely used features from a platform, such as complicated filters or excessive customization options, can streamline the user experience and make navigation easier.

Reverse

The reverse step involves challenging conventional assumptions by flipping or inverting processes, roles, or traditional ways of thinking. By asking *What if we did the opposite?* Or *What if we flipped this process on its head?* Entrepreneurs can uncover innovative perspectives and unorthodox solutions. This step helps in breaking free from habitual thinking and exploring paths that may not have been considered otherwise.

Example: Instead of upfront payments, *what if the marketplace implemented a pay-as-you-sell model for artisans, reducing entry barriers for smaller sellers and encouraging participation?*

This step also includes reverse, which involves flipping assumptions or rethinking traditional roles and methods. This approach can lead to groundbreaking ideas by challenging the status quo and exploring unorthodox solutions.

Example: For the marketplace, a reverse perspective might involve creating a subscription model where buyers receive curated artisan goods each month, instead of a traditional one-off purchase model. Another reversal could be incentivizing buyers to promote artisans' products, flipping the usual dynamic where sellers handle all marketing.

When Tara learnt about SCAMPER, she organized her learning and plans into substitute, combine, adapt, modify (also magnify or minify), put to another use, eliminate, and reverse (also rearrange).

She found this analysis invaluable for sharing with prospective investors and engaging friends and family to support her entrepreneurial journey. Recognizing the importance of prioritization, Tara made the deliberate decision to de-prioritize certain options for her MVP. She clearly struck them out to ensure transparency and demonstrate her focus on building an MVP that was feasible, achievable, and aligned with delivering value to her target customers. The following table is the result of her detailed exploration:

	Actions	How it helps
Substitute	• Replace artisan-managed shipping with logistics partnerships. • Explore social commerce integrations instead of building a full platform initially.	• Simplifies operations and ensures reliable delivery. • Lowers initial costs and tests the market.
Combine	• Merge storytelling with product listings. • Combine artisan training with onboarding. • Enable bulk buying for corporate buyers alongside individual sales.	• Enhances emotional appeal and builds customer connection. • Improves listing quality and artisan engagement. • Attracts diverse customer segments and increases revenue streams.
Adapt	• Introduce gamification techniques (e.g., badges for artisans). • Offer a subscription model for exclusive deals or early access. • Use influencer marketing to promote artisan products.	• Encourages quality and sustained engagement. • Creates recurring revenue and customer loyalty. • Expands reach and builds brand credibility.

Modify (Magnify/ Minify)	• Magnify reach by including international shipping. • Minify onboarding by simplifying product listing processes. • Magnify product range to include artisan services (e.g., custom commissions). • Minify catalog by starting with niche product categories (e.g., handmade jewelry).	• Expands market potential and visibility for artisans. • Ensures ease of use for artisans, especially those new to technology. • Diversifies offerings and adds high-value options for customers. • Reduces complexity during the MVP phase.
Put to another use	• Position the platform for corporate gifting. • Promote artisan-led workshops for customers. • Collaborate with tourism boards to promote artisan villages as cultural destinations.	• Opens new revenue streams and attracts business clients. • Creates unique experiences and adds to the platform's versatility. • Enhances artisan visibility and connects with a broader audience.
Eliminate	• Remove categories that take away focus from high-demand artisan goods. • Simplify user verification steps. • Avoid unnecessary features (e.g., live chat) during the MVP phase.	• Maintains quality and relevance of offerings. • Reduces friction in onboarding. • Conserves resources and ensures focus on core functionality.
Rearrange (or Reverse)	• Rearrange the payment model to allow deposits with full payment on delivery. • Reverse product discovery by letting customers post wish lists for artisans to fulfill. • Rearrange priority listings to highlight newer artisans or trending products.	Reduces risk for buyers and builds trust in the platform. Encourages personalized shopping experiences and supports artisan creativity. Keeps the platform dynamic and encourages participation from all artisans.

Table 4.3: Tara's SCAMPER analysis

Six Thinking Hats

The Six Thinking Hats technique, introduced by *Edward de Bono*[6] in his 1985 book *Six Thinking Hats*, is a structured approach to enhance creative thinking, problem-solving, and decision-making. It encourages entrepreneurs to analyze a problem statement or opportunity from multiple distinct perspectives, ensuring a comprehensive and well-rounded evaluation. The

---

6 De Bono, Edward. Six Thinking Hats. United Kingdom, Penguin, 2008.

core principle behind the technique is that effective solutioning requires deliberate shifts in thinking, each represented by a metaphorical hat. These hats symbolize specific modes of thought—ranging from factual analysis to emotional intuition and creative brainstorming—allowing for a focused yet diverse exploration of any situation.

For entrepreneurs, particularly those working independently or without immediate access to a sounding board, the Six Thinking Hats technique serves as a powerful tool. It fosters clarity and balance, helping to evaluate ideas, identify risks, and uncover innovative solutions. By systematically guiding their thought process, entrepreneurs can make confident, informed decisions even in challenging or high-stakes scenarios.

The following are the six steps of the Six Thinking Hats technique, along with guidance for entrepreneurs on how to execute each step effectively:

1. **White Hat: Focus on facts**: The White Hat emphasizes objective data and factual information, helping to establish a foundation of knowledge.

   - **Action:**
     o Collect all relevant data and statistics related to the problem or opportunity.
     o Identify gaps in knowledge and plan to acquire missing information.
     o Avoid personal opinions or assumptions; focus solely on verified facts.

2. **Yellow Hat: Highlight benefits and opportunities**: The Yellow Hat shifts the focus to optimism, exploring the potential benefits and positive outcomes of the idea.

   - **Action:**
     o Identify all possible advantages and opportunities associated with the idea.
     o Discuss how the solution could succeed and bring value to stakeholders.
     o Brainstorm ways to enhance the positive aspects of the idea.

3. **Black Hat: Address risks and caution**: The Black Hat is focused on identifying potential risks, challenges, and negative outcomes. It ensures critical thinking and proactive problem-solving.

   - **Action:**
     o Critique the idea constructively by highlighting potential weaknesses and risks.
     o Consider what could go wrong and explore worst-case scenarios.
     o Use this step to prepare mitigation strategies for identified risks.

4. **Red Hat: Explore emotions**: The Red Hat allows participants to express feelings, intuitions, and emotional reactions without the need for justification.

   - **Action:**
     o Encourage open and honest sharing of emotional responses.

- o Avoid analyzing or critiquing feelings during this step.
- o Use this phase to gauge instinctive reactions and emotional resonance with the idea.

5. **Green Hat: Foster creativity and innovation**: The Green Hat emphasizes creativity and brainstorming to generate innovative ideas and solutions.

- **Action:**
  - o Encourage free-flowing ideas without judgment or constraints.
  - o Explore unconventional approaches and build on others' suggestions.
  - o Challenge traditional assumptions and think outside the box.

6. **Blue Hat: Manage the thinking process**: The Blue Hat serves as the control hat, guiding the overall process and ensuring productive and balanced discussions.

- **Action:**
  - o Assign a facilitator to guide the conversation and maintain focus.
  - o Summarize the key insights and outcomes from each hat.
  - o Plan actionable steps based on the collective input from all perspectives.

For entrepreneurs, the Six Thinking Hats technique offers a practical and structured framework for uncovering opportunities, addressing challenges, and making well-informed, balanced decisions. It helps align their actions with their business vision while minimizing the influence of preconceived notions, biases, and gaps in critical thinking. By encouraging diverse perspectives, this method ensures that decisions are thorough, objective, and innovative, even in the face of uncertainty or limited experience.

Here is an example of how Tara used the Six Thinking Hats method to analyze her business opportunity:

Hat	Perspective	Insights for Tara's marketplace initiative
White Hat (Facts)	Focus on objective data, facts, and information.	• India's upper and middle-class demographics represent a SAM of INR 25,435 crores annually. • Online shoppers express strong demand for unique, handmade goods. • Survey results confirm a willingness to pay a 10% premium for authenticity and quality.
Red Hat (Feelings)	Consider emotions, intuition, and gut feelings.	• Customers are frustrated with a lack of trustworthy platforms and poor quality. • Artisans feel overwhelmed by logistics and limited market access. • Tara feels passionate about empowering local artisans and sees the festival season as a timely opportunity.

Hat	Perspective	Insights for Tara's marketplace initiative
Black Hat (Caution)	Identify risks, weaknesses, and potential obstacles.	• Strong competition from Amazon Karigar. • Logistical challenges for consistent delivery and maintaining product quality. • Dependency on influencers for brand awareness may not guarantee success.
Yellow Hat (Benefits)	Highlight the potential advantages and opportunities.	• Creating a unique marketplace fills a clear gap. • Storytelling and authenticity can be strong differentiators. • A well-targeted demographic with disposable income is likely to embrace this concept.
Green Hat (Creativity)	Explore creative ideas, alternative approaches, and solutions.	• Introduce storytelling features to connect artisans with buyers. • Collaborate with NGOs or government initiatives supporting local artisans. • Offer loyalty programs for repeat buyers and subscription models for curated products.
Blue Hat (Process)	Maintain an overview of the thinking process, ensuring focus and direction.	• Ensure all hats are explored thoroughly to gain a 360-degree view. • Establish clear next steps for MVP development based on insights. • Use findings to refine the business pitch and prepare for investor discussions.

Table 4.4: Tara's Six Thinking Hats analysis

This exercise reinforced her confidence in the business opportunity while preparing her to tackle challenges proactively.

How Might We technique

The **How Might We (HMW)** technique is a powerful tool for reframing challenges into opportunities for innovative solutions. Rooted in the design thinking methodology pioneered by the *Stanford d.school* and popularized by *IDEO*, this approach fosters optimism and constructive problem-solving. It shifts the focus from limitations and obstacles to possibilities and actionable steps, enabling a mindset of exploration and creativity.

HMW transforms seemingly overwhelming or insurmountable problems into manageable opportunities. By framing challenges as open-ended questions, entrepreneurs can break free from mental blocks, approach issues with clarity, and encourage brainstorming in a structured yet flexible manner. This process not only drives innovation but also helps unlock pathways to meaningful solutions.

Here are the steps for the How Might We method:

1. **Identify the core problem**: The first step involves gathering insights from research, customer feedback, and market analysis to define the central challenge. If the problem is too broad or complex, break it down into more specific areas of focus to make it actionable. This step is covered extensively in *Chapter 1, Understanding Customer Pain Points,* and *Chapter 2, Market Analysis and Validation,* which provide entrepreneurs with the tools to dissect problems and lay the groundwork for informed decision-making.

   For instance, Tara identified the overarching problem of local artisans struggling to reach urban buyers. To focus her efforts, she broke this down into issues such as limited visibility, lack of trust in product authenticity, and challenges in delivery logistics.

2. **Reframe the problem as a question**: Using the How Might We phrasing, entrepreneurs can turn a challenge into an opportunity for innovation. Begin by understanding the context of the problem, and then convert it into a positive, action-oriented question.

   For example, instead of saying, *Local artisans can't reach urban buyers,* Tara reframed it as, *How Might We help local artisans connect with urban buyers in meaningful ways?* This shift opens the door to brainstorming creative solutions rather than being stuck in problem-focused thinking.

3. **Narrow the scope**: Ensure the HMW question is specific enough to provide clear direction but broad enough to inspire diverse ideas. Techniques from *Chapter 3, Opportunity Prioritization,* can help refine the problem into a well-defined challenge.

   For example, when tackling delivery logistics, Tara narrowed her focus by asking, *How Might We make delivery of artisan goods faster and more reliable?* This specific framing ensured that her team could brainstorm targeted solutions without straying into unrelated territory.

4. **Generate further HMW questions**: Create multiple variations of HMW questions to explore different aspects of the challenge. This step encourages lateral thinking and opens up possibilities for addressing the problem from various angles.

   For example, Tara expanded her exploration with questions like:

   - How Might We make shopping for handmade goods an engaging experience?
   - How Might We ensure buyers trust the authenticity of artisan products?
   - How Might We streamline communication between artisans and buyers?

   Each variation highlights a distinct dimension of the problem, encouraging comprehensive ideation.

5. **Prioritize and refine**: Once a set of HMW questions is generated, prioritize them based on relevance, feasibility, and alignment with business goals. Review and refine the phrasing to ensure clarity and focus. This iterative process continues until a satisfactory

problem statement emerges—one that is actionable, specific, and conducive to innovative solutioning.

For example, after reviewing her questions, Tara prioritized *How Might We make delivery of artisan goods faster and more reliable?* and refined it further into, *How Might We create an affordable, reliable logistics network tailored to artisans' needs?*

6. **Iterate to achieve clarity**: Continue the process of refining and generating HMW questions until the problem statement achieves an optimal level of specificity and clarity. This step ensures the entrepreneur has a well-scoped challenge that leads naturally into brainstorming actionable solutions.

Mind Mapping

A Mind Map is a powerful visual brainstorming tool that organizes ideas and information around a central theme or concept. It is an ideal method for entrepreneurs when they face difficulty identifying patterns or structure in their thoughts. This technique allows them to freely jot down all seemingly chaotic ideas without worrying about immediate organization, enabling analysis and structure to emerge naturally at a later stage.

Using a radial layout, a Mind Map branches out from a central core idea, extending into key topics, related concepts, and finer details. Each main branch can further divide into sub-branches, which in turn can delve deeper into specific aspects or additional ideas. This iterative process helps entrepreneurs systematically explore each topic until all associated ideas are captured.

Mind Maps offer flexibility—some branches may develop into extensive and intricate sub-maps, while others might remain relatively simple. This adaptive structure helps entrepreneurs focus deeply on areas of interest, prioritize key elements, and uncover connections between seemingly disparate ideas, ultimately leading to well-rounded and innovative solutions.

The evolution of Mind Maps from ancient methods to *Tony Buzan's* structured approach[7] and their subsequent digitization underscores their enduring relevance. Today, they serve as a versatile and powerful tool for entrepreneurs, educators, and professionals alike, bridging the gap between creative ideation and structured planning. Their growing integration with technology ensures they remain a cornerstone of innovation and productivity.

Tara liked the Mind Map techniques as it helps her put onto paper the sprawl of tasks. The following is her version of Mind Map:

---

7 TED. Tony Buzan: The Power of Mind Mapping. YouTube, 17 Dec. 2013, **www.youtube.com/watch?v=EgG8GuQHHIs**. Accessed 3 Jan. 2025.

Figure 4.5: Tara's Mind Map created using xmind.app

Summary

This summary enables a direct comparison, helping entrepreneurs decide the most appropriate technique for their specific solutioning needs based on shared scenarios:

When to use	SCAMPER technique	Six Thinking Hats	How Might We method	Mind Mapping
Early ideation stages	Ideal for brainstorming innovative solutions by systematically modifying or combining existing elements.	Useful for team-based evaluations of early ideas from multiple perspectives.	Effective for reframing problems into actionable opportunity questions to guide ideation.	Encourages free-flowing creativity, capturing and organizing scattered ideas visually.
Improving existing products	Helps refine or differentiate a product by exploring alternative features, functions, or approaches.	Can evaluate improvement ideas by considering risks, opportunities, and feasibility comprehensively.	N/A	Visually maps enhancements and their impacts, revealing interconnections and priorities.

Pivoting	Facilitates exploring new directions by rethinking components or adapting ideas to new contexts.	Assesses potential pivots holistically, balancing creative and critical viewpoints.	Frames pivot opportunities as manageable, well-scoped How Might We questions.	Breaks down pivot options, showcasing how each aligns with the core problem and priorities.
Complex challenges	Encourages looking at problems from alternative angles to uncover new possibilities.	Provides structure for tackling multifaceted issues with collaborative, detailed analysis.	Helps break overwhelming problems into manageable questions to inspire focused ideation.	Dissects complex problems into interconnected components for deeper analysis and solution mapping.
Team collaboration	Can be adapted for group brainstorming sessions to foster diverse contributions.	Perfect for fostering alignment and exploring diverse viewpoints in team discussions.	Aligns team members around shared opportunities framed as collaborative questions.	Provides a shared visual framework for brainstorming and building alignment among team members.
Strategic planning	Generates creative strategies by reimagining existing processes or structures.	Facilitates balanced evaluation of strategies, considering risks, opportunities, and emotional factors.	Frames strategic priorities as actionable opportunities to guide focused planning.	Maps out strategic pathways, showing dependencies, timelines, and milestones visually.
Breaking down complex problems	N/A	N/A	Breaks into manageable opportunities for which a path forward is visible.	Simplifies multifaceted issues into smaller parts, revealing relationships and helping focus efforts.
Creative roadblocks	Stimulates fresh thinking by suggesting modifications, adaptations, or eliminations of components.	Shifts thinking by prompting exploration of alternative perspectives or angles.	Revitalizes ideation by reframing roadblocks into opportunities for innovation.	Encourages new idea generation by expanding or rearranging thought processes visually.

Identifying gaps and opportunities	Highlights areas for improvement or innovation by systematically exploring product elements.	N/A	N/A	Reveals gaps in the competitive landscape or customer experience through detailed mapping.
Iterative solution development	Encourages continuous refinement and adaptation of ideas through systematic exploration.	Balances iterative refinements with critical evaluations, ensuring no angle is overlooked.	N/A	Tracks evolving solutions and captures feedback-driven changes, keeping development organized.

Table 4.5: Which common brainstorming techniques is best suited for a scenario

Legal, compliance, and regulatory review

Navigating the legal, compliance, and regulatory landscape is an essential aspect of building and scaling a successful e-commerce or digital business. Entrepreneurs must understand that while their primary focus might be on innovation, market entry, and customer acquisition, adhering to legal and regulatory requirements is equally critical. Non-compliance can lead to hefty fines, business disruptions, reputational damage, or even complete shutdowns, making this area a cornerstone of sustainable business operations.

India's regulatory environment for e-commerce and digital businesses is comprehensive and continually evolving, reflecting the dynamic nature of technology and market practices. Entrepreneurs need to familiarize themselves with a range of laws and guidelines, from data protection and consumer rights to taxation and intellectual property. These regulations not only govern the operational aspects of the business but also set ethical and fair-play standards by which businesses are expected to operate.

Given the complexity and scope of applicable regulations, entrepreneurs must engage professionals to ensure comprehensive compliance. A **chartered accountant** (**CA**) and a lawyer are indispensable members of an entrepreneur's advisory team:

- **CA**: Provides guidance on tax compliance, financial reporting, and adherence to indirect tax laws such as **Goods and Services Tax** (**GST**). They can also assist in understanding the financial implications of laws like the Equalization Levy and other direct tax requirements.

- **Lawyer**: Offers expert advice on contracts, intellectual property, data protection, consumer protection laws, and regulatory frameworks. A lawyer can help draft compliant terms of service, privacy policies, vendor agreements, and ensure adherence to critical laws like the *Consumer Protection (E-commerce) Rules 2020* and the *Information Technology Act, 2000*.

An entrepreneur should familiarize themselves with the key regulations governing e-commerce and digital businesses in India to provide educated and meaningful inputs when consulting with their CA and lawyer. A strong understanding of these regulations not only ensures compliance but also empowers entrepreneurs to make informed decisions, proactively address risks, and align their strategies with legal and ethical standards.

The **Information Technology (IT)** Act, 2000, forms the cornerstone of digital commerce in India, addressing electronic transactions, data protection, and cybersecurity. Complementing this, the *Consumer Protection (E-commerce) Rules, 2020,* mandate transparency, including seller disclosures, return policies, and grievance mechanisms, while prohibiting practices like misleading advertisements and unfair trade.

Taxation laws such as the GST ensure that e-commerce operators comply with taxation on goods and services, including the collection of **Tax Collected at Source (TCS)**. Simultaneously, the **Foreign Direct Investment (FDI)** Policy governs marketplace e-commerce models, allowing 100% FDI but prohibiting inventory-based operations.

Data protection is a significant focus, with the proposed **Personal Data Protection Bill (PDPB)** introducing stringent GDPR-like regulations on data processing, localization, and user rights. Similarly, the *Payment and Settlement Systems Act, 2007,* mandates compliance for payment gateways and wallets to ensure secure online transactions.

Ensuring fair market practices, the *Competition Act, 2002*, prohibits anti-competitive behavior such as predatory pricing and exclusivity clauses, safeguarding healthy competition. Transparency in product labeling is governed by the *Legal Metrology Act, 2009*, while the *Shops and Establishments Act* ensures compliance with labor laws for physical operations like warehouses and offices.

Contracts, advertising, and intellectual property are governed by the *Indian Contract Act, 1872,* **Advertising Standards Council of India (ASCI)** Guidelines, and **Intellectual Property Rights (IPR)** regulations, respectively. These laws protect against misleading claims, ensure fair digital agreements, and safeguard trademarks, copyrights, and patents.

Sustainability is increasingly critical, with environmental laws such as the *Plastic Waste Management Rules* promoting eco-friendly packaging. Additionally, the *Income Tax Act, 1961,* and Equalization Levy govern direct tax implications for e-commerce revenues and digital advertisements. Finally, Cybersecurity Guidelines by CERT-In mandate breach reporting and robust security measures.

By staying informed about these regulations, entrepreneurs can better collaborate with their CA and Lawyer, build trust with customers, and lay a legally sound foundation for their MVPs.

Risk analysis

Understanding risk and planning to mitigate or reduce it is a vital component of the solutioning process, enabling entrepreneurs to build viable, resilient solutions. Risk is an inherent part of any entrepreneurial journey, particularly when launching new products or services. By identifying, assessing, and proactively planning for potential risks early in the process, entrepreneurs can protect their MVP from unforeseen challenges, reduce resource wastage, and enhance the likelihood of achieving success.

A deep understanding of risks—whether arising from market dynamics, regulatory changes, or technological dependencies—provides clarity and strategic context. This understanding allows entrepreneurs to evaluate trade-offs, prioritize actions, and design solutions that are robust and minimally susceptible to distractions or setbacks when addressing the core problem statement. By addressing risks systematically, entrepreneurs ensure that their efforts remain focused on creating value for their target audience.

Incorporating risk analysis and mitigation into the solutioning phase also promotes efficient resource allocation. Building a solution requires significant investments of time, capital, and effort. Identifying risks early helps entrepreneurs avoid unnecessary expenditure on features or initiatives that may derail progress or overextend the business. This ensures that resources are channeled into the most impactful areas, maximizing the MVP's potential and minimizing financial and operational strain.

Entrepreneurial endeavors are rarely linear; external factors such as market shifts, competitive pressures, or supply chain disruptions can impact even the best-laid plans. Proactively identifying and preparing for these risks enables entrepreneurs to build contingency plans, allowing their solutions to adapt to changing circumstances. This foresight ensures continuity and stability, even in the face of unexpected challenges, and enhances the resilience of the solution.

Ultimately, understanding and managing risks is about balancing ambition with realism. While innovation demands bold thinking, the ability to anticipate and mitigate potential downsides ensures that visionary ideas are implemented practically, are scalable, and in alignment with market realities. By embedding risk planning into the solutioning process, entrepreneurs not only increase the likelihood of their MVP's success but also position their ventures for sustainable growth and long-term impact.

Even with thorough planning, entrepreneurs will inevitably encounter unknown unknowns—risks that are unforeseen and without clear precedent. Preparing for unknown unknowns isn't about predicting every scenario; it is about establishing a risk management flow.

Risk management flow

Risk management begins with risk identification, which helps entrepreneurs uncover potential threats across market dynamics, regulatory changes, and technological shifts. The next step, risk assessment, analyzes these risks to prioritize actions based on their likelihood and impact. Risk mitigation involves proactive measures to prevent or reduce risks, ensuring compliance, resource efficiency, and business continuity. Lastly, risk reduction focuses on minimizing the impact of unavoidable risks, fostering resilience through market validation, cost optimization, and contingency planning. Let us look deeper into each step.

Risk identification

Risk identification is the initial step in understanding potential threats and uncertainties that could impact a product or service. It is particularly crucial for entrepreneurs as they navigate the complexities of launching a new venture. A focused subset of risk analysis, market risk analysis, examines external factors such as demand fluctuations, competitive dynamics, economic conditions, regulatory changes, technological disruptions, and social or cultural shifts. These elements shape the market environment and can directly influence the viability and success of a business model.

For example, changes in customer preferences or buying behavior may result in demand fluctuations that entrepreneurs need to anticipate. Similarly, technological advancements or the entry of new competitors can disrupt the market, requiring adjustments to the solution or business strategy. Regulatory changes, such as new compliance requirements, can add layers of complexity, while shifts in societal values, like the rising preference for sustainable products, may open new opportunities or present challenges.

To systematically identify these risks, entrepreneurs can leverage several analytical tools. SWOT analysis allows them to evaluate internal strengths and weaknesses alongside external opportunities and threats, helping prioritize risks that need attention. PESTEL analysis provides a comprehensive examination of political, economic, social, technological, environmental, and legal factors influencing the market. Additionally, scenario planning enables entrepreneurs to envision different potential futures—worst-case, best-case, and most likely scenarios, allowing for strategic preparation.

Effective risk identification goes beyond simply listing threats; it involves contextualizing these risks within the broader business landscape. This helps entrepreneurs assess the interplay of different factors, enabling a clearer understanding of how and when risks might manifest. By proactively identifying risks, they can better align their strategies, ensuring that their solutions are robust, adaptable, and poised to address market challenges effectively.

Risk assessment

Risk assessment is the next critical phase after risk identification, where entrepreneurs analyze potential risks in greater detail to understand their likelihood, impact, and potential fallout. This process helps prioritize risks based on their severity and prepares the entrepreneur to address them effectively. Unlike risk identification, which focuses on listing and understanding risks, risk assessment involves deeper analysis, categorization, and actionable insights to manage these risks strategically.

One of the primary tools in risk assessment is the risk matrix, which plots risks based on their likelihood and impact. This visual tool helps entrepreneurs prioritize risks, focusing on those that are both highly probable and have significant consequences. For example, a high-probability risk such as a regulatory change that could impact operations would be prioritized for immediate action, while low-impact risks might only require monitoring.

Entrepreneurs can also use benchmarking to compare their business or solution against industry standards or competitors, identifying gaps that may pose risks. A risk checklist ensures no critical area is overlooked by systematically evaluating the business against a list of common risks, from operational inefficiencies to cybersecurity vulnerabilities.

The insights gained from risk assessment allow entrepreneurs to develop targeted mitigation strategies, ensuring that resources are allocated efficiently. By understanding how and when risks might manifest and their potential fallout, entrepreneurs can plan proactively, safeguarding their business from avoidable disruptions and strengthening their ability to adapt to unforeseen challenges.

Risk mitigation

Risk mitigation involves taking proactive steps to prevent identified risks from materializing or reducing their likelihood and impact. For entrepreneurs, effective risk mitigation is essential to building a stable foundation for their ventures and ensuring long-term success. This phase is rooted in the insights gained from the earlier stages of risk identification and assessment, transforming theoretical risks into actionable strategies.

One crucial aspect of risk mitigation is ensuring regulatory compliance. Entrepreneurs must assess legal and compliance risks early in the process to ensure that their solutions meet all relevant standards. By addressing regulatory requirements from the outset, such as data privacy laws or industry-specific regulations, entrepreneurs can avoid penalties, delays, and reputational damage. Consulting legal experts and staying updated on policy changes can further strengthen compliance efforts.

Right prioritization of efforts, covered in *Chapter 3, Opportunity Prioritization*, is another cornerstone of risk mitigation. Entrepreneurs should focus on initiatives with the highest potential impact and the lowest risk, ensuring that limited resources are allocated efficiently. This approach minimizes the chances of spreading efforts too thin or investing heavily in areas with uncertain returns. Similarly, when developing an MVP, prioritizing capabilities that do not introduce additional risks helps create a lean and secure foundation for further growth.

Market validation plays a pivotal role in risk mitigation by ensuring alignment between the proposed solution and market demands. Testing concepts through surveys, prototypes, or pilot launches allows entrepreneurs to identify potential misfits early, reducing the risk of product-market disconnect. Cost optimization also mitigates financial risks by identifying areas where expenses can be controlled, helping entrepreneurs stay within budget and avoid cost overruns.

Finally, contingency planning ensures that entrepreneurs are prepared for adverse scenarios. By developing backup plans and allocating resources for unforeseen circumstances, entrepreneurs can navigate challenges more effectively. Whether it is a sudden market downturn or a supply chain disruption, having contingency measures in place helps maintain business continuity.

In essence, risk mitigation transforms potential threats into manageable challenges, enabling entrepreneurs to move forward with confidence. By adopting a structured approach, entrepreneurs can safeguard their ventures against avoidable pitfalls and position themselves for sustainable growth.

Risk reduction

Risk reduction focuses on minimizing the impact of risks that cannot be entirely avoided or eliminated. Unlike mitigation, which seeks to prevent risks from occurring, risk reduction accepts the inevitability of certain risks and emphasizes proactive strategies to lessen their consequences. For entrepreneurs, this phase is critical in ensuring that their ventures remain resilient in the face of challenges, enabling smoother execution of their business strategies.

A key element of risk reduction is the prioritization of efforts. Entrepreneurs must concentrate on initiatives and features that offer the greatest potential for success while posing the least amount of risk. By channeling resources toward these low-risk, high-value areas, they can efficiently allocate their time, budget, and energy. This strategy not only reduces exposure to significant risks but also ensures that the business progresses steadily toward its goals.

Another important aspect is the right prioritization of MVP capabilities. When designing an MVP, entrepreneurs should focus on core features that address the primary customer pain points without adding unnecessary risks. Avoiding overly complex or resource-intensive capabilities at this stage allows entrepreneurs to validate their ideas more effectively and with fewer obstacles. This lean approach ensures a streamlined development process while maintaining the flexibility to adapt based on market feedback.

Market validation is a powerful tool for risk reduction. By testing their solutions with real customers through prototypes, surveys, or pilot launches, entrepreneurs can confirm alignment with market needs and identify potential misalignments early. This feedback-driven approach minimizes the risk of product-market fit issues, ensuring that resources are invested in solutions that resonate with the target audience.

Cost optimization also plays a significant role in reducing financial risks. By closely monitoring expenses and identifying areas for cost-saving, entrepreneurs can avoid budget overruns that could jeopardize their operations. This involves implementing efficient processes, negotiating favorable terms with suppliers, and continuously evaluating spending to ensure alignment with business priorities.

Finally, contingency planning provides a safety net for navigating unforeseen circumstances. Entrepreneurs can develop alternative strategies to address adverse scenarios, such as supply chain disruptions, regulatory changes, or economic downturns. Having backup plans in place not only reduces the potential fallout of these risks but also instills confidence among stakeholders, including investors and team members.

In summary, risk reduction equips entrepreneurs with the tools and strategies to face inevitable challenges with preparedness and resilience. By prioritizing efforts, validating market fit, optimizing costs, and planning for contingencies, they can ensure their ventures remain adaptable and poised for sustainable growth. This proactive approach transforms potential vulnerabilities into manageable components of the entrepreneurial journey.

Risk matrix

The risk matrix is a high-level analysis tool that visually maps risks based on two key dimensions: the likelihood of occurrence and the potential impact. This simple yet effective framework enables entrepreneurs to prioritize risks systematically, ensuring that their attention and resources are directed toward the most critical threat. Here is a visual representation:

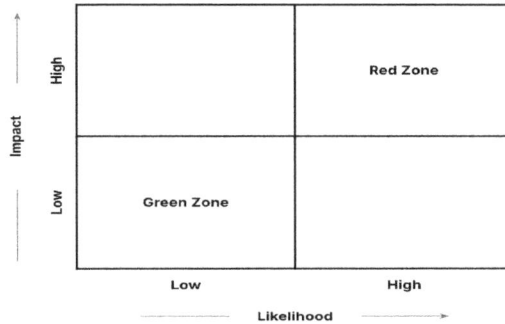

Figure 4.6: *2x2 risk matrix*

By plotting risks on a 2x2 matrix—where one axis represents likelihood and the other represents impact—entrepreneurs can categorize risks into zones of priority. High-probability, high-impact risks, such as logistical delays or regulatory changes, fall into the red zone, signaling an urgent need for mitigation strategies. On the other hand, low-probability, low-impact risks fall into the green zone, requiring only periodic monitoring and minimal intervention.

The risk matrix empowers entrepreneurs to assess and focus on avoiding or mitigating risks that pose significant threats to their solution while avoiding unnecessary distractions from minor or unlikely issues. This approach helps entrepreneurs anticipate challenges and reduce the chances of being caught off guard by underestimated threats.

SWOT analysis

SWOT analysis is a more detail-oriented tool that offers entrepreneurs a structured framework to evaluate strengths, weaknesses, opportunities, and threats. This approach facilitates a comprehensive understanding of both opportunities and potential solutions, providing actionable insights that guide decision-making and enhance solutioning. By dissecting internal and external factors, entrepreneurs can refine their strategies and create more effective, market-aligned offerings.

The SWOT framework originates from the field of strategic planning and business management, pioneered by *Albert S. Humphrey* in the 1960s at the *Stanford Research Institute* (now *SRI International*). Its precursor, SOFT analysis, categorized factors into satisfactory, opportunities, faults, and threats for evaluating present and future operations. *Humphrey's* evolution of SOFT into SWOT refined these categories into internal factors (strengths and weaknesses) and external factors (opportunities and threats), making it more actionable and widely applicable.

Let us see how an entrepreneur applies SWOT Analysis to build a better solution:

- **Strengths**: Identifying strengths is crucial for entrepreneurs as it showcases the unique aspects of their solution that can set it apart in the market. Strengths may include robust technical capabilities, a well-defined value proposition, cost efficiency, or a strong personal reputation. Entrepreneurs can leverage these strengths to build confidence among stakeholders, differentiate themselves from competitors, and focus their efforts on areas that drive competitive advantage.

- **Weaknesses**: Recognizing weaknesses allows entrepreneurs to pinpoint areas of disadvantage or vulnerability within their solution or business model. These could range from resource constraints to gaps in product features or limited market reach. By addressing weaknesses, entrepreneurs can proactively reduce risks and improve their solution's robustness.

- **Opportunities**: Opportunities represent external factors that entrepreneurs can exploit to enhance their solution or gain a competitive edge. These may include unmet customer needs, emerging technologies, regulatory changes, or shifts in consumer behavior. By identifying and acting on these opportunities, entrepreneurs can align their solutions with market trends and create additional value for their customers.

- **Threats**: Understanding threats is essential for entrepreneurs to anticipate challenges that could hinder their solution's success. These threats might arise from competitive pressures, economic fluctuations, technological disruptions, or regulatory changes. By preparing contingency plans and risk mitigation strategies, entrepreneurs can navigate these challenges effectively.

The following SWOT analysis highlights the strategic landscape Tara faces as she builds her venture, emphasizing her strengths, potential growth opportunities, and areas to mitigate risks effectively:

Strengths:	Weaknesses:
• **Personal expertise**: Tara's extensive experience and domain knowledge provide her with a strong foundation.	• **Limited initial resources**: As a new venture, Tara may face constraints in funding and team bandwidth.
• **Clear problem identification**: Focus on the lack of marketplaces for local artisans, a specific and relevant gap.	• **Dependence on third parties**: Heavy reliance on logistics, packaging, and regulatory partners introduces potential vulnerabilities.
• **Comprehensive stakeholder insights**: Detailed Empathy Maps for both online shoppers and local artisans offer in-depth understanding of target groups.	• **High competition**: Established competitors like Amazon Karigar may make market penetration challenging.
• **Large market potential**: Estimated SAM of INR 25,435 crores indicates significant opportunity.	• **Tech expertise gap**: While Tara has domain knowledge, scaling the tech aspects might require external expertise.
• **Strategic planning**: Tara has already mapped out regulatory compliance and logistical partnerships, ensuring a solid foundation.	

Opportunities:	Threats:
• **Rising consumer interest**: Growing preference for authentic, handmade products aligns with Tara's platform vision. • **Festival season demand**: High demand during festive periods provides an opportunity to launch and gain traction. • **Niche differentiation**: A platform emphasizing storytelling, authenticity, and uniqueness can stand out in a competitive market. • **Support for local artisans**: Increasing societal focus on supporting local economies provides a strong value proposition. • **Collaborative partnerships**: Opportunities to collaborate with influencers, artisan cooperatives, and urban retailers to amplify reach and credibility.	• **Regulatory risks**: Any changes to FDI or e-commerce-specific regulations could impact operations. • **Competitive price wars**: Established players with economies of scale might undercut pricing, affecting Tara's profitability. • **Technological challenges**: Ensuring platform reliability, scalability, and cybersecurity might strain resources initially. • **Artisan awareness and adoption**: Convincing local artisans to adopt and use the platform effectively may require significant effort and education. • **Customer trust issues**: Overcoming skepticism around authenticity, quality, and delivery for handmade products is critical to gaining market trust.

Table 4.6: Tara's SWOT analysis

PESTEL analysis

Political, Economic, Social, Technological, Environmental, and Legal (**PESTEL**) analysis is a strategic framework that examines six key external factors that can influence a business environment. It provides entrepreneurs with a holistic understanding of the macro-environment in which their solution operates. By analyzing these factors, entrepreneurs can identify potential opportunities and threats that might impact their solution's success and sustainability.

PESTEL analysis originated as an evolution of the **Political, Economic, Social, and Technological** (**PEST**) framework, a tool initially developed in the 1960s by American academic *Francis J. Aguilar* in his book *Scanning the Business Environment*[8]. *Aguilar* introduced it as ETPS, a concept of environmental scanning, emphasizing the importance of analyzing external factors that impact organizational decision-making. It later expanded into PESTEL by adding Environmental and Legal dimensions to reflect the growing significance of ecological concerns and regulatory complexities in modern business environments.

The acronym PESTEL stands for:

- **Political**: Government policies, trade regulations, political stability, taxation, and other political influences.

---

8 Aguilar, Francis J. Scanning the Business Environment. Macmillan, 1967.

- **Economic**: Market trends, inflation, unemployment rates, consumer spending power, and economic growth patterns.
- **Social**: Cultural trends, demographics, consumer behavior, and societal attitudes.
- **Technological**: Advances in technology, innovation trends, and access to technological resources.
- **Environmental**: Sustainability concerns, ecological regulations, and climate-related factors.
- **Legal**: Compliance with laws, regulations, intellectual property rights, and labor laws.

By systematically applying PESTEL analysis, Tara proactively addressed risks, enhanced the viability of her solution, and positioned her marketplace to succeed in a dynamic environment.

- **Political**: Benefit from government's **Pradhan Mantri Vishwakarma Kaushal Samman (PM-VIKAS)** for marketplace models.
- **Economic**: Design an affordable pricing structure for middle-class customers.
- **Social**: Highlight storytelling and authenticity to align with cultural trends favoring local artisans.
- **Technological**: Invest in a scalable e-commerce platform with secure payment systems.
- **Environmental**: Offer sustainable packaging solutions to appeal to eco-conscious customers.
- **Legal**: Ensure adherence to e-commerce-specific regulations, including GST and consumer protection rules.

Technical feasibility analysis

A technical feasibility analysis evaluates whether a proposed solution can be developed and implemented using the available technology, resources, and expertise. For entrepreneurs, particularly those without a technical background, conducting such a study can initially appear overwhelming. However, with a structured approach, a willingness to learn the basics, and the ability to ask pertinent questions, entrepreneurs can effectively assess feasibility and identify potential risks without excessive complexity or resource investment.

Process of a technical feasibility analysis

These are the steps in conducting a technical feasibility study:

1. **Define the core functionalities**: The first step is defining the core functionalities of the solution. Using methods such as those outlined the *Chapter 3, Opportunity Prioritization*, entrepreneurs should start by clearly articulating the primary features the solution must deliver. This clarity is foundational, ensuring that all subsequent evaluations are aligned with the solution's intended purpose.

2. **Consult with technical experts**: Consulting with technical experts is a crucial phase in this study. Entrepreneurs can engage freelancers, consultants, or software development companies for an initial assessment. Providing comprehensive details about the solution, including its intended functionalities and underlying problem statement, helps these experts offer accurate feedback on feasibility. Asking for cost estimates at this stage can also provide insights into budgeting and potential financial requirements.

3. **High-level solution architecture diagram**: To further evaluate technical feasibility, entrepreneurs should create a high-level solution architecture diagram. If needed, the entrepreneur should collaborate with a technical expert to build one. This diagram visualizes how different components of the solution will interact, highlighting potential integrations or dependencies. Tools like Lucidchart, Draw.io, or even a simple pen-and-paper approach can be used for this purpose. The diagram not only simplifies communication with technical experts but also acts as an artifact to start conversations with technologists.

4. **Validate technical requirements against budget**: Validating technical requirements against the available budget is another critical step. Entrepreneurs should map out the cost implications of their chosen technologies, including licenses, infrastructure (e.g., cloud hosting), and development resources. Comparing these costs with the budget ensures that the solution remains financially viable and avoids overextension of resources.

5. **Leverage low-code or no-code platforms**: Once the core functionalities of the solution are clearly defined, the next logical step is to explore platforms, tools, and technologies that can support its development.

    For entrepreneurs without a technical background, leveraging low-code or no-code platforms can be a game-changer. No-code platforms allow non-technical users to build applications entirely through visual tools, drag-and-drop interfaces, and pre-configured modules, eliminating the need for coding.

    Platforms like *Bubble, OutSystems,* and *Webflow* enable the development of functional MVPs with little to no coding knowledge.

    Platforms like *Shopify* and *WooCommerce* offer ready-to-use frameworks for e-commerce ventures. They provide a seamless way to build marketplaces without requiring deep technical expertise. Entrepreneurs can rely on e-commerce related low-code platforms to manage critical technical aspects such as payment processing, inventory management, and user interface design, allowing them to allocate their time and energy toward refining their business strategies and customer experiences.

Tips for entrepreneurs without a technical background

For entrepreneurs who may feel intimidated by technical feasibility studies, a few practical strategies can help:

- **Ask questions freely**: Never hesitate to ask technical experts for simplified explanations. This approach fosters understanding and prevents miscommunication. Remember there is nothing like a stupid question.

- **Focus on the why**: Clearly articulating the problem statement helps technical experts propose the most effective solutions.

- **Start small**: Prioritize essential features for the MVP to keep technical complexity manageable. Avoid overloading the initial solution with non-essential capabilities.

- **Learn basic concepts**: Familiarize yourself with fundamental technical terms like APIs, databases, and cloud hosting to participate meaningfully in technical discussions.

- **Minimize costs and efforts**: Platforms like *Upwork* or *Fiverr* can connect entrepreneurs with affordable technical consultants for short-term engagements.

Meanwhile, Tara develops a comprehensive risk checklist to systematically assess and address potential risks as she builds her platform. This proactive approach ensures that critical aspects are not overlooked, preventing issues from slipping through the cracks due to oversight or evolving circumstances.

She begins by identifying key risk areas and outlining potential risks associated with each. For every identified risk, she documents her current mitigation strategies, recognizing that these strategies will require regular review and updates to stay aligned with changing realities and market dynamics. This iterative approach enables Tara to adapt effectively and maintain a robust risk management framework as her platform evolves.

Risk area	Potential risks	Mitigation strategies
Market risks	Market demand fluctuations due to shifting customer preferences.	Conduct regular customer surveys and monitor market trends.
	Intense competition from platforms like Amazon Karigar.	Differentiate with unique value propositions such as storytelling, authenticity, and artisan exclusivity.
Regulatory risks	Non-compliance with e-commerce regulations or tax laws.	Consult with a CA and legal expert to ensure adherence to all relevant laws, such as GST and FDI policies.
	Data privacy violations under emerging regulations (e.g., PDPB).	Implement strong data protection measures and align with upcoming data laws.

Operational risks	Delays in logistics and order fulfillment.	Partner with reliable logistics providers and build contingency plans for delays.
	Issues with packaging quality, leading to product damage.	Source high-quality packaging materials and perform regular quality checks.
Technological risks	Platform outages or bugs affecting customer experience.	Use a stable, scalable e-commerce platform and plan for periodic testing and updates. Establish a customer support and technical operations team at right moment.
	Integration challenges with third-party services (e.g., payment gateways).	Select widely compatible technologies and test integrations thoroughly.
Financial risks	Overspending on technology or marketing without returns.	Set a clear budget and track expenses regularly to avoid overruns.
	Difficulty in securing additional funding.	Strengthen investor network, increase her visibility, and keep updating the investor pitch highlighting market potential and scalability.
Customer experience risks	Poor user experience due to unclear navigation or lack of trust-building elements (e.g., reviews, policies).	Focus on UI/UX design and include clear refund/return policies and trust indicators like certifications.
	Customer dissatisfaction with quality or authenticity.	Vet artisans thoroughly and introduce a product authenticity certification.
Artisan onboarding risks	Difficulty in convincing artisans to join the platform.	Showcase the platform's benefits, such as wider reach and better margins, through testimonials, demos and offer incentives.
	High churn rate among artisans due to dissatisfaction in early days as the platform takes off.	Offer regular feedback on how to improve and support services for artisans (e.g., training, logistics assistance).
Economic risks	Recession or reduced consumer spending impacting sales.	Diversify product categories and focus on premium as well as affordable handmade products.
Cultural risks	Misalignment with cultural shifts or values, e.g., sustainability trends.	Emphasize sustainable practices in packaging and sourcing.
Technological disruptions	New entrants leveraging advanced technology (e.g., AI-driven personalization).	Invest in innovation and stay updated on technology trends.

Table 4.7: Tara's risk checklist

Actions for the entrepreneurs

The following actionable steps are recommended to help entrepreneurs apply the key concepts covered in this chapter:

- Using insights from the previous chapter, describe the comprehensively detailed idea using the Idea Canvas.

- Map the ecosystem of products and systems within which the solution for the opportunity will exist.

- Conduct a risk analysis of building a solution for the identified opportunity.

- Identify all legal, compliance, and regulatory requirements that would be applicable.

Conclusion

By applying the structured techniques outlined in this chapter, entrepreneurs can move beyond the randomness of unstructured brainstorming and the pitfalls of preconceived ideas to develop innovative, impactful solutions. The tools and frameworks, such as the Double Diamond approach, design thinking, SCAMPER, and the How Might We method, offer a disciplined yet creative pathway to ideation. Techniques like Mind Mapping and the Idea Canvas empower entrepreneurs to explore, refine, and articulate their ideas, ensuring clarity and alignment with market needs.

Additionally, leveraging insights from market trends, customer feedback, and competitive analysis ensures that solutions are not only innovative but also grounded in real-world relevance. The integration of the Ecosystem Mapping Canvas and risk analysis methods equips entrepreneurs to assess their ideas within the broader market landscape, accounting for potential opportunities and challenges.

As entrepreneurs move forward, it is essential to maintain a mindset of adaptability. Ideas should not be rigid but evolve through continuous iteration and validation. By embracing structured ideation and solution-generation techniques, entrepreneurs position themselves to build solutions that are not only visionary but also practical, scalable, and capable of delivering promised value in the marketplace.

In the next chapter, the entrepreneur will learn to ensure the solution addresses the problem identified.

Join our Discord space

Join our Discord workspace for latest updates, offers, tech happenings around the world, new releases, and sessions with the authors:

https://discord.bpbonline.com

CHAPTER 5
Problem-solution Fit

Introduction

After generating and refining potential solutions during the ideation phase, the next critical step for entrepreneurs is to ensure alignment between the identified problems and the proposed solutions. This stage, known as achieving problem-solution fit, is where entrepreneurs validate whether their solution effectively addresses the core needs of their target customers. Without this alignment, even the most innovative solutions risk failing to resonate with customers or create meaningful value.

Problem-solution fit focuses on systematically evaluating the proposed solutions against customer needs, pain points, and business goals. This process ensures that the entrepreneur is solving the right problem in a way that is feasible, impactful, and scalable. To achieve this, entrepreneurs must develop clear problem statements, leverage structured frameworks like the Value Proposition Canvas, and explore tools such as the Elevator Pitch Canvas to articulate their solutions concisely and compellingly.

This chapter equips entrepreneurs with the methods and tools to align their solutions with the problems they aim to solve. Techniques such as Customer Journey Mapping, **Jobs to be Done** (**JTBD**) analysis, and prototyping help entrepreneurs deeply understand their customers' experiences and validate the relevance and efficacy of their solutions. By systematically evaluating fitment, entrepreneurs can prioritize efforts that address high-impact problems while reducing risks and optimizing resource allocation.

Problem-solution fit is a pivotal milestone in the entrepreneurial journey. Achieving it not only validates the solution's viability but also lays the foundation for building an MVP that delivers measurable value. This chapter provides entrepreneurs with actionable strategies to assess, iterate, and strengthen their solutions, ensuring a clear and compelling path forward.

Structure

In this chapter, we will cover the following topics:

- Problem statement canvas
- User persona
- Value Proposition Canvas
- User Journey Maps
- Solution architecture
- Elevator pitch

Objectives

By the end of this chapter, entrepreneurs will have the tools and frameworks necessary to validate and strengthen the alignment between identified problems and proposed solutions. They will learn to craft precise problem statements and develop hypotheses to address these problems effectively. Entrepreneurs will gain the skills to use tools like the Value Proposition Canvas, Customer Journey Mapping, and JTBD analysis to ensure their solutions resonate with customer needs and expectations.

Additionally, they will explore prototyping techniques to test and refine their ideas, while tools like the Elevator Pitch Canvas will help them articulate their problem-solution fit concisely and persuasively. By mastering these methodologies, entrepreneurs will be equipped to optimize resource allocation, reduce risks, and lay a robust foundation for building a successful MVP.

Problem statement canvas

Defining the problem statement clearly is a foundational step for any entrepreneur because it provides clarity, focus, and direction. It ensures that all efforts are aligned toward solving the core challenge, preventing miscommunication among team members and stakeholders. A well-articulated problem statement helps entrepreneurs concentrate limited resources on the most pressing issues, guiding solution development and enabling measurable outcomes. By centering on genuine customer needs and pain points, it fosters a customer-centric approach that enhances product-market fit while reducing the risk of developing irrelevant solutions. Furthermore, a clear problem statement prevents solution bias, encourages adaptability, and builds confidence among stakeholders, such as investors and partners, by showcasing the entrepreneur's deep understanding of the market.

Whenever an entrepreneur engages with an investor, a potential team member, or a user, their ability to clearly articulate the problem and its impact can significantly influence the response they receive. Investors are more likely to fund a venture when they understand the urgency and scope of the issue being addressed. Similarly, users and potential employees are more inclined to connect with a vision when they see how the solution directly alleviates a genuine pain point. Being crisp and clear about the problem not only builds credibility but also fosters emotional resonance with the audience. Tools like the Problem Canvas can help entrepreneurs structure and refine their problem statements, ensuring they are concise, compelling, and impactful. By doing so, entrepreneurs can effectively communicate their vision and rally support from all key stakeholders.

The Problem Canvas is a practical tool for entrepreneurs, helping you craft a concise and easy-to-remember version of the problem statement you are working to solve.

The canvas is presented in the following figure:

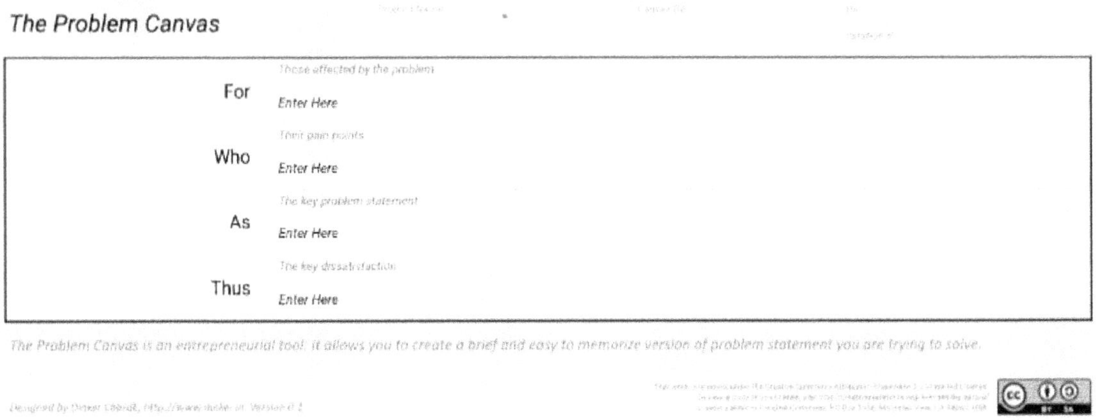

Figure 5.1: The Problem Canvas

The various sections of the Problem Canvas are outlined as follows:

- **For**: This section identifies the key stakeholders affected by the problem.

- **Who**: Here, you detail their specific pain points, using phrases like *unable to, cannot, find it hard to*, or *has to spend a lot to*, to clearly articulate their challenges.

- **As**: This is where you define the core problem statement, capturing the essence of the issue.

- **Thus**: In this section, you highlight the resulting dissatisfaction, such as *are unable to complete their task, are very dissatisfied*, or *are unable to earn*, emphasizing the impact of the problem.

Let us recap Tara's journey so far. Tara, a 36-year-old with extensive expertise in her domain, decided to embark on her entrepreneurial journey to tackle meaningful societal and economic challenges. She began by compiling a comprehensive list of problem statements, ranging from water supply issues to concerns about digital privacy. To narrow her focus, she conducted a self-assessment by asking critical questions about her passion, awareness, network, and engagement capabilities for each idea. This process led her to identify two promising opportunities: addressing restrictions on farmers trading grain freely and creating marketplaces for local artisans. Ultimately, she chose the latter, as it presented a more feasible and impactful venture with fewer barriers to entry.

Focusing on the *lack of marketplaces for local artisans*, Tara conducted a detailed stakeholder analysis. She identified online shoppers, local artisans, logistics providers, e-commerce platforms, and influencers as key players in the ecosystem. To deepen her understanding, she created Empathy maps that revealed online shoppers' frustrations with finding authentic, handmade products and local artisans' struggles with visibility, fair pricing, and logistics. These insights laid the groundwork for developing a solution tailored to the needs of both groups.

Tara validated the market opportunity through thorough research. She estimated the TAM at ₹1,33,308 crores and the SAM at ₹25,435 crores, targeting urban, middle-class demographics aged 25-54. By analyzing competitors like *Etsy, Craftsvilla,* and *Amazon Karigar,* she identified a clear differentiation opportunity in emphasizing storytelling, authenticity, and direct artisan support. To ensure a comprehensive perspective, she also engaged experts in e-commerce, logistics, customer support, digital marketing, and design to map and optimize the current value stream for artisans and shoppers.

Through Value Stream Mapping, Tara identified inefficiencies in artisan onboarding, product listing, marketing, and logistics. Key pain points included the lack of tools for artisans to create high-quality product images and packaging, poor search and discovery experiences for shoppers, and delays in delivery. A SWOT analysis revealed her strengths in domain expertise and problem clarity, weaknesses in tech scalability and competitive pressure, opportunities in niche differentiation, and threats from market saturation and regulatory challenges.

With these insights, Tara used tools like an Experiment Canvas covered in *Chapter 2, Market Analysis and Validation,* and SCAMPER analysis covered in *Chapter 4, Ideation and Solution Generation,* to ideate solutions. Her Experiment Canvas outlined the goal of creating a trustworthy platform that connects artisans and shoppers while ensuring authenticity, quality, and reliable delivery. SCAMPER analysis helped her explore innovative approaches such as merging storytelling with product listings, introducing gamification for artisan engagement, and expanding reach through international shipping. Using the Six Thinking Hats method, she balanced facts, risks, opportunities, and creative strategies to refine her concept.

Tara also built a strategic roadmap to mitigate risks and ensure success. She addressed market, operational, and technological risks with strategies like forming reliable partnerships for logistics, maintaining compliance with regulations, and vetting artisans to build customer trust. Ecosystem mapping highlighted the value her marketplace would deliver, such as curated product catalogs, artisan training, and seamless logistics. She also identified opportunities for innovation, including authenticity verification using AI, subscription models for curated goods, and corporate gifting services.

Tara chose to use the Problem Canvas to craft a concise and memorable version of the problem she is aiming to address.

Here is what Tara's Problem Canvas looks like:

For online shoppers searching for unique, artisan-made products and local artisans seeking better platforms to sell their creations,

Who struggle to connect with each other, making it difficult to buy or sell authentic, handmade products,

As there is a significant lack of marketplaces dedicated to local artisans,

Thus, both groups are left dissatisfied—shoppers miss out on genuine, high-quality products that support artisans, while artisans lose potential customers.

User persona

A user persona is a semi-fictional profile of a target user group, created using a mix of real data and thoughtful assumptions. These personas are essential tools for entrepreneurs and product teams, offering a clear way to understand their audience. By defining who the users are, their needs, challenges, and motivations, personas help guide product decisions during development. They remind teams that every feature or solution is meant for real people with specific expectations, making it easier to prioritize what truly matters.

Personas also help make stakeholders more relatable by putting a name and face to the abstract concept of a user. When stakeholders are easily identifiable, personas can serve as a valuable tool for anonymizing sensitive details while keeping the focus on their needs and behaviors.

As part of establishing problem-solution fit, personas are instrumental in activities like creating Customer Journey Maps and JTBD, filling out a Value Proposition Canvas, and guiding the prototyping process.

A user persona typically includes:

- **Persona name**: The persona's name is usually a blend of a common first name and an attribute reflecting their role in the solution. The common name aids recall, while the descriptive element subtly highlights their role. Using diverse names, including different genders, ethnicities, or geographic origins, can help broaden the solution's perceived audience. Tools like **name-generator.org.uk** can be useful for this. It is also important to verify that the chosen name does not belong to a real person (a quick Google search can help) and does not carry negative connotations (check sites like **urbandictionary.com**).

  Example: Tara named one persona *Channapatna Kishore,* to represent a local artisan. The name reminded her of the handmade wooden toys and dolls made by artisans she wanted to promote. It felt authentic, sweet, and memorable, adding a cultural touch.

For the persona of an online shopper, Tara chose *Digital Divya* to reflect a buyer who is tech-savvy, purpose-driven, culturally conscious, and responsible. The name captures ease with technology and a dynamic personality, aligning perfectly with the target user group.

- **Brief description**: A one-liner that highlights the core of the persona's life and their relevance to the solution being designed.

    Example: For *Channapatna Kishore*, Tara chose: *A skilled artisan crafting timeless handmade treasures, striving to reach appreciative buyers in a broader market.*

- **Photo**: To make a persona tangible and relatable, entrepreneurs often add photographs to represent a user persona. These foster a stronger emotional connection and provide a mental image, putting a face to the name. While some teams may use photos of colleagues or stock images, tools like DALL-E offer AI-generated profile pictures tailored to the persona's description, ensuring uniqueness and alignment with the intended audience.

- **Demographics**: Demographics often play a crucial role in why a particular persona is prioritized or represents an important user segment. Key demographic attributes typically include factors such as age, gender, occupation, education level, and location, whether urban, suburban, or rural. Additionally, marital or family status and specific job titles can provide deeper insights into the persona's context, making them more relatable and relevant to the solution being designed. These attributes help entrepreneurs and teams ground their personas in reality and ensure they align closely with the target audience's needs.

    Example: Tara chose the following demographics for *Channapatna Kishore* to represent the median characteristics:

    o **Age**: 42

    o **Gender**: Male

    o **Occupation**: Artisan specializing in handmade wooden toys and crafts

    o **Education level**: High school graduate

    o **Location**: Rural area near *Channapatna, Karnataka*

    o **Marital/Family status**: Married with two children

- **Behaviors and preferences**: A persona's behaviors and preferences provide valuable insights into their intentions, thought processes, and actions that are relevant to the problem statement and solution. These details can help entrepreneurs prioritize user needs or represent an important user segment effectively.

    o **Tech-savviness**: Personas can range across the spectrum from innovation seekers and early adopters to trend followers, latecomers, or even laggards.

o **Preferred communication channels**: These could include various modes of interaction, such as email, social media, or face-to-face engagement, depending on their habits and comfort levels.

o **Buying habits**: Personas may range from avid online shoppers to steadfast supporters of brick-and-mortar stores, providing cues about how they interact with purchasing platforms.

o **Hobbies and interests**: Interests can span a wide array, offering additional context about their lifestyle, preferences, and motivations.

Example: Based on her conversation with many local artisans, Tara assigned the following behaviors and preferences for *Channapatna Kishore*:

o Minimal exposure to technology; comfortable with basic mobile usage but finds online platforms challenging.

o Prefers face-to-face interactions or phone calls over digital communication. Comfortable with messaging apps for basic inquiries.

o Primarily reliant on local markets, artisan fairs, and aggregators for selling products. Limited experience or trust in online marketplaces.

o Enjoys creating intricate designs and innovating on traditional techniques. Passionate about preserving cultural heritage and storytelling through craft.

- **Pain points and challenges**: Highlight the specific pain points that intersect with the persona's broader life or career goals and relate directly to the problem statement and proposed solution. Additionally, address general challenges within the domain that affect their ability to achieve their objectives or fulfill their needs. These insights help entrepreneurs align their solutions to the most pressing issues faced by their target audience.

Example: Tara surfaced following pain points and challenges for *Channapatna Kishore*:

o Struggles to connect with buyers who value and are willing to pay for handmade products.

o Limited knowledge and access to platforms for effectively showcasing products online.

o Difficulty managing logistics like packaging and shipping often results in product damage or delays.

- **Motivations, goals, and needs**: Identify how the problem statement reflects a key pain point (need) for the persona, what issues they prioritize solving first (motivation), and the outcomes they aim to achieve (goals). Explore why they currently use (or would consider using) the proposed solution, linking it to their broader life or career aspirations that align with the problem and solution. Understanding these drivers provides a clear framework for tailoring the solution to their needs and fostering long-term engagement.

Example: Tara surfaced following motivations, goals, and needs for *Channapatna Kishore*:

- o Aspire to connect directly with buyers who value handcrafted products, ensuring fair recognition and sustainable income for their artistry.

- o Build a dependable sales channel that provides visibility, logistical support, and an authentic platform to showcase their craft.

- o A straightforward, supportive marketplace that handles marketing, quality assurance, and delivery logistics to alleviate operational burdens.

These sections will help an entrepreneur draw out a sufficiently complete user persona, as shown in the following figure:

Digital Divya

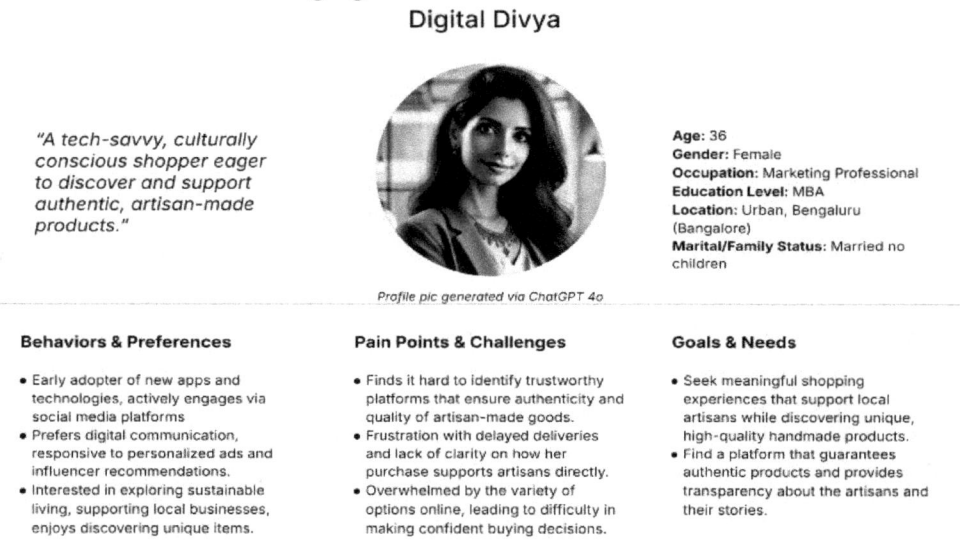

"A tech-savvy, culturally conscious shopper eager to discover and support authentic, artisan-made products."

Age: 36
Gender: Female
Occupation: Marketing Professional
Education Level: MBA
Location: Urban, Bengaluru (Bangalore)
Marital/Family Status: Married no children

Profile pic generated via ChatGPT 4o

Behaviors & Preferences

- Early adopter of new apps and technologies, actively engages via social media platforms
- Prefers digital communication, responsive to personalized ads and influencer recommendations.
- Interested in exploring sustainable living, supporting local businesses, enjoys discovering unique items.

Pain Points & Challenges

- Finds it hard to identify trustworthy platforms that ensure authenticity and quality of artisan-made goods.
- Frustration with delayed deliveries and lack of clarity on how her purchase supports artisans directly.
- Overwhelmed by the variety of options online, leading to difficulty in making confident buying decisions.

Goals & Needs

- Seek meaningful shopping experiences that support local artisans while discovering unique, high-quality handmade products.
- Find a platform that guarantees authentic products and provides transparency about the artisans and their stories.

Figure 5.2: Tara's version of persona slide

Jobs to be Done

JTBD is a powerful methodology for understanding customer actions, behaviors, and decisions. It shifts the focus from merely observing what customers do to uncovering the deeper motives and objectives that drive their choices. At its core, JTBD emphasizes the task or job the customer is trying to accomplish, providing a perspective that uncovers aspects of a solution that are most relevant and beneficial to the end user. This, in turn, increases the likelihood of MVP adoption and long-term product success.

This approach gained prominence through the work of *Professor Clayton Christensen* of *Harvard Business School*[1], who popularized JTBD in his research on innovation[2]. *Christensen* identified

---

1 https://sloanreview.mit.edu/article/finding-the-right-job-for-your-product/. Accessed 12 Jan, 2025.
2 https://hbr.org/2016/09/know-your-customers-jobs-to-be-done. Accessed 12 Jan, 2025.

a significant gap in traditional market segmentation—such as demographics, geography, psychographics, and behaviors—and product-focused strategies, noting that they often failed to address the core reasons people made purchasing decisions, namely, the real-life goals, tasks, and problems they aim to solve. His insight was that customers essentially hire products or services to perform specific jobs in their lives. This perspective represented a paradigm shift, moving beyond demographic-based strategies to a deeper understanding of real-life tasks and challenges faced by users.

For example, consider a drill. Traditional thinking might suggest that people buy drills because they need a drill. However, through the JTBD lens, customers do not necessarily want the drill itself—they want a hole in the wall to hang a picture. The job to be done here is *create a hole to hang a picture,* and the drill is just one potential means to achieve that outcome.

Once entrepreneurs understand this concept, they can begin to innovate beyond the obvious. For instance, *what if there was a way to make holes without a drill? Or what if a drill could be designed to require less effort, create less mess, or offer unmatched precision?* This perspective can lead to breakthrough solutions.

Take adhesive hooks as an example. By reframing the job—hanging something on a wall—entrepreneurs developed a product that eliminated the need for drilling altogether. Customers could now simply stick adhesive hooks or strips to the wall, achieving the same outcome more quickly, easily, and without the noise or expense of buying new equipment.

The job—hanging something—remained constant, but the method (or product) used to get the job done evolved, resulting in a more user-friendly, efficient, and innovative solution. This example demonstrates the essence of JTBD: identifying the deeper purpose behind customer behavior and leveraging it to develop solutions that address the real needs and aspirations of users.

For entrepreneurs, adopting the JTBD framework is transformative. It encourages them to move beyond surface-level observations and understand the why behind customer behavior. By doing so, they can design solutions that resonate deeply with their audience, stand out in competitive markets, and ultimately drive lasting success.

To assist entrepreneurs in crafting a structured and actionable JTBD statement, adopting a popular format can be immensely helpful. A structured approach ensures clarity, focus, and alignment with customer motivations. The following is one widely used JTBD format[3] that can guide entrepreneurs through the process:

When [Situation], I want to [Motivation/Action], so I can [Desired Outcome].

This format breaks the JTBD into three sections:

- **Situation**: The context or circumstance that triggers the job. This is the problem or need the customer encounters.

---

3 **https://www.intercom.com/resources/books/intercom-jobs-to-be-done**. Accessed 12 Jan, 2025.

- **Motivation/Action**: The action the customer wants to take to address the situation or problem.

- **Desired outcome**: The result or benefit the customer aims to achieve by completing the job.

Example:

When I move into a new home, I want to find an easy way to hang pictures, so I can personalize my space without damaging the walls.

Based on the problem statement and the persona *Channapatna Kishore's* pain points, challenges, motivations, goals, and needs, Tara wrote JTBD stories. Here are the top prioritized ones:

- **JTBD story 1**: *When I create intricate, handcrafted products that reflect my cultural heritage, I want to reach buyers who value and are willing to pay for the uniqueness of handmade items, so I can ensure fair recognition and a sustainable income for my artistry.*

- **JTBD story 2**: *When I try to expand beyond local markets and fairs, I want to find an easy-to-use platform that helps me effectively showcase my work to a broader audience, so I can gain visibility, attract more customers, and grow my business sustainably.*

- **JTBD story 3**: *When I receive orders from distant customers, I want to have reliable support for packaging, shipping, and handling, so I can deliver my products safely and on time without worrying about damage or delays.*

Following up, based on the problem statement and the persona *Digital Divya's* pain points, challenges, motivations, goals, and needs, Tara wrote additional JTBD stories. Here are the top prioritized ones:

- **JTBD story 4**: *When I want to purchase unique, artisan-made products, I want to discover a trustworthy platform that guarantees authenticity and quality, so I can shop confidently knowing my purchase supports local artisans and aligns with my values.*

- **JTBD story 5**: *When I browse for handmade products, I want to know how my purchase directly benefits the artisans who created them, so I can feel assured that I'm contributing to their livelihood and promoting sustainable craftsmanship.*

- **JTBD story 6**: *When I explore online platforms with a variety of options, I want to easily navigate, compare, and select items without feeling overwhelmed, so I can make confident decisions and enjoy a seamless shopping experience.*

Now armed with a well-defined persona and a clear understanding of the jobs they want to accomplish, she is now ready to take the next steps towards finalizing the solution.

Value Proposition Canvas

With a well-defined persona and a clear understanding of the jobs they aim to accomplish, the entrepreneur is now poised to take the next step: linking these jobs to the value her solution will provide. This is where the Value Proposition Canvas becomes indispensable. By aligning the JTBD with the solution's components, the canvas serves as a bridge that connects the problem to the solution. This structured approach ensures that the entrepreneur designs a solution that not only addresses customer challenges but also creates meaningful value, laying a strong foundation for product-market fit.

The Value Proposition Canvas, developed by *Dr. Alexander Osterwalder*[4] co-founder of *Strategyzer*, is a practical tool that helps entrepreneurs align their solutions with the needs, expectations, and pain points of their target audience. Derived from persona research, it provides a structured approach to ensure the solution resonates with its intended customers by addressing their challenges and creating meaningful value.

Following is the visualization of the canvas:

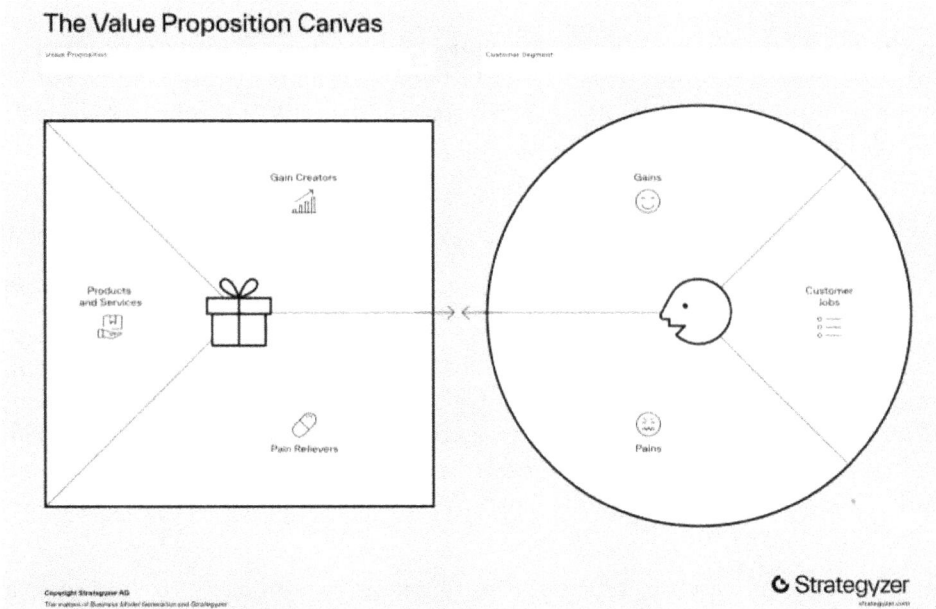

Figure 5.3: *The Value Proposition Canvas by Strategyzer*
Source: *Strategyzer AG*

The Value Proposition Canvas is divided into two key sections: **Customer Segment** and **Value Proposition**. Each section provides actionable insights to help entrepreneurs refine their solution to better serve their target audience.

Value proposition

This section captures the solution's value proposition and its relevance to the customer's needs and challenges. It consists of the following:

---

4 **https://www.strategyzer.com/library/the-value-proposition-canvas**. Accessed 12 Jan, 2025.

- **Gain creators**: Gain creators outline how the solution adds value for the customer, offering benefits or advantages that make their experience better. This is where innovation thrives—by not only meeting expectations but also creating unexpected delights. For example, a marketplace platform might provide additional features such as personalized recommendations or a portion of sales directly benefiting artisans, distinguishing itself from competitors.

- **Pain relievers**: Pain relievers focus on how the solution addresses the identified customer pains. Every feature or functionality should have a clear purpose in alleviating these challenges. For entrepreneurs, this means ensuring the solution reduces or eliminates barriers, frustrations, or risks associated with the customer's current journey. For instance, a transparent shipping policy with tracking updates could ease a shopper's anxiety about delayed deliveries.

- **Products and services**: This component lists the core offerings—products, features, and services—that form the foundation of the value proposition. These are the tangible and intangible elements that help create gains and relieve pain, establishing the solution's role in the customer's life.

Customer segment

This section captures a detailed understanding of the customer's functional, social, and emotional needs and challenges. It includes:

- **Customer jobs**: These are the tasks customers are trying to accomplish, problems they want to solve, or needs they aim to fulfill. Understanding customer jobs goes beyond surface-level tasks; it involves understanding the emotional, social, and functional drivers behind their decisions. For example, an artisan might seek to showcase their craftsmanship, while also wanting to build a reputation and connect with buyers who value handmade products.

- **Pain points**: Pain points describe the negative experiences, frustrations, and risks customers face while trying to get their jobs done. Identifying these pains enables entrepreneurs to design solutions that address specific barriers. For instance, customers may feel overwhelmed by the lack of authentic artisan platforms or frustrated by unclear delivery timelines.

- **Expected gains**: Gains represent the positive outcomes, benefits, and delights customers expect or desire. This is an opportunity for entrepreneurs to innovate by delivering benefits that exceed expectations. For example, a platform that guarantees authenticity and transparency while sharing artisans' stories can create a strong emotional connection with users.

Aligning the value proposition and customer segment

Each component of the customer segment directly correlates with a component in the Value Proposition:

- **Customer jobs <=> Products and services**: The solution's offerings should align with the tasks customers aim to accomplish.

- **Pain points <=> Pain relievers**: Pain relievers should be designed to address the specific challenges customers face.

- **Expected gains <=> Gain creators**: Gain creators should enhance or deliver the outcomes customers desire, fostering satisfaction and loyalty.

This alignment helps prioritize features, refine the offering, and ultimately deliver a value proposition that stands out in the market.

Tara took the help of the Value Proposition Canvas to ensure that her solution directly addresses the pain points and the issues they are facing. Here is her version for *Digital Divya*:

Value proposition		Customer segment
Gain creators: • Provide artisan stories and transparency about how purchases benefit artisans. • Guarantee authenticity and quality certifications for products. • Curate collections or provide recommendation features to simplify decision-making.		**Gains:** • Confidence in the authenticity and quality of the products purchased. • Seamless online experience with clear product descriptions and artisan stories. • Satisfaction from supporting artisans directly and aligning her shopping with her values.
Products and services: • Marketplace platform connecting artisans and buyers. • Logistics and packaging solutions for artisans. • Storytelling and artisan profiles integrated with product listings. • Training and onboarding support for artisans. • Filters, curation, and recommendations for buyers to simplify shopping.	<=>	**Customer jobs:** • Shop for unique, authentic, and artisan-made products that align with her values. • Ensure her purchases directly support artisans and contribute to sustainable practices. • Navigate online platforms seamlessly to discover and compare products without feeling overwhelmed.

Pain relievers:		Pains:
• Use storytelling to connect artisans with buyers and build trust in the platform. • Provide clear filters, comparisons, and reviews to simplify product selection. • Ensure fast, reliable delivery with clear return and refund policies.		• Finds it difficult to trust platforms for authenticity and quality of handmade goods. • Frustrated by unclear artisan stories and the lack of transparency on how purchases support artisans. • Overwhelmed by too many choices and poorly designed online experiences.

Table 5.1: *Tara's Value Proposition Canvas for Digital Divya*

Here is her version for *Channapatna Kishore*:

Value proposition		Customer segment
Gain creators: • Offer training sessions and support to onboard artisans easily onto the platform. • Partner with logistics providers to streamline shipping and delivery. • Highlight artisan products through storytelling and marketing campaigns.		**Gains:** • Reliable platform that handles marketing, logistics, and payments efficiently. • Access to a wider audience that appreciates and values handmade products. • Recognition for craftsmanship and a dependable income stream.
Products and services: • Marketplace platform connecting artisans and buyers. • Logistics and packaging solutions for artisans. • Storytelling and artisan profiles are integrated with product listings. • Training and onboarding support for artisans. • Filters, curation, and recommendations for buyers to simplify shopping.	<=>	**Customer jobs:** • Reach a broader audience of buyers who value handmade, culturally rich products. • Simplify logistics like packaging, shipping, and handling. • Gain visibility and recognition for craftsmanship while achieving sustainable income.

Pain relievers:	Pains:
• Handle packaging and logistics to reduce the artisan's operational burden. • Provide a simple interface for listing products and managing orders. • Create a certification system to ensure authenticity and attract more buyers.	• Struggles to find reliable buyers and showcase products effectively online. • Overwhelmed by logistics, such as packaging and shipping, leading to damage or delays. • Faces challenges with technology, making online selling intimidating and complicated.

Table 5.2: Tara's Value Proposition Canvas for Channapatna Kishore

User Journey Maps

Understanding users deeply is essential for any entrepreneur, and a key part of this understanding is analyzing their current journey. This journey represents the process users go through when encountering the problem, the entrepreneur aims to solve. Addressing this journey—whether by simplifying, shortening, optimizing, or completely reimagining it—is critical to delivering value.

VSM is a powerful tool for these scenarios. It is a lean management technique designed to visualize, analyze, and improve the flow of information and materials within a process. For entrepreneurs, VSM helps pinpoint inefficiencies, bottlenecks, and areas of waste, enabling better optimization of operations, reduction of costs, and enhanced value delivery. Here, value refers to the benefit customers receive and are willing to pay for.

While a typical value stream outlines the full journey across all users, the focus should shift to specific personas once the primary target users are identified. For these personas, entrepreneurs can create detailed Customer Journey Maps—subsections of the overall value stream—that highlight key touchpoints and serve as a foundation for optimizing cost and value delivery.

Though each persona and solution may lead to unique user journeys, common stages often emerge in a User Journey Map:

- **Awareness**: This stage marks when a user first becomes aware of the problem or the proposed solution. The focus here is on understanding how effectively the solution is reaching and resonating with its intended audience.

- **Consideration**: At this stage, users are evaluating their options and exploring potential solutions to their problem. The goal is to ensure the solution provides compelling reasons for users to proceed further.

- **Purchase decision**: This is the critical moment when users commit to the solution by making a purchase or signing up for a service. Metrics at this stage reflect how effectively the solution convinces users to act.

- **Usage**: Once users begin interacting with the product or service, it is crucial to measure how effectively it delivers value and meets their expectations.

- **Loyalty, advocacy, and feedback**: In this stage, the focus is on building lasting relationships with users, encouraging advocacy, and collecting feedback for continuous improvement.

Building on all the components she has identified throughout her journey; Tara systematically organizes them by aligning each with the appropriate stage of the user journey. Within each stage, she further categorizes the components based on the products and services defined in her Value Proposition Map. This structured approach ensures clarity and a direct connection between the user journey, the value being delivered, and the solution's core offerings.

This is what the User Journey Map looks like now:

User journey stage	Products and services	Solution components
Awareness	Filters, curation, and recommendations for buyers to simplify shopping.	• Conduct regular customer surveys and monitor market trends.
		• Differentiate with unique value propositions such as storytelling, authenticity, and artisan exclusivity.
		• Use influencer marketing to promote artisan products.
	Storytelling and artisan profiles integrated with product listings.	• Introduce storytelling features to connect artisans with buyers.
Consideration	Marketplace platform connecting artisans and buyers.	• Filters, curation, and personalized recommendations for buyers.
		• Rearrange priority listings to highlight newer artisans or trending products.
		• Reverse product discovery by letting customers post wishlists for artisans to fulfill.
	Storytelling and artisan profiles integrated with product listings.	• Merge storytelling with product listings.
		• Showcase the platform's benefits, such as wider reach and better margins, through testimonials and demos.

Purchase decision	Filters, curation, and recommendations for buyers to simplify shopping.	• Start with niche product categories (e.g., handmade jewelry).
	Logistics and packaging solutions for artisans.	• Rearrange the payment model to allow deposits with full payment on delivery.
	Marketplace platform connecting artisans and buyers.	• Focus on high-demand artisan goods, removing redundant categories.
		• Simplify user verification steps.
Usage	Filters, curation, and recommendations for buyers to simplify shopping.	• Focus on UI/UX design and include clear refund/return policies and trust indicators like certifications.
	Logistics and packaging solutions for artisans.	• Partner with reliable logistics providers and build contingency plans for delays.
		• Replace artisan-managed shipping with logistics partnerships.
	Training and onboarding support for artisans.	• Combine artisan training with onboarding.
		• Minify onboarding by simplifying product listing processes.
		• Whet artisans thoroughly and introduce a product authenticity certification.
Loyalty, advocacy and feedback	Marketplace platform connecting artisans and buyers.	• Offer loyalty programs for repeat buyers and subscription models for curated products.
		• Magnify product range to include artisan services (e.g., custom commissions).
	Storytelling and artisan profiles integrated with product listings.	• Promote artisan-led workshops for customers.
	Training and onboarding support for artisans.	• Emphasize sustainable practices in packaging and sourcing.

Table 5.3: Tara's User Journey Map

Here are the values Tara deprioritized from her first draft of the User Journey Map based on her decision to not focus on partners and corporates:

User journey stage	Products and services	Solution components
Awareness	Storytelling and artisan profiles integrated with product listings.	Collaborate with NGOs or government initiatives supporting local artisans.
	Storytelling and artisan profiles integrated with product listings.	Collaborate with tourism boards to promote artisan villages as cultural destinations.
Purchase decision	Marketplace platform connecting artisans and buyers.	Integrate bulk buying for corporate buyers alongside individual sales.
Usage	Filters, curation, and recommendations for buyers to simplify shopping.	Introduce gamification techniques (e.g., badges for artisans).
	Logistics and packaging solutions for artisans.	Magnify reach by including international shipping.
	Logistics and packaging solutions for artisans.	Source high-quality packaging materials and perform regular quality checks.
	Training and onboarding support for artisans.	Offer regular feedback mechanisms and support services for artisans (e.g., training, logistics assistance).
Loyalty, advocacy and feedback	Marketplace platform connecting artisans and buyers.	Position the platform for corporate gifting.

Table 5.4: Deprioritized Items from Tara's first draft

Solution architecture

Solution architecture (**SA**) serves as the strategic blueprint that guides the development of a solution tailored to the problem statement. It bridges the gap between identifying what needs to be solved and determining how to address it. For entrepreneurs, SA provides a structured framework to ensure their MVP aligns with user needs while being scalable, efficient, and adaptable for future growth. The SA, often leading this effort, ensures the design phase focuses on delivering immediate value while setting the foundation for long-term sustainability.

Key considerations in solution architecture

While there are many possible solutions, at a high level, there are a few common aspects of a solution architecture.

Digital components

A well-designed solution starts by evaluating existing tools, software, and services that can be leveraged. Entrepreneurs must decide:

- **Platforms and touchpoints**: *Will the solution primarily cater to desktop users, mobile users, or other modes such as kiosks or smart devices?*

- **Pre-built tools**: Off-the-shelf solutions, like *Shopify* for e-commerce or *Slack* for team collaboration, can reduce development costs and time to market.

- **User accessibility**: Ensure the design is user-friendly across all customer touchpoints, aligning with personas and their needs.

System integration

Most modern solutions require seamless integration of multiple systems, such as:

- **Customer relationship management** (**CRM**) tools for managing customer data.

- Payment gateways for secure transactions.

- Workplace Suites like *Office 365, Google Workspace*, or *Zoho* for operational workflows. SA ensures these systems communicate effectively, reducing inefficiencies and enhancing overall user experience.

Custom software development

In cases where off-the-shelf solutions cannot meet specific needs, custom development becomes essential. The SA outlines:

- **Purpose and capabilities**: What the custom software will achieve.

- **Workflows and data flow**: How users will interact with the system and how data will be managed.

- **Alignment with value delivery**: Ensuring the development directly addresses the core problem statement.

Operational tools

Beyond the customer-facing components, a solution must support day-to-day business operations. The examples include:

- **Email campaign tools**: For marketing and communication.

- **User support platforms**: Chatbots, ticketing systems, or help desks.

- **Analytics tools**: To monitor performance and customer behavior. SA identifies and integrates these tools to streamline operations, ensuring entrepreneurs can focus on strategic growth.

Defining MVP architecture

For entrepreneurs, especially those without a technical background, it is essential to understand the differences between solution architecture, enterprise architecture, and technical architecture. Misunderstanding these roles can lead to misaligned expectations and inefficiencies.

Enterprise architecture

Enterprise architecture (**EA**) emphasizes the long-term strategic alignment of technology with an organization's overarching business goals. It provides a macro-level perspective, ensuring that all IT initiatives support the company's vision and objectives. By focusing on strategic alignment, EA enables organizations to leverage technology as a key driver of growth, efficiency, and competitive advantage.

The scope of enterprise architecture extends across the entire IT infrastructure and business processes of the organization. It addresses large-scale initiatives such as **enterprise resource planning** (**ERP**) transformations, application modernization, and IT integration following mergers or acquisitions. To structure these complex initiatives, EA often relies on established frameworks like **The Open Group Architecture Framework** (**TOGAF**) or the Zachman Framework. These methodologies offer structured approaches to organizing, analyzing, and managing technology investments, ensuring cohesive and sustainable solutions.

Technical architecture

Technical architecture (**TA**) focuses on the detailed implementation and configuration of individual components within a solution. It explores the technical specifications, ensuring that software, hardware, and networks work seamlessly together to support the system's overall functionality. TA bridges the gap between high-level designs and hands-on execution, translating architectural plans into actionable technical configurations.

The scope of TA includes specifying and managing how various technologies interact. This can involve designing cloud infrastructure, implementing data security protocols, or creating efficient network designs. The ultimate goal of TA is to ensure that systems are performant, scalable, and secure, enabling reliable operations even as demands evolve. For instance, when deploying a cloud-based application, TA addresses aspects like server configurations, encryption methods, and bandwidth optimization to guarantee a seamless user experience. By focusing on technical precision, TA plays a critical role in turning strategic plans into operational success.

Solution architecture

Solution architecture (**SA**) serves as the critical bridge between business strategies and technical execution, translating high-level objectives into actionable and tangible plans. It focuses on designing specific solutions that address well-defined problems, such as developing an MVP or creating a platform for a new service. By taking a targeted approach, SA ensures that technical initiatives are directly aligned with the business's value proposition and broader goals.

The scope of SA encompasses all aspects of the solution's design, from its functional requirements to its integration with existing systems. This includes defining workflows, identifying tools and technologies, and mapping out how components will interact. The ultimate goal of SA is to create solutions that not only fulfill customer needs but also integrate seamlessly into the organization's operations, reducing friction and enabling scalability. Whether it is enabling smooth payment processing or optimizing customer interactions, SA plays a vital role in bridging strategic intent and real-world functionality.

While EA defines the strategy, SA creates actionable blueprints to realize that strategy, and TA executes these plans at a granular technical level. Together, these disciplines create a cohesive approach to building and maintaining technology-driven initiatives.

Building a solution architecture

As an entrepreneur, developing these high-level design diagrams, the Solution Architecture, is a vital step in crafting their solution. It acts as a key reference and a valuable artifact for communication, providing a clear and visual representation of how systems, tools, and components will work together to address the problem statement and deliver meaningful value to users represented by the prioritized personas.

A well-crafted solution architecture diagram does not require intricate technical knowledge to create. It is about clarity, organization, and highlighting the connections between key components. Here is how you can build one:

- **Identifying systems and tools**: The first step in crafting a SA diagram is identifying all the systems, tools, and technologies involved in the solution. This includes:

  o **User-facing systems**: Websites, mobile apps, customer portals.

  o **Internal systems**: Databases, analytics tools, and CRM platforms.

  o **External integrations**: Payment gateways, logistics systems, and third-party APIs.

    For example, a retail solution might encompass an e-commerce platform, inventory management tools, **point of sale** (**POS**) systems, and logistics tracking software.

- **Using shapes and lines to represent relationships**: To visualize the identified components, simple shapes such as rectangles, circles, or icons are used to represent systems. These shapes are connected with lines to illustrate relationships and interactions. Lines may signify data flows, communication protocols, or user interactions, making the diagram intuitive and easy to interpret.

- **Grouping systems into logical categories**: Logical groupings enhance clarity in SA diagrams. Systems are commonly organized into layers such as:

  o **User-facing layer**: Includes mobile apps, websites, and customer dashboards.

  o **Internal processing layer**: Comprises middleware, databases, and back-end logic.

  o **Integration layer**: Encompasses third-party APIs, payment processors, and logistics systems.

    For example, an omnichannel retail solution might include a *Customer Interaction Layer* (e-commerce site, mobile app), a *Business Operations Layer* (inventory management, CRM), and a *Logistics Layer* (shipping and returns). Each group is clearly labeled to show the logical flow of the solution.

- **Adding details and annotations**: Annotations provide valuable context and make the diagram more informative. Key details to include are:

  o Roles and responsibilities of each system.

  o Security considerations for sensitive data flows, such as in payment systems.

  o Data flow descriptions using arrows to show how information moves between systems (e.g., orders flowing from the website to inventory systems).

  o Dependencies between components to clarify integration points.

    For instance, an annotation might state, *Order details flow from the* e-commerce *platform to the logistics system for fulfillment.*

- **Highlighting data movement**: Data flow is a critical component of Solution Architecture. Directional arrows or visual markers are used to indicate how data travels, such as:

  o Customer data moving from a sign-up form to the CRM.

  o Payment details flowing securely to the payment gateway.

  o Order status updates returning to customers via notifications.

  o Visualizing these movements helps identify inefficiencies or potential bottlenecks.

- **Keeping the diagram simple**: Simplicity is essential for an effective SA diagram. The goal is to present a high-level overview, not to recreate technical blueprints. Overloading the diagram with excessive details or jargon can reduce its effectiveness. Instead, focus on providing a clear, concise representation of the solution's structure and functionality.

Let us try to see this concept in action.

Example: The following is an example of a Solution Architecture for an e-commerce website. This architecture serves as a blueprint, detailing how various systems, tools, and components collaborate to deliver a seamless and efficient online shopping experience. It encompasses multiple layers, each tailored to address specific user-facing functionalities, business operations, integrations, data management, and infrastructure requirements.

Here is the visual representation:

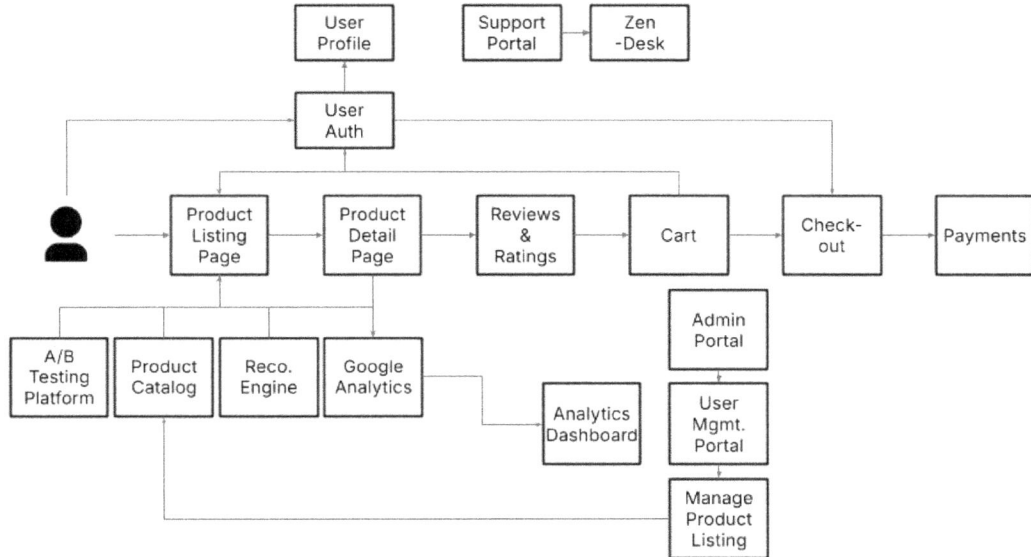

Figure 5.4: *Solution architecture of an e-commerce website*

Example: Roo Kids app was the flagship product of the now-defunct startup *Gungroo Software*. Designed as a safe and fun instant messaging app for kids, it aimed to provide a digital communication platform with essential parental controls. Often referred to as *WhatsApp for Kids* or *WhatsApp for Kids with Safety*, *Roo Kids* caters to children aged 6–12, addressing the growing need for a secure and child-friendly alternative in the digital world.

The app emerged from the belief that kids should be able to explore and master digital communication while addressing two critical concerns of parents: the risks of talking to strangers and distractions during homework or bedtime. Roo Kids tackled these issues directly with features such as parental review of contact lists, the ability for kids to block unwanted users or messages instantly, and curfew settings to restrict chat during designated times.

Roo Kids stood out by ensuring user safety with minimal data retention, removing messages from servers once delivered. Available on iPhone, iPad, and Android, the app offered a transitional experience for children before they ventured into less secure social networking platforms. Roo Kids was a bold attempt to blend fun, learning, and safety, reflecting a vision of preparing kids for the digital age while keeping them protected.

The following figure is the solution architecture used by the Founder (the author of this book) used in investor deck:

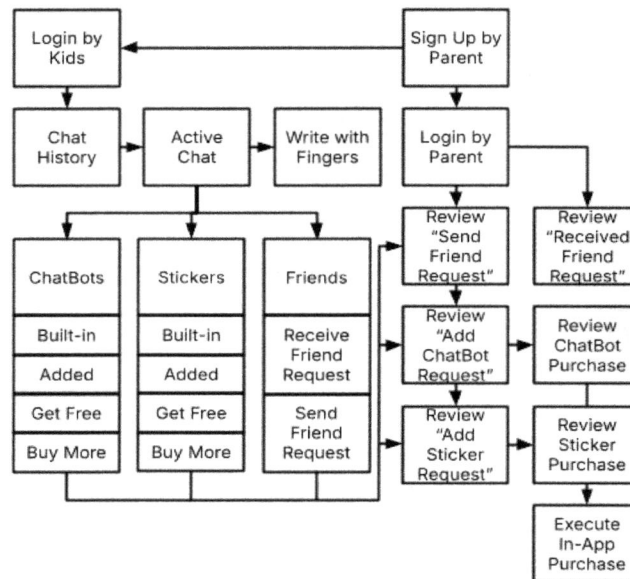

Figure 5.5: Solution architecture of Roo Kids app

To create a comprehensive SA, Tara meticulously identified all the systems and tools required for her marketplace. She began by mapping out the functional needs of her platform, ensuring every aspect of the solution was connected to the right software, platforms, and technologies. This strategic approach not only aligned with her vision but also laid the foundation for a scalable and efficient marketplace. Here is a detailed breakdown.

User-facing systems

User-facing systems are the applications and interfaces that directly interact with customers and artisans. For building IndicOcean, Tara identified:

- **Customer facing mobile application**: Offers a seamless shopping experience for smartphone users, enabling easy browsing, product discovery, and secure purchasing. Customers can track their orders, leave reviews, and manage preferences effortlessly. The platform also helps users explore artisan products through intuitive filters such as categories, price ranges, and other criteria, ensuring a personalized and enjoyable shopping journey.

- **Artisan facing mobile application**: Provides artisans with a user-friendly mobile application designed to simplify and streamline their online selling experience. The app enables artisans to upload products with detailed descriptions and high-quality images, manage their inventory, and track orders in real-time. It also facilitates seamless communication with buyers, offers insights into sales performance, and provides notifications for new orders or important updates. By integrating tools for logistics coordination, payment tracking, and customer feedback, the application empowers artisans to focus on their craft while effectively managing their digital storefront. This solution bridges the gap between artisans and buyers, fostering greater reach and recognition for their work.

Internal systems

Internal systems support the behind-the-scenes operations. For building IndicOcean, Tara identified:

- **Inventory management system**: Tracks artisan product availability and helps manage stock levels.
- **Order management system (OMS)**: Ensures smooth processing of orders and manages their status.
- **CRM**: Maintains customer profiles, purchase history, and engagement metrics.
- **Marketing automation**: Sends personalized email campaigns and promotional offers.

External integrations

External integrations connect the platform with essential third-party services that enable core functions such as payments, logistics, and marketing. For building IndicOcean, Tara identified:

- **Payment gateways**: Facilitate secure transactions.
- **Logistics and shipping**: Manages delivery from artisans to customers.
- **Social media integrations**: Promotes products through influencer marketing and social commerce.

Security and data privacy

Security and data privacy frameworks are foundational to user trust and regulatory compliance. For building IndicOcean, Tara identified:

- **Authentication and authorization**: Ensures secure user login and access controls.
- **Data encryption**: Protects sensitive customer and artisan data.
- **Compliance systems**: Aligns with data protection regulations (e.g., GDPR, local data laws).

Analytics and insights

Analytics and insights tools help the entrepreneur understand how users interact with the platform and where there are opportunities for improvement. For building IndicOcean, Tara identified:

- **App analytics**: Tracks user behavior and platform performance.
- **Feedback analysis**: Aggregates customer reviews and ratings for quality improvement.

Collaboration and operational tools

Collaboration and operational tools facilitate internal coordination and external stakeholder management. For building IndicOcean, Tara identified:

- **Artisan onboarding system**: Simplifies registration and training for artisans.
- **CMS**: Manages product descriptions, artisan stories, and blog content.
- **Communication tools**: Facilitates collaboration among team members and external stakeholders.

Data flow overview

The data flow overview illustrates how different systems and components interact with one another, from customer actions to backend processing and external services. For building IndicOcean, Tara identified:

- Customers access the *Customer Facing Mobile Application* to browse products.
- The app queries the *Inventory Management System* for stock details and the *Content Management System* for product descriptions and artisan profiles.
- Orders placed by customers are routed to the *Order Management System*, triggering updates in the *Inventory Management System* and notifying the artisan via the *Artisan Facing Mobile Application*.
- The *Payment Gateway* processes transactions, while the *CRM* logs customer data for engagement and loyalty programs.
- The *Marketing Automation* system uses analytics from the *App Analytics* tool to target customers with personalized campaigns.
- The *Compliance Systems* and *Data Encryption* layer ensures regulatory and data protection requirements are met.

Elevator pitch

Imagine this scenario: an entrepreneur finds themselves sharing an elevator ride with a top-tier executive or a venture capitalist. In the span of just a minute or two, they have the opportunity to present an innovative idea, justify its potential, and capture the interest of this influential individual enough to open doors for funding or collaboration. The question is: *are they ready for this moment?*

This scenario perfectly illustrates the purpose of an elevator pitch—the ability to succinctly convey vision and value in the short duration of an elevator ride. However, the true importance of an elevator pitch extends far beyond these rare chance encounters. Its real power lies in the clarity it brings to founders and their teams.

Crafting an elevator pitch requires founders to engage in a disciplined and structured thought process, distilling their vast knowledge, insights, opportunities, and overarching vision into a concise and compelling narrative. This process ensures that everyone involved in the venture, from the founder to the core team, is aligned and able to clearly articulate the value proposition of their product or service.

For many entrepreneurs, synthesizing their big ideas into a brief, impactful pitch can feel overwhelming. This is where the elevator pitch becomes a vital tool—not only as a communication device but also as a way to crystallize the essence of the venture. It compels founders to focus on the why and how of their solution, making it easier to communicate its relevance and potential impact.

To simplify this process, tools like the Elevator Pitch Canvas are invaluable. This lean innovation framework helps entrepreneurs craft a concise, memorable, and impactful description of their product and its purpose. By using this tool, founders can ensure their pitch resonates with stakeholders, investors, and potential partners, leaving a lasting impression in even the shortest of conversations.

The Elevator Pitch Canvas provides a structured and efficient framework to distill the core value of a solution, the value it brings, and who whom into a concise, compelling message. This tool is especially useful for entrepreneurs, enabling them to articulate their vision clearly and persuasively in just a few moments. Entrepreneurs can use the following format to build an Elevator Pitch:

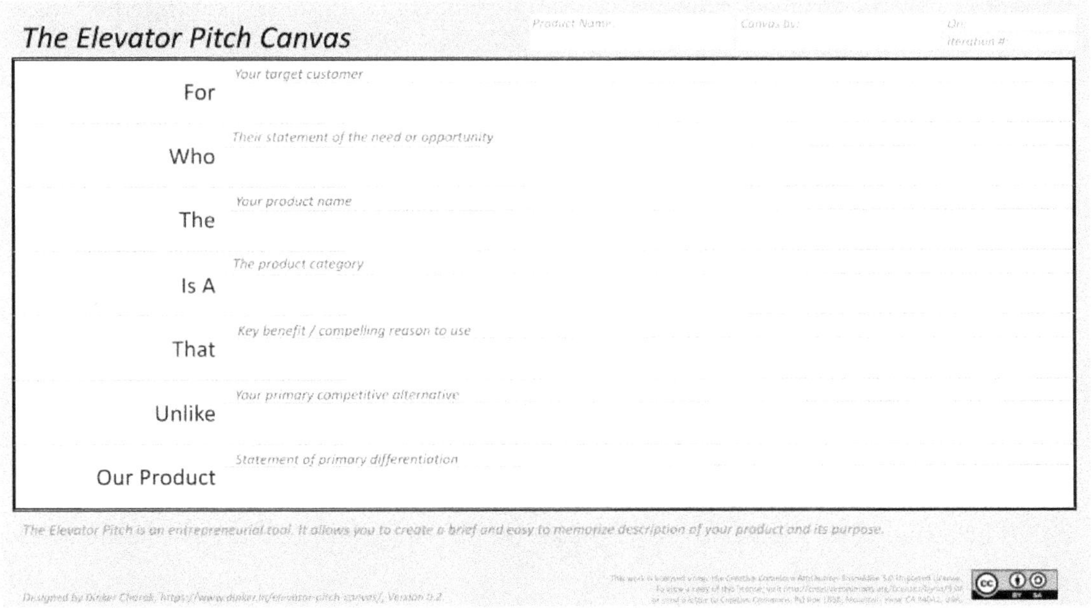

Figure 5.6: Elevator Pitch Canvas

Here is a breakdown of its sections, each designed to guide the entrepreneur toward crafting a pitch that resonates with their audience:

- **For (Target customer)**: This section identifies the primary audience or demographic for the product. The focus should be on specifying a well-defined customer segment to ensure the pitch resonates directly with those who will benefit most from the solution.

- **Who (Need or opportunity)**: Here, the entrepreneur articulates the main need, pain point, or opportunity that the product addresses. This step is vital as it sets the context for the pitch, showcasing the problem or gap in the market that the product aims to solve.

- **The (Product name)**: State the name of the product clearly and succinctly. A memorable product name enhances recognition and helps the audience connect the solution to its identity.

- **Is a (Product category)**: Define the product's category to provide clarity about its nature or purpose. This categorization places the offering within a familiar framework, making it easier for the audience to understand its function and relevance.

- **That (Key benefit)**: Highlight the standout benefit of the product that directly addresses the identified need or opportunity. Instead of listing multiple features, this section focuses on a singular, compelling capability that aligns closely with customer pain points.

- **Unlike (Primary competitive alternative)**: Identify the primary alternatives or competitors currently addressing the same need. By referencing existing products, solutions, or services, this section helps establish a baseline, setting the stage for differentiation.

- **Our product (Primary differentiation)**: This is where the entrepreneur highlights what makes their product unique. Emphasizing the key differentiator or USP reinforces the product's value and demonstrates why it outshines the competition.

Crafting and refining the pitch

Once all sections are completed, the next step is to combine them into a seamless, cohesive sentence. Reading the pitch aloud ensures it flows naturally and sounds conversational rather than overly scripted. Practicing repeatedly, refining the language, and delivering with confidence are essential to perfecting the pitch.

Keeping *Digital Divya* persona in focus, Tara crafted the following elevator pitch:

- **For** tech-savvy, culturally conscious shoppers like Digital Divya
- **Who** struggle to find trustworthy platforms offering authentic, artisan-made products
- **The** artisan connect marketplace
- **Is a** curated e-commerce platform

- **That** delivers unique, high-quality handmade items while supporting local artisans directly
- **Unlike** generic marketplaces that lack transparency or personalization
- **Our platform** features artisan stories, authenticity certifications, and seamless shopping experiences to align purchases with values and purpose

Actions for the entrepreneur

1. Identify key personas for each stakeholder and outline the key JTBD for each.
2. Build a Value Proposition Canvas to map how the solution aligns with user needs.
3. Develop a solution architecture for the opportunity.
4. With a high-level solution in place, craft a short pitch using the Elevator Pitch Canvas.

Conclusion

Achieving problem-solution fit is a critical milestone in the entrepreneurial journey, bridging the gap between identifying customer pain points and crafting solutions that resonate. This chapter has provided entrepreneurs with the tools and frameworks necessary to ensure their solutions align with real-world needs and expectations. By leveraging structured methodologies such as the Value Proposition Canvas, JTBD analysis, and Customer Journey Mapping, entrepreneurs can develop a deep understanding of their target audience, ensuring their solutions are both relevant and impactful.

The introduction of prototyping techniques equips entrepreneurs to validate and refine their ideas in a practical and iterative manner. Tools like the Elevator Pitch Canvas enable entrepreneurs to distill their ideas into compelling narratives, facilitating communication with stakeholders, investors, and customers. Through these techniques, entrepreneurs can test assumptions, minimize risks, and focus resources on the most critical aspects of their solutions.

Ultimately, the process of achieving problem-solution fit is about more than just validating ideas—it is about building a foundation for long-term success. By aligning solutions with customer needs and business goals, entrepreneurs set the stage for developing an MVP that delivers measurable value.

In the next chapter, the entrepreneur will learn how to choose the right metrics.

Join our Discord space

Join our Discord workspace for latest updates, offers, tech happenings around the world, new releases, and sessions with the authors:

https://discord.bpbonline.com

CHAPTER 6
Defining Metrics

Introduction

In the entrepreneurial journey, defining and tracking metrics is critical to transforming a vision into measurable progress. Metrics act as a compass, guiding the MVP toward its goals by providing tangible data to evaluate performance and identify areas for improvement. As the adage goes, *what is measured can be managed*. For entrepreneurs, defining clear metrics is not just about numbers—it is about accountability, alignment, and adaptability.

Metrics serve as an antidote to the extremes of over-optimism or over-pessimism. They offer a reality check, providing an unbiased perspective on whether an MVP is truly on the path to achieving its objectives or veering off course. Furthermore, well-defined metrics make it easier for entrepreneurs to explain, convince, and onboard stakeholders, whether investors, team members, or early adopters, by demonstrating clear progress and aligning efforts around shared goals.

Structure

In this chapter, we will cover the following topics:
- Leading and lagging indicators
- KPIs and Fitness Metrics
- AARRR pirate metrics

- The Viability Spectrum
- Concept of a fully modeled metric

Objectives

By the end of this chapter, entrepreneurs will have the knowledge and tools to define and implement **key performance indicators** (**KPIs**) that effectively measure the success of their MVP and align with their strategic objectives. They will learn to distinguish between outcome and output metrics, leading and lagging indicators, and track progress effectively.

Entrepreneurs will gain the ability to build comprehensive metric models by defining success indicators, failure thresholds, and baseline values, ensuring their measurements are actionable and insightful.

Through this chapter, entrepreneurs will develop the skills to manage their progress objectively, use metrics to safeguard against over-optimism or over-pessimism, and craft a compelling narrative that builds trust and simplifies stakeholder communication. These abilities will enable them to iterate confidently, optimize their efforts, and make data-driven decisions that support sustainable growth.

Leading and lagging indicators

As entrepreneurs strive to achieve their goals and measure performance, they rely on key metrics known as **leading and lagging indicators**. These indicators provide essential insights into both future potential and past performance, enabling informed decision-making and strategic planning.

Leading indicators signal what is likely to happen, while lagging indicators reflect what has already happened.

Leading indicators are forward-looking metrics that offer early insights into trends or changes, allowing entrepreneurs to anticipate outcomes and take proactive steps to influence success. Think of a leading indicator as a compass, guiding your journey by showing the direction you are heading. These metrics are proactive and predictive, helping stakeholders optimize strategies and address potential issues before they become critical.

Examples of leading indicators include customer engagement levels, product adoption rates, or the number of qualified leads generated. For an MVP, metrics like feature usage, customer satisfaction scores, or early sign-ups can provide valuable signals about how well the solution resonates with its target audience. By focusing on these early trends, entrepreneurs can fine-tune their product offerings, address customer concerns, and capitalize on emerging opportunities.

Lagging indicators, on the other hand, are retrospective metrics that measure the results of past actions or decisions. They function like a rear-view mirror, providing a historical perspective on performance. These indicators assess whether objectives were met and offer insights into the outcomes of completed initiatives.

Examples include total revenue, churn rates, and customer retention. While lagging indicators lack the ability to prompt proactive action, they are crucial for understanding the effectiveness of past efforts and learning from successes or failures.

The combination of leading and lagging indicators is a powerful framework for entrepreneurs. Leading indicators enable proactive adjustments while lagging indicators validate past performance. Together, they provide a comprehensive view of the MVP's performance, ensuring that entrepreneurs can monitor progress, refine strategies, and achieve their strategic objectives effectively.

A comparison to help understand them better:

Leading indicators	Lagging indicators
Future-oriented, helps anticipate potential changes or trends	Historical performance, assess past outcomes
Actionable, offering insights that support timely decisions	Measure actual results or outcomes
Early warning signals to detect changes or trends before they become critical	Evaluate the success or failure of completed initiatives or goals
Proactive, drive actions, and optimize strategies	Retrospective, provide a benchmark for performance evaluation
Examples: Sales leads, customer engagement, product adoption	**Examples**: Historical sales data, customer retention rate, product returns

Table 6.1: Comparison between leading and lagging indicators

KPIs and Fitness Metrics

KPIs are measurable values that provide entrepreneurs with insights into how effectively their MVP is addressing the identified pain points and meeting business objectives. These metrics enable founders to track performance, identify trends, and make data-driven decisions to refine their product strategy.

The specific KPIs chosen depend on the nature of the product, the business goals, and the stage of the product lifecycle. For example, a social media MVP might prioritize user acquisition metrics, such as the number of new sign-ups per month and engagement metrics like **daily active users** (**DAU**). For an e-commerce MVP, conversion rates (percentage of visitors making a purchase) and **average order value** (**AOV**) could be key metrics. A SaaS MVP might focus on customer retention rates and **monthly recurring revenue** (**MRR**) to evaluate success. KPIs are typically quantitative, offering clear numerical targets to track performance over time.

KPIs also operate across organizational levels. For instance, a marketing team might monitor **cost per acquisition (CPA)**, while a customer support team could track average response time or **customer satisfaction scores (CSAT)**. By aligning these KPIs with broader business goals, entrepreneurs ensure all teams work toward a unified vision.

In addition to KPIs, entrepreneurs can also track Fitness Metrics—contextual indicators that ensure the system remains healthy even if core KPIs fluctuate. Fitness Metrics extend the concept of KPIs by offering a holistic measure of how effectively a process or activity contributes to achieving a desired business outcome. Unlike KPIs, which are often narrowly focused on specific numerical targets, Fitness Metrics evaluate broader efficiencies and outcomes, incorporating qualitative and multivariate aspects.

In the book, *Building Evolutionary Architectures*, fitness functions are described as *an objective evaluation reflecting specific architectural attributes*.[1] Fitness Metrics in product development serve a similar purpose—they assess whether a team's actions align with overarching business goals and deliver meaningful results.

A Fitness Metric should have the following attributes:

- **Multivariate**: Draws from multiple data sources to provide a comprehensive view. For example, a Fitness Metric for customer satisfaction could combine CSAT scores, customer retention rates, and feedback trends to avoid manipulation.

- **Holistic**: Focuses on the overall process effectiveness rather than isolated outcomes. For instance, instead of merely tracking feature usage, a Fitness Metric could evaluate how well the feature improves user workflows and satisfaction.

- **Transparent**: Every team member should understand the metric and its connection to business goals. For example, a Fitness Metric tied to revenue growth could show how product enhancements directly increase conversion rates.

AARRR pirate metrics

The **acquisition, activation, revenue, retention, and referral (AARRR)** framework, famously coined by *Dave McClure*[2] and affectionately known as **pirate metrics**, simplifies this process into five pivotal stages. Each stage marks a successful outcome in the customer's journey.

Let us explore these stages.

Acquisition

Acquisition marks the successful transition from the awareness stage of the customer journey to tangible user interaction with the product. It focuses on attracting potential users and identifying the most effective channels for reaching them.

1 Parsons, Rebecca, et al. Building Evolutionary Architectures: Support Constant Change. O'Reilly, 2017.
2 **https://www.slideshare.net/dmc500hats/startup-metrics-4-pirates-may-2010**. Accessed 14 Jan, 2025.

For entrepreneurs, acquisition is about asking critical questions:

- *Where are users coming from?*
- *Which marketing channels are yielding the best results?*

Analyzing acquisition metrics helps refine marketing strategies and ensures that resources are invested in the most impactful avenues.

The following are the example metrics:

- **Traffic source analysis**: Tracks the number and percentage of visitors from various channels such as organic search, paid ads, social media, or referrals.

- **Brand mentions**: Measures how often the product or brand is mentioned across platforms, reflecting growing visibility.

- **Impressions**: Counts how often advertisements or content are viewed, providing insights into overall exposure.

Focusing on these metrics enables entrepreneurs to optimize outreach efforts and establish a strong user base early on.

Activation

Activation is the outcome of the consideration stage, where users take their initial steps with the product. It is about creating a strong first impression and ensuring users engage meaningfully with the product's core features.

The critical questions include:

- *Are users successfully completing the sign-up process?*
- *Are they interacting with key features of the product?*

A successful activation phase significantly increases the chances of users evolving into loyal, high-value customers, making this stage pivotal in the user journey. Effective onboarding experiences—like walkthroughs or tutorials—also play a crucial role in guiding users toward activation success.

The following are the example metrics:

- **Engagement rate**: Tracks time spent on the website, pages visited per session, and bounce rates to assess user interaction.

- **Content interaction**: Measures how often users engage with informational content like FAQs, reviews, or testimonials.

- **Cart abandonment rate**: Identifies obstacles by calculating the percentage of users who add items to their cart but fail to complete the purchase.

Revenue

Revenue indicates a successful outcome of the purchase decision stage in the customer journey, where user engagement translates into monetary value. For entrepreneurs, this phase is about understanding what drives users to pay for features, services, or products and optimizing those revenue streams.

The key questions include:

- *Which features or offerings are users willing to pay for?*
- *Are there opportunities for upselling or cross-selling?*

Revenue metrics offer insights into user preferences, the perceived value of the solution, and areas for potential growth or improvement.

The following are the example metrics:

- **Conversion rate**: Measures the percentage of visitors who complete desired actions, such as signing up for a service or making a purchase.

- **AOV**: Tracks the average amount spent per transaction, reflecting user trust and perceived value.

- **Checkout drop-off rate**: Measures how many users abandon the checkout process, helping identify friction points and areas for improvement.

Retention

Retention represents the usage stage of the customer journey, where the focus is on encouraging users to return and engage consistently. It is a clear indicator of long-term value and the product's ability to meet user expectations.

Following are key questions to consider:

- *What percentage of users are returning after their first interaction?*
- *Are users actively engaging with key features over time?*

High retention rates signify a product's relevance and effectiveness, while low retention often points to gaps in user experience or functionality.

The following are the example metrics:

- **DAU/monthly active users (MAU)**: Assesses user engagement and the frequency of interactions.

- **Feature adoption rate**: Tracks the percentage of users leveraging specific features, highlighting areas of success and underperformance.

- **Customer support tickets**: Tracks the volume and nature of support requests to identify pain points and enhance the user experience.

- **Cohort analysis:** Helps understand user retention trends over time by grouping users based on when they first interacted with the product.

Referral

Referral is the pinnacle of the loyalty, advocacy, and feedback stage, where satisfied users become evangelists for the product. It focuses on how often users recommend the product, helping to expand reach and lower acquisition costs.

The key questions are:

- *Are users sharing their positive experiences?*
- *How effective are referral programs in driving new user acquisition?*

Referrals are a testament to the product's value and its ability to exceed user expectations.

The following are the example metrics:

- **Net promoter score (NPS)**: Measures user loyalty and the likelihood of recommending the product.
- **Referral rate**: Tracks how often current users bring in new users, indicating the success of referral programs.
- **Retention rate**: Evaluates long-term satisfaction and continued use of the product.

The Viability Spectrum

The Viability Spectrum is a decision-making framework that helps entrepreneurs assess where their product stands based on measurable performance metrics. It spans three zones—the measure of success, the zone of struggle, and the threshold of failure—each representing a distinct phase in the product's journey toward market fit.

Measure of success

The measure of success is typically customer-centric, reflecting how well the product aligns with user needs and expectations. The examples include:

- Our customer retention score is 90%
- Our net promoter score is 80%
- Our churn rate has never crossed 10%

These metrics should be well-defined and carefully crafted. They not only quantify success but also guide the organization toward desired user behaviors and outcomes.

Understanding the zone of struggle

Consider an entrepreneur who identifies a 50% conversion rate from trial users to paying customers as the benchmark for success. If the actual conversion rate hits 49%, it does not indicate failure. Instead, it signals the need for incremental improvements.

Now, imagine the conversion rate dips to 45%. While concerning, it does not signify failure. It suggests lagging performance that calls for refinement. A drop to 40% conversion rate introduces uncertainty, requiring a more critical evaluation of whether minor setbacks are compounding into significant issues.

At 30%, the situation becomes serious. Here, an entrepreneur must determine whether foundational elements are flawed and whether a strategic pivot or return to basics is warranted. A further decline to 20% triggers comprehensive reviews: user studies, market analyses, and a re-evaluation of the go-to-market strategy. At this point, the product's viability is in jeopardy, but giving up is premature. Instead, a radical transformation may be necessary.

If the conversion rate remains below 5% for three months despite concerted efforts, falling beneath the defined failure threshold, the entrepreneur should critically assess whether to continue investing in the project or consider a hard pivot—or even a shutdown. This disciplined approach ensures that success metrics provide a clear path forward while also establishing thresholds for action.

Threshold of failure

While success metrics are often the focus, defining failure metrics is equally critical. Failure metrics establish clear thresholds that signal when a product is no longer viable. For example, consider a product with a conversion rate below 10% over a sustained period despite significant iterations. This would trigger discussions about whether the product is a sunk cost or whether a transformative pivot could salvage it.

Failure metrics serve as a compass, delineating the boundaries between success, struggle, and failure. Falling short of success metrics places the product in the zone of struggle, where it has not aligned with the market but has not failed either. This zone is an opportunity for iteration, but without well-defined failure metrics, entrepreneurs risk staying too long in a state of diminishing returns. Clarity on when to pivot or persevere often separates resilient founders from those who burn out chasing a fading vision.

Let us summarize using the above example:

Metrics	Measure band	Duration	Action
Measure of Success	Conversion rate > 50%	–	Keep going. Keep learning. Keep improving.
Zone of Struggle	Conversion rate <= 50%	–	Renewed product analysis, user research, market research, ecosystem research, and competition research to find the root cause of low conversation rates.
Threshold of Failure	Conversion rate <= 5%	Over 3 months	Record learning and wind up or pivot.

Table 6.2: *Action plan based on success and failure metrics*

Concept of a fully modeled metric

Metrics, in their basic form, provide raw numbers and their unit. While these figures are essential, their true value lies in the depth and context they offer to an entrepreneur. To achieve this depth, the concept of a fully modeled metric emerges as a comprehensive framework for understanding and applying metrics in a meaningful way.

Let us use this visualization of the Viability Spectrum—showing the progression of a key metric over time—to explore the details of fully modeled metrics.

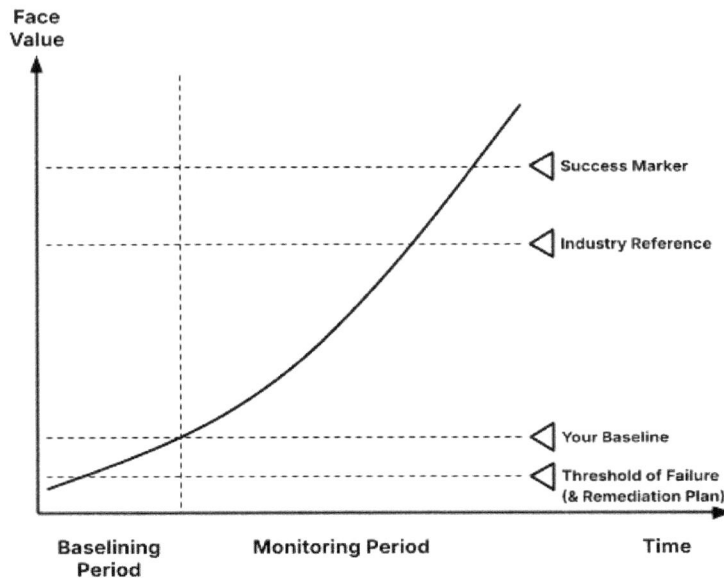

Figure 6.1: *Fully modeled metrics*

Let us explore the key elements that make a metric fully modeled:

- **Success marker**: A success marker is a predefined benchmark that defines the desired outcome or goal for a metric. It serves as a clear indicator of when the metric has achieved its intended purpose, aligning the team's efforts with measurable objectives.

- **Industry reference**: Metrics gain relevance when contextualized within industry standards or competitor benchmarks. Comparing performance to these references provides valuable insights into where the team stands in the broader market and identifies areas needing improvement.

- **Team's current baseline**: A baseline establishes the current performance level of a metric. This starting point is essential for tracking progress and evaluating the impact of interventions.

- **Failure thresholds**: Failure thresholds set the boundaries beyond which a metric's performance is deemed unsatisfactory. Identifying these limits allows the team to act swiftly, mitigating risks and preventing further negative outcomes.

- **Baselining period**: The baselining period refers to the specific timeframe chosen to measure the baseline. This period offers a snapshot of performance and sets a reference for future evaluations.

- **Directionality**: Understanding whether a metric should trend higher or lower is critical. For instance, lower defect rates signal improvement, while higher engagement rates indicate success. Directionality ensures metrics are interpreted correctly.

- **Remediation plans**: Metrics must be actionable. A fully modeled metric includes pre-established remediation plans that outline steps to address underperformance. These plans enable teams to respond effectively and minimize disruptions.

- **Ownership matrix**: Clarity on roles and responsibilities is vital for effective metric management. Using frameworks like **responsible, accountable, consulted, informed (RACI)** ensures every metric has a clear owner. This structure prevents confusion, blame games, and reactive decision-making when metrics fall short of expectations.

A fully modeled metric is more than just a number—it is a strategic tool that provides actionable insights, fosters accountability, and drives continuous improvement. By layering metrics with context and structure, product teams can align their efforts, optimize decision-making, and ensure sustained success.

Actions for the entrepreneur

1. Define key metrics to measure the MVP's progress toward success.
2. Set clear success markers and failure thresholds for each metric.

3. Benchmark your metrics against industry standards and past baselines.

4. Regularly monitor and iterate based on metric trends, not gut feelings.

Conclusion

Defining and tracking metrics is an indispensable aspect of an entrepreneur's journey, transforming ambitions into measurable progress and aligning efforts toward strategic goals. Metrics, whether leading or lagging, output or outcome, KPIs or Fitness Metrics, offer a structured way to navigate the complexities of developing and scaling an MVP. They provide clarity and direction at every stage of the customer journey, from acquisition to advocacy, ensuring that every step is purposeful and data driven.

A well-defined metric is not just a number—it is a fully modeled system with clearly established success markers, failure thresholds, and baseline values. These metrics offer insights that are both actionable and insightful, enabling entrepreneurs to measure progress, iterate confidently, and optimize their efforts. By using metrics effectively, entrepreneurs can avoid the pitfalls of over-optimism or over-pessimism and make informed decisions rooted in reality.

However, the power of metrics extends beyond measurement. They provide a narrative that simplifies stakeholder communication, making it easier to onboard investors, team members, and customers. Metrics instill accountability and adaptability, ensuring that entrepreneurs remain Agile in responding to challenges and opportunities.

Yet, metrics also require courage. When key metrics fall below failure thresholds, entrepreneurs must confront hard truths, considering pivots or even exits to avoid the sunk cost fallacy. This disciplined approach ensures that resources are used wisely, and efforts remain aligned with meaningful outcomes.

Ultimately, metrics serve as a compass for entrepreneurs, guiding them toward sustainable growth, informed decision-making, and a resilient foundation for success. By embracing metrics as a tool for alignment, evaluation, and iteration, entrepreneurs position themselves to build products that not only meet expectations but also deliver exceptional value in an ever-changing marketplace.

In the next chapter, the entrepreneur will learn how to start developing an MVP.

Join our Discord space

Join our Discord workspace for latest updates, offers, tech happenings around the world, new releases, and sessions with the authors:

https://discord.bpbonline.com

Section 3:
MVP Creation

CHAPTER 7

Building Successful MVP

Introduction

In the journey of turning an idea into a viable product, building an MVP serves as a pivotal milestone. The MVP represents the simplest version of a product that effectively addresses core customer needs while validating key business hypotheses. By focusing on the essential features and functionalities, an MVP allows entrepreneurs to test their assumptions, gather valuable user feedback, and adapt quickly, all without investing excessive time, effort, or resources.

For many entrepreneurs, the challenge lies not in imagining the final product but in distilling their vision into its most critical components. Cluttering an MVP with unnecessary features risks diluting its value and delaying market entry, while under-delivering can fail to capture customer interest or validate the solution. Striking the right balance between simplicity and utility is the key to building a successful MVP.

This chapter introduces a range of MVP development techniques, from clickable prototypes to models like the Single Feature App, Concierge MVP, and Wizard of Oz MVP. These approaches provide entrepreneurs with flexible frameworks to test and refine their ideas efficiently. Additionally, the chapter gets into real world feature prioritization strategies to focus on delivering maximum value through minimal effort, ensuring that every feature included in the MVP aligns with solving the most pressing customer problems.

Embracing a user-centric approach is crucial for MVP success. User feedback sessions, coupled with iterative development, help entrepreneurs build rapport with their target audience, prioritize user satisfaction, and foster long-term customer retention. A well-executed MVP not only validates the product's potential but also builds a strong foundation for future growth and market success.

By mastering the principles and techniques of MVP development, entrepreneurs position themselves to test their ideas effectively, make data driven decisions, and embark on a pathway to delivering impactful solutions in the marketplace.

Structure

In this chapter, we will cover the following topics:

- Prototyping
- MVP definition
- Gathering user feedback

Objectives

By the end of this chapter, entrepreneurs will have a comprehensive understanding of how to define an MVP that validates their core business hypotheses and resonates with their target audience.

Entrepreneurs will understand various MVP models, including clickable prototypes, Single Feature Apps, Concierge MVPs, Wizard of Oz MVPs, and **Minimal Operable Product** (**MOP**), and select the most suitable strategy for their product and market.

Entrepreneurs will also understand how to prioritize essential systems and features that address critical customer needs while maintaining focus on efficiency and resource optimization.

Prototyping

At this stage, a high-level solution captured in a comprehensive solution architecture is already in place. The problem has also been clearly defined, with strong evidence of problem-solution fit backed by thorough research and analysis. The next logical step for an entrepreneur is to validate this alignment. This step ensures that the proposed solution effectively addresses the problem and resonates with the target audience before investing significant resources in full-scale development. The most effective way to achieve this validation is through prototyping.

Prototyping is a critical step in the solutioning phase, where solution ideas and concepts are transformed into tangible, testable, usable minimal representations. This process enables entrepreneurs to explore, validate, and refine their solutions by creating models or simulations of their proposed MVP.

Prototyping serves as a bridge between ideation and implementation, ensuring that ideas are actionable and aligned with user needs. Often, verbal descriptions of a concept fail to convey its essence effectively. There is a risk of entrepreneurs explaining one thing while potential users interpret it as something entirely different. Additionally, it is challenging for individuals to articulate what they want in abstract terms. However, humans are inherently visual, making it easier to react to something they can see. With a prototype, stakeholders can provide credible feedback by pointing out what does not work for them. Prototypes act as visual aids, offering clarity and fostering a shared understanding among stakeholders, team members, and investors, while providing a solid foundation for discussions.

Prototyping is inherently iterative, evolving through cycles of creation, testing, feedback, and refinement. Entrepreneurs often begin with basic, low-fidelity prototypes—simple sketches or wireframes—and progressively move toward more detailed, high-fidelity versions. This iterative approach allows for the early identification of issues, minimizing the risk of costly rework during later development stages.

By testing solutions early through prototypes, entrepreneurs can uncover potential flaws or areas for improvement, reducing the likelihood of failure during full-scale development. Prototyping not only refines the solution but also builds confidence in its feasibility and alignment with user expectations.

Types of prototyping

Prototyping comes in various forms, each catering to specific stages of solution development, objectives, and complexity. Choosing the right type of prototype depends on the purpose of the validation, the resources available, and the level of fidelity required.

Low-fidelity prototypes

Low-fidelity prototypes are simple, abstract representations of the solution, focusing on the structure and basic functionality without the polish of high-fidelity versions. These are cost-effective and quick to create, making them perfect for early-stage testing and ideation.

Examples: Sketches and diagrams are hand-drawn or digital sketches that outline the primary flow, structure, and layout of the product. Tools like Balsamiq can help create such prototypes.

Wireframes are basic layouts that show the structure of a solution without visual design elements, focusing on user navigation and content hierarchy.

Storyboards

Storyboards are narrative tools that visualize how users would interact with a product or solution. Presented as a series of images or sketches, they are excellent for early-stage ideation and communication.

Storyboards showcase the user journey step-by-step. These are ideal for presenting the product experience to stakeholders or testing the concept with users. Often likened to a comic strip, with panels depicting key actions or moments in the user's experience.

Video prototypes

Video prototypes use visual storytelling to explain and showcase the functionality and value of a product or solution. They are particularly useful for pitching to stakeholders or communicating complex ideas in a clear and engaging manner.

Video prototypes combine animation, voiceovers, and screen recordings. They are ideal for demonstrating user journeys, feature functionality, or potential use cases.

Physical prototypes

For products that include physical components, prototypes can be built as tangible models. They are easy to share and help to construct a better view of the user journey. These physical representations are used to test usability, ergonomics, and functionality in real-world scenarios.

Examples: A 3D-printed version of a product or a mockup made from readily available materials.

Concierge MVP

The Concierge MVP delivers the product or service manually rather than relying on automated systems. By handling processes manually, entrepreneurs can iterate quickly based on real-time customer feedback. This method is resource-efficient for testing hypotheses without building full-scale systems. This approach allows entrepreneurs to directly engage with customers, providing personalized experiences while validating the demand and value of the offering.

Example: A meal subscription service where the entrepreneur personally curates meal selections based on prior conversations with customers, gathering their preferences and expectations. Meals are then delivered directly to customers without the need for an app or platform, providing a highly personalized and streamlined experience.

The method gives deep insights into customer preferences and pain points. It allows the entrepreneur the flexibility to adapt and refine the service iteratively without major technological investments.

Wizard of Oz prototypes

In Wizard of Oz prototypes, users interact with a seemingly functional solution, but behind the scenes, the processes are manually controlled. This approach is used to test concepts and gather feedback without developing full functionality.

Example: A chatbot interface where responses are manually typed by a human operator instead of AI-driven automation.

Feasibility prototypes

Feasibility prototypes are built to test specific technical features or challenging aspects of the solution. They are less about user experience and more about proving that certain features or integrations are possible.

They help focus on validating high-risk or complex features. Examples include testing API integrations, hardware compatibility, or data-processing capabilities.

Single Feature App

A Single Feature App focuses on delivering one key feature that solves the core problem for the target audience. This type of MVP is streamlined to avoid distractions and allows entrepreneurs to validate the most critical functionality of their product. It is especially effective in assessing user adoption and engagement for the feature that defines the product's value proposition.

The goal is simplicity and clarity, making it easier to gather feedback and iterate quickly. Once the core feature gains traction, additional features can be developed and integrated based on user feedback and business priorities.

Example: A photo-sharing app where the sole functionality is uploading and sharing photos with friends to validate that instant upload and single-click share to a group is a valuable proposition to the target audience.

High-fidelity prototypes

High-fidelity prototypes are detailed, interactive representations of the final solution. These prototypes closely mimic the design, interactions, and functionalities of the completed product. They are ideal for showcasing the user interface, user experience, and core features to stakeholders or testing with end-users. Tools like **Figma**, **Adobe XD**, or **Axure** are commonly used for creating high-fidelity prototypes.

Example: Clickable Prototypes allow users to navigate through the product interface as if it were live, enabling detailed testing of the design and user interactions.

Minimum operable product

The MOP[1] focuses on delivering a functional version of the product that demonstrates operational feasibility and scalability. This approach emphasizes backend processes, technical capabilities, and operational workflows rather than user-facing features.

---

1 **https://www.thoughtworks.com/en-in/insights/blog/product-innovation/minimum-operational-product-model**. Accessed 19 Jan, 2025.

MOP is ideal for startups working on complex systems or technologies where the primary risk lies in operational execution. It ensures that the foundational systems are robust and capable of supporting future expansions.

Example: A fintech solution that tests payment processing and regulatory compliance while offering minimal user interface functionality.

This method validates the feasibility of core operations before investing in user experience enhancements. This reduces the risks associated with scalability and technical complexity. It allows the entrepreneur to adapt and refine services, especially when building for enterprises.

MVP definition

A MVP must be fully and meticulously defined to ensure clarity of purpose and alignment with business goals. A well-defined MVP acts as a roadmap, helping entrepreneurs focus their efforts on delivering a solution that effectively addresses the target audience's core needs while avoiding unnecessary complexities. By articulating the MVP's scope and success criteria clearly, entrepreneurs can maximize their chances of validating key hypotheses, attracting early adopters, and gaining valuable feedback without overinvesting in unproven ideas.

Capability vs. feature

Before we go deeper into the process of defining an MVP, it is essential to first understand the concept of an MVP's capability as compared to its feature, as capabilities form the foundation of its definition and purpose.

The distinction between capability and feature is key to understanding product design and user outcomes.

Capability represents the broad outcome or potential a user achieves through the product. It focuses on the *what;* what the user can accomplish or how they benefit. Capabilities align with the higher-level value the product delivers and often tie directly to user goals or desired outcomes.

Example: Tara decided to call her venture IndicOcean. So, on IndicOcean.com, a user can discover the story behind a product. This is the capability that aligns with the user's goal of supporting and connecting with artisans.

Feature represents the specific functionality or characteristic that enables the capability. It focuses on the how; the tangible action or tool provided by the product to deliver the capability. Features are the practical enablers designed to fulfill user needs.

Example: IndicOcean.com includes a video on the product detail page that allows users to watch the artisan describe the creation process while standing at the production site. This is the specific feature supporting the capability of discovering the story behind the product.

This distinction helps ensure that product development aligns with user outcomes (capabilities) while delivering actionable functionalities (features). It ensures the solution stays both user-centered and technically feasible.

Identifying key systems

An MVP is often mistakenly thought of as just the customer-facing website or mobile app. However, an MVP encompasses much more, it is a focused slice of everything the entrepreneur needs to put in place to address the identified problem statement effectively. This includes not just the app or website but also systems and processes for marketing, manual operations, setting up partnerships, customer onboarding, product information management, payment processing, customer support, and handling returns or cancellations. Each of these elements contributes to delivering a functional, end-to-end solution.

The first step in defining the MVP is identifying the key systems required to support its functionality. Building on the Value Stream Map, entrepreneurs should revisit and refine it based on new learnings and priorities identified throughout their journey. For each step in the Value Stream Map, key supporting systems are identified. It is common for a single system to support multiple steps in the process.

Once the necessary systems are outlined, the entrepreneur must evaluate each one to determine whether it should be built in-house, purchased, or subscribed to as a service. This decision depends on factors like cost, complexity, scalability, and the strategic value of the system. By taking this holistic approach, entrepreneurs ensure their MVP is not just a prototype but a robust framework capable of validating their business hypothesis effectively.

Tara revisited her Value Stream Map and listed the key supporting systems needed. Her analysis was summarized as this table:

Value Stream Map	Key supporting system
Artisan onboarding and training	Artisan facing app
Artisan creates product	-
Product documentation and photography	Artisan facing app
	Content management system (CMS)
Product listing on e-commerce platform	**Inventory management system (IMS)**
	Social media integration
	Analytics system
Product marketing and promotion	CRM
	Analytics system

Customer browsing and discovery	Customer facing app
	Analytics system
Customer decision-making	Customer facing app
	Analytics system
Customer adds product to cart	Customer facing app
	Order management system (OMS)
	Analytics system
Order placement and payment	Customer facing app
	OMS
	Logistics and shipping support
	Payment gateway
	Analytics System
Order notification to artisan	Artisan facing app
	IMS
	OMS
	Logistics and shipping support
	Analytics system
Product packaging	OMS
	Logistics and shipping support
	Analytics system
Shipping and delivery	OMS
	Logistics and shipping support
	Analytics system
Order tracking by customer	Customer facing app
	OMS
	Logistics and shipping support
	Analytics system
Product delivery	IMS
	OMS
	Logistics and shipping support
	Analytics system

Customer feedback and reviews	Customer facing app
	CRM
	Analytics system
Customer support (when needed)	CRM
	Support helpdesk management
	Customer facing app
	Social media integration
	Analytics system
Payment to artisan	Artisan facing app
	Payment gateway
	Analytics system
Replenishment and inventory management	IMS
	Analytics system
Post-purchase engagement	Customer facing app
	CRM
	Marketing platform
	Social media integration
	Analytics system

Table 7.1: Tara's value stream system analysis

Build, buy, or subscribe

In the context of MVP development, the decision to build, buy, or subscribe refers to how an entrepreneur acquires or creates the systems, tools, or functionalities necessary to deliver the MVP. Each option carries strategic implications for cost, speed, scalability, and long-term adaptability. Here is a detailed breakdown.

Build

Build involves developing the system or feature in-house, either from scratch or by customizing existing code. This approach is ideal when the system is central to the MVP's unique value proposition and no off-the-shelf solution adequately meets specific requirements. It offers full control over design, functionality, and updates, ensuring the solution aligns perfectly with business needs. However, this approach is often the most time-consuming and expensive, requiring significant technical expertise and resources.

Buy

Buy refers to purchasing a ready-made product, system, or software license. This option is best when the functionality is not unique to the MVP but is essential for operations. Buying enables quick implementation with proven reliability and industry-standard features. However, it may offer limited customization and can involve higher upfront costs for licensing.

Subscribe

Subscribe typically involves leveraging **software as a service (SaaS)**, where an entrepreneur pays a monthly or annual fee for access to a cloud-based tool. This approach is ideal when the requirement is short-term or subject to change as the MVP evolves. Subscribing allows for quick deployment with minimal technical expertise and scales easily with business needs. The trade-off is reduced control over customization and the potential for recurring costs to add up over time.

To summarize, in order to determine the best approach, entrepreneurs should evaluate each system based on:

- Criticality to the MVP's core value proposition
- Cost and budget considerations to build or buy, or subscribe
- Speed of deployment, the solution needs to be in place
- Future scalability and adaptability to support long-term growth and flexibility

This decision-making framework ensures that resources are optimally allocated while aligning the MVP with its strategic goals.

Now that Tara has identified each system, she does a build, buy, or subscribe analysis. This is shown in the following table:

Key system	Suggested non-exhaustive options	Key stakeholder	Decision
Analytics system	Adobe Analytics, Amplitude, AppsFlyer, Firebase, Google analytics, Kissmetrics, Matomo, Mixpanel, Pendo, quantum analytics, UXCam	Entrepreneur and team	Subscribe
Artisan facing app	Custom software	Suppliers	Build
CMS	Adobe Commerce (formerly Magento), Craft CMS, Drupal, Ghost, Grav, HubSpot CMS, Joomla, OctoberCMS, PrestaShop, Strapi, WooCommerce, WordPress	Suppliers, influencers	Subscribe
Customer facing app	Custom software	Customers	Build

CRM	Freshsales, HubSpot, LeadSquared, Pipedrive, Salesforce, SugarCRM, Zoho CRM	Entrepreneur and team	Subscribe
IMS	Cin7, Fishbowl Inventory, Inciflo, Increff, inFlow, Katana, Ordoro, ShipBob, Sortly, Zoho Inventory	Suppliers	Subscribe
Logistics and shipping support	Delivery, Ecom Express, Ekart Logistics, Freightwalla, Safexpress, Shadowfax, Shiprocket	Partners, suppliers	Subscribe
Marketing platform	Agorapulse, AWeber, Brightedge, Conductor, Drip, Later, Mailchimp, Marketo, Nozzle, Omnisend, Pipedrive, Semrush	Partners, suppliers	Subscribe
OMS	NetSuite, QuickBooks Commerce (formerly TradeGecko), Shiprocket, Unicommerce	Partners, suppliers	Subscribe
Payment gateway	CCAvenue, Instamojo, PayPal India, Paytm, PayU, Razorpay, Stripe	Entrepreneur and team	Subscribe
Social media integration	Hootsuite, Sprout Social, Buffer, Sendible, SocialPilot, Loomly, Emplifi	Supporters	Subscribe
Support helpdesk management	AzureDesk, Faveo Helpdesk, Freshdesk, Front, Gorgias, HappyFox, Help Scout, Hiver, LiveAgent, ServiceDesk Plus, ProProfs, Spiceworks, Zendesk, Zoho Corporation	Entrepreneur and team	Subscribe

Table 7.2: Tara's build, buy, or subscribe analysis

Then, there were platforms such as *Shopify* that have many of these systems already out of the box. With help from a technologist friend, Tara was able to decide which SaaS offering she will go for.

Defining customer software

Fully defining custom software is a multifaceted and often complex task, requiring specialized expertise in design, development, and technology integration. It involves understanding user needs, translating them into actionable requirements, and ensuring that the software aligns with the business's goals and value proposition. While this process may seem daunting, entrepreneurs are not expected to be technical experts or proficient in software development themselves.

What entrepreneurs can, and should, do is provide a clear, meaningful description of what the software should accomplish. This is where structured methodologies, such as the JTBD framework, come into play. Covered in *Chapter 5, Problem-solution Fit*, JTBD is a powerful tool that helps entrepreneurs articulate the goals and outcomes their users want to achieve. By focusing on the customer's needs and the jobs they are trying to get done, entrepreneurs can effectively communicate the desired functionality and purpose of the software to their development team.

For instance, instead of vaguely requesting a *user-friendly interface*, an entrepreneur can define a specific job like, *When a user wants to discover artisan products, they should be able to filter by category, price, and artisan story easily, so they can quickly find what aligns with their preferences.* This level of clarity ensures that the development team has actionable insights to work with.

By leveraging frameworks like JTBD, entrepreneurs bridge the gap between their vision and the technical execution, ensuring the resulting software is aligned with user expectations and business objectives. While professionals handle the technical intricacies, the entrepreneur's role in shaping the software's purpose and priorities remains critical to its success. With the right tools and communication, entrepreneurs can confidently contribute to the development process without needing to master every technical detail.

Drawing from her research and prioritization efforts, Tara outlined the key capabilities for the customer-facing mobile application in the form of the following table:

Capability	JTBD
Product discovery	When browsing for unique handmade products, I want to easily search and filter by category, price, or artisan, so I can find items that suit my preferences quickly.
Authenticity assurance	When considering a purchase, I want to see artisan stories, so I can feel confident that the product is genuine and handmade.
Seamless purchasing experience	When I decide to buy a product, I want a smooth and secure checkout process, so I can complete my purchase without hassle.
Order tracking	When waiting for my purchase to arrive, I want to track my order in real-time, so I can know its status and estimated delivery date.
Review and feedback	When I have received my order, I want to leave a review or rating, so I can share my experience and help other buyers.
Social sharing	When I find something I love, I want to share it with friends or on social media, so I can get opinions or spread awareness about artisan-made products.
Transparent pricing	When deciding to buy, I want to see clear pricing, including taxes and delivery charges, so I can avoid surprises at checkout.
Customer support	When I face an issue, I want quick access to customer support, so I can resolve my concerns efficiently.

Table 7.3: Capabilities for customer-facing mobile application for IndicOcean

The following are the capabilities Tara deprioritized:

Capability	JTBD
Personalized recommendations	When exploring the platform, I want to receive curated recommendations based on my preferences, so I can discover products that align with my taste.
Wishlist and favorites	When I find a product I like but am not ready to buy, I want to save it to a wish list, so I can revisit it later.

Table 7.4: *Deprioritized capabilities for customer-facing mobile application for IndicOcean*

Tara then outlined the essential capabilities for the artisan-facing mobile application, carefully refining the list by striking out those that were deprioritized:

Capability	JTBD
Training and onboarding	When I join the platform, I want access to tutorials and guidance, so I can quickly learn how to list and sell my products.
Product upload	When I create a new product, I want to upload images and descriptions easily, so I can showcase my work to potential buyers.
Product storytelling	When I list my product, I want to add my story or process as a narrative, so I can connect with buyers emotionally and highlight the uniqueness of my craft.
Inventory management	When I sell products online or offline, I want to update stock levels in real-time, so I can avoid overselling or stockouts.
Order notifications	When I receive an order, I want instant notifications, so I can prepare and ship the product on time.
Order management	When processing multiple orders, I want an organized view of pending, shipped, and completed orders, so I can manage them efficiently.
Packaging guidance	When preparing an order for shipping, I want recommendations on packaging, so I can ensure the product reaches the buyer intact.
Logistics integration	When fulfilling an order, I want a streamlined way to coordinate shipping and delivery, so I can ensure timely and safe delivery to the customer.
Payment tracking	When I sell a product, I want to track my payments and payouts, so I can manage my finances effectively.

Table 7.5: *Capabilities for artisan-facing mobile application for IndicOcean*

Follow are the capabilities Tara deprioritized:

Capability	JTBD
Sales performance insights	When reviewing my business, I want to access sales trends and analytics, so I can understand what products are popular and improve my offerings.
Communication with buyers	When a buyer has a question, I want a simple way to respond, so I can build trust and provide excellent service.
Simplified returns	When a product is returned, I want a straightforward process to manage it, so I can handle customer concerns effectively.
Bulk order handling	When I receive a corporate or bulk order, I want dedicated support, so I can fulfill large requests without complications.
Gamification and recognition	When I achieve sales milestones, I want badges or recognition on the platform, so I can feel motivated and gain visibility among buyers.

Table 7.6: Capabilities for artisan-facing mobile application for IndicOcean

Gathering user feedback

In *Chapter 2, Market Analysis and Validation* on *Primary Research*, entrepreneurs were introduced to a range of techniques for gathering direct feedback from their target audience, enabling them to resonate with their users and ensure satisfaction. Building on these methods, entrepreneurs can iteratively use these techniques to refine their MVP and align it with user needs effectively.

Primary research is a powerful tool that allows entrepreneurs to collect firsthand data. From surveys at malls to feedback forms after a purchase, businesses rely on these insights to make data-driven decisions. For entrepreneurs, such research is crucial for understanding customer preferences, validating product ideas, and assessing market needs.

To ensure research efforts are both effective and ethical, entrepreneurs should adhere to best practices. Defining objectives clearly helps ensure that the collected data is purposeful. Taking comprehensive notes, or recording interactions (with consent), ensures accuracy and captures subtle insights. Informed consent and maintaining confidentiality build trust and ensure ethical conduct. Additionally, respecting participants' time by sticking to agreed-upon durations reflects professionalism.

Entrepreneurs can gather user feedback through methods like interviews, focus groups, and surveys, as previously discussed. Iterating these methods ensures continuous learning. For example, interviews provide in-depth qualitative insights, while surveys allow entrepreneurs to collect broader quantitative data. Focus groups offer real-time discussions among diverse users, revealing group dynamics and shared pain points. Each method should be tailored to specific research objectives and combined for comprehensive insights.

Avoiding biases is equally critical. Leading questions and observer effects can distort research findings, steering responses towards preconceived notions. Neutral questioning and minimizing observer influence ensure authentic feedback.

By employing these iterative primary research techniques, entrepreneurs can consistently refine their MVP to meet user expectations and validate its market fit, fostering a stronger connection with their audience and enhancing the product's chances of success.

Consider Tara's thoughtful approach to shaping her vision into a viable product. She began by crafting an Elevator Pitch to gauge interest and gather feedback from her network of friends and family:

For tech-savvy, culturally conscious shoppers like Digital Divya who struggle to find trustworthy platforms offering authentic, artisan-made products, IndicOcean.com is a curated e-commerce platform that delivers unique, high-quality handmade items while supporting local artisans directly.

Unlike generic marketplaces that lack transparency or personalization, our platform features artisan stories, authenticity certifications, and seamless shopping experiences to align purchases with values and purpose.

After refining her pitch, Tara moved on to creating storyboards to map the journey for both the customer and the artisan. This helped her visualize key touchpoints and challenges for each stakeholder.

Recognizing the value of expertise, she collaborated with a product manager she met at a **National Association of Software and Services Companies** (**NASSCOM**) event (NASSCOM is a trade association representing the Indian IT-BPM and tech industry). The product manager, eager for light-weight consulting projects, assisted Tara in building a clickable prototype. They recommended tools like Figma, Adobe XD, InVision, Sketch, Proto.io, UXPin, Axure RP, Justinmind, Marvel, and Webflow as popular options for creating such prototypes.

Once the clickable prototype was ready, Tara sought iterative feedback from *Digital Divya*. Through trial and error, they refined the prototype together, ensuring that the user journey met Divya's expectations without unnecessary complexity.

For the artisan's journey, Tara took the help of ChatGPT to create the following storyboard:

Figure 7.1: *Artisan onboarding, training, creation of toys, and social media presence*

The following figure shows the journey as it continues:

Figure 7.2: Order placement and packaging

The following figure shows the journey as it completes:

Figure 7.3: Shipping and payment

Tara worked closely with *Channapatna Kishore*, adding details with each iteration. Despite multiple iterations, she found his feedback inconsistent. While he often asked for simplicity, his input lacked clear direction. Recognizing the need for a deeper understanding, Tara decided to adopt the Concierge MVP approach. Instead of automating the entire process upfront, she chose to manage the journey manually. This hands-on method would allow her to gain invaluable insights into artisan needs and refine the process post-MVP for optimal results.

Actions for the entrepreneur

1. List all systems needed to support the MVP.
2. Decide what to build, buy, or subscribe to for optimal efficiency.

3. Define the product backlog as a prioritized list of capabilities.

4. Gather user feedback on the high-level MVP design developed so far.

Conclusion

Building a successful MVP is critical in transforming entrepreneurial visions into tangible solutions. By focusing on the core functionalities that address the most pressing customer problems, an MVP allows entrepreneurs to validate their hypotheses, gain valuable user insights, and establish a place in the market—all while optimizing resources and time-to-market.

Throughout this chapter, we explored various techniques and models for MVP development, including clickable prototypes, Single Feature Apps, Concierge MVPs, Wizard of Oz MVPs, and more. These approaches offer entrepreneurs the flexibility to test their ideas effectively, tailoring their strategies to fit specific market needs and product goals. From low-fidelity prototypes for early-stage ideation to high-fidelity prototypes for detailed user interaction testing, each technique underscores the importance of aligning the MVP with user expectations and business objectives.

Defining an MVP goes beyond the user-facing application; it involves identifying and prioritizing key systems, capabilities, and features that underpin the solution. The decision to build, buy, or subscribe further empowers entrepreneurs to balance speed, cost, and scalability while maintaining alignment with their core value proposition.

Equally essential is adopting a user-centric approach to MVP development. Iterative feedback sessions, informed by techniques discussed in earlier chapters, ensure that the MVP resonates with its target audience, fostering user satisfaction and retention. By continuously engaging with users and integrating their feedback, entrepreneurs can refine their solutions and build a strong foundation for future growth.

In the next chapter, the entrepreneur will learn how to validate their business model.

Join our Discord space

Join our Discord workspace for latest updates, offers, tech happenings around the world, new releases, and sessions with the authors:

https://discord.bpbonline.com

CHAPTER 8
Business Model Validation

Introduction

Entrepreneurs often find themselves navigating uncharted territory when developing a **minimum viable product** (**MVP**) for a market that is either not well understood or entirely new. These ventures typically operate under constraints—limited funding, time, and team resources. The stakes are high, and the margin for error is narrow, which means entrepreneurs cannot afford to endlessly experiment with various business models. Instead, they are forced to make decisions based on incomplete information, taking calculated risks to discover the elusive business model market fit. Even if a business model proves viable on a small scale, the challenge of scaling it to a larger audience remains significant. For instance, a strategy like heavy discounting might attract early adopters but is unlikely to be sustainable in the long term. Entrepreneurs must validate whether the initial success was driven by unique, one-time factors or if it reflects a repeatable and scalable pattern.

Despite these challenges, early-stage startups have a unique advantage: the ability to learn directly from their first few customers. These early adopters provide invaluable feedback that can reshape an entrepreneur's understanding of customer needs, preferences, and behaviors. This dynamic learning process empowers entrepreneurs to iteratively refine their business model, aligning it more closely with market realities and setting the stage for long-term success.

Validating and evolving a business model requires more than intuition; it demands deliberate, data-driven experimentation. Entrepreneurs can leverage tools like the Business Model

Canvas to structure their approach, ensuring that critical aspects such as costing, pricing, and revenue streams are well-defined. They can also use customer interviews, surveys, polls, A/B pricing tests, and other market experiments to test their assumptions and refine their strategy. This iterative process not only mitigates risks but also ensures the business model is adaptable to changing market dynamics. Validating the business model is not a one-time checkpoint but a continuous process, where each stage of growth brings new assumptions that must be tested and refined to ensure long-term viability.

Structure

In this chapter, we will cover the following topics:

- Product costing
- Product pricing
- Business Model Canvas
- Unit economics
- Go-to-market
- Product launch
- Collaterals for product launch
- Digital advertising

Objectives

By the end of this chapter, entrepreneurs will have a comprehensive understanding of how to define, evaluate, and refine the business model based on real-world data and customer behavior that aligns with their startup's goals and market needs. They will learn to use frameworks such as the Business Model Canvas to map out key components, including revenue streams, cost structures, value propositions, and customer segments. This structured approach will enable them to articulate the foundational elements of their business effectively. This clarity is essential not only for internal alignment but also for communicating with investors, partners, and other stakeholders.

Entrepreneurs will gain insights into various business models, such as subscription, freemium, e-commerce, marketplace, licensing, advertising, and direct sales. They will develop an understanding of the strengths, limitations, and best applications of these models, empowering them to make informed decisions about the one that aligns best with their startup's product, market, and strategic goals.

The chapter will also guide entrepreneurs on how to validate their chosen business model through iterative processes. Techniques such as customer interviews, surveys, polls, A/B testing, and other market experiments will be explored, providing a framework for testing assumptions, gathering feedback, and refining the business model based on real-world data.

This iterative approach ensures that entrepreneurs can continuously adapt their strategies to meet customer needs and market expectations. Ultimately, this chapter equips entrepreneurs with the tools and mindset to treat their business model as a living hypothesis, one that must be continually tested, validated, and evolved as their startup grows.

Product costing

Understanding product costs plays a pivotal role in identifying the right business model and setting a foundation for financial viability. Product costing refers to the process of determining the total expenses involved in producing or offering an MVP. This process goes beyond just direct costs, such as materials and labor, to include overheads, operational costs, and other indirect expenses. For software products, these costs span the entire lifecycle, from initial ideation and development to testing, deployment, maintenance, and customer support. These costs also include opportunity costs—what the startup foregoes in terms of alternative investments or features, especially when resources are limited.

For entrepreneurs, having an accurate understanding of product costs is essential for several reasons. First, it aids in setting realistic budgets and allocating resources effectively. Second, it helps forecast financial outcomes and set the appropriate selling price, which directly impacts market positioning and competitiveness. Lastly, a clear grasp of costs enables entrepreneurs to assess the profitability of their products, helping them decide whether to continue, modify, or discontinue an offering. In essence, product costing is a key driver of informed decision-making and long-term success. Additionally, understanding variable vs. fixed costs can help entrepreneurs model different growth and revenue scenarios, providing better insights into scaling strategies and funding requirements.

Common costing techniques

While it may seem straightforward for an entrepreneur to track the total cost of their spending, after all, they are closely managing their budget, the challenge arises when assigning these costs to individual units that a customer might purchase. This process introduces significant complexity as it requires accurately breaking down and allocating overall expenses across products or services.

To achieve this, a more systematic and structured approach is essential. Entrepreneurs must systematically analyze all cost components, including direct costs like materials and labor, as well as indirect costs like overhead, tools, and subscriptions. The intangible nature of software and its intricate development process make accurate costing a challenge. Entrepreneurs will gain better clarity on product costs when they maintain control over scope, time, and proactively address risks early in the development cycle.

However, several well-established techniques can provide clarity and precision in estimating costs. Choosing the right costing technique enhances financial accuracy and influences strategic decisions, such as pricing models, outsourcing choices, and investment needs.

Activity-based costing

This method allocates costs to specific activities involved in MVP development, such as research, design, coding, testing, deployment, and support. By breaking down the process into these distinct activities, entrepreneurs can accurately identify resource-intensive areas and allocate associated costs, overhead expenses (e.g., legal fees, rent, utilities), and indirect costs (e.g., software licenses, subscriptions, cloud services). This detailed cost analysis provides a clearer understanding of the total production cost of the MVP, enabling entrepreneurs to make informed decisions about resource allocation, pricing strategies, and areas for optimization. Moreover, activity-based costing supports better forecasting and scalability planning, helping startups anticipate how costs will evolve as usage or complexity increases.

Entrepreneurs can follow these steps to effectively apply the activity-based costing method in MVP development:

1. **Identifying activities**: Activity-based costing begins by pinpointing all activities involved in the MVP development process. These can range from the initial stages of ideation and research to post-deployment support and maintenance. Each activity is treated as a distinct cost center.

2. **Assigning cost drivers**: For each activity, a cost driver is defined, which quantifies how much of that activity is consumed by a specific task or deliverable. For instance, design hours might be the cost driver for the design phase, while the number of tests executed could drive testing costs.

3. **Allocating costs**: The actual input costs of tools, labor, and subscriptions associated with each activity are calculated and assigned to the respective products or features based on their consumption of the activity. This ensures a detailed and accurate cost breakdown.

   For example, an entrepreneur can break down resource needs by grouping them according to development phases. This granular allocation also highlights cost-heavy stages, enabling targeted decisions on whether to optimize, outsource, or automate certain activities.

4. **Research phase**:
   a. **Activities**: Conducting surveys, analyzing customer feedback, or identifying market trends.
   b. **Cost drivers**: Number of surveys sent, or hours spent on analysis.
   c. **Costs**: Researchers' salaries, tools for distributing surveys (e.g., Google Forms, SurveyMonkey), and data collection tools like **Typeform**.

5. **Design phase**:
   a. **Activities**: UI/UX design, prototyping, and user testing.
   b. **Cost drivers**: Design hours or the number of prototypes created.

    c. **Costs**: Software tools such as Adobe XD or Figma, external design agencies, and user testing expenses.

6. **Coding phase**:

    a. **Activities**: Developing the MVP, integrating APIs, and addressing bugs.

    b. **Cost drivers**: Development hours or the number of features coded.

    c. **Costs**: Salaries of developers, outsourced development fees, or vendor pricing models.

    d. **Time and material (T&M) pricing**: Charges based on actual hours worked and materials used.

    e. **Fixed pricing**: A predetermined cost for a specific task or deliverable.

    f. **Cost-based pricing**: Vendor's input costs plus a profit margin.

7. **Testing phase**:

    a. **Activities**: QA testing, bug fixing, and user acceptance testing.

    b. **Cost drivers**: Number of tests conducted, or hours spent on testing.

    c. **Costs**: Internal QA salaries, external testing services, and testing tools like Selenium or BrowserStack.

8. **Deployment phase**:

    a. **Activities**: Server setup, app store submission, and live environment monitoring.

    b. **Cost drivers**: Number of deployments or server usage hours.

    c. **Costs**: Server hosting fees (e.g., AWS, Azure), app store listing fees, and bandwidth costs.

This method not only supports effective costing but also budgeting and strengthens decision-making as the MVP evolves.

Feature-based costing

This method assigns costs to individual features or components of the MVP. It is especially useful for modular software, allowing entrepreneurs to prioritize or omit features based on their cost implications and alignment with user needs.

Example: Feature-based costing involves using historical data and statistical relationships to predict costs. For example, if developing a mobile app typically costs ₹50,000 per feature based on historical project data, and the MVP has five planned features, the estimated total cost would be ₹250,000. This method relies on established cost-per-unit metrics. This approach also enables more flexible budgeting and roadmap planning, as entrepreneurs can easily adjust the scope based on cost-benefit analysis at the feature level.

Expert judgment

Involving experienced professionals, either internal or external, provides valuable insights into cost estimation. Experts draw on knowledge from similar projects to predict costs and identify potential challenges. Expert judgment is particularly valuable in early-stage startups where historical internal data is limited, and rapid estimation is needed for quick decision-making.

Example: An entrepreneur seeks the help of an experienced project manager who estimates the cost of developing a mobile app based on their knowledge of similar past projects, factoring in team expertise, complexity, and timelines. Their insights guide budgeting decisions, especially when precise data is unavailable, leveraging their judgment to set realistic expectations and allocate resources more effectively.

Analogous estimating

This approach involves comparing the current project to past similar projects. By analyzing historical data, entrepreneurs can generate more accurate cost estimates. It is particularly effective when an organization has a strong database of previous projects.

Example: An entrepreneur can connect with another entrepreneur who recently developed a similar e-commerce platform with their software development team. By discussing the project's scope, complexity, and overall development process, they can identify key similarities, such as the number of features, user interfaces, or integrations required. They can also account for differences, like newer technologies, advanced functionalities, or unique requirements for their project. By leveraging these insights and adapting the cost structure based on these variables, the entrepreneur can derive a more informed and realistic cost estimate. This collaborative method not only yields valuable benchmarking insights but also opens the door to practical advice on common pitfalls, cost-saving strategies, and more efficient development practices.

Additionally, analogous estimating helps in reducing the uncertainty associated with MVP budgeting, especially when precise cost breakdowns are difficult due to a lack of internal benchmarks or historical records. It offers a fast, relatively low-effort method to establish a ballpark figure and make early-stage financial decisions.

Product costing, especially for software, is a nuanced field that often requires specialized accounting expertise. At the early stages of MVP validation, entrepreneurs must rely heavily on judgment, which can result in rough estimates rather than precise calculations. Costing estimates are susceptible to change due to several factors. For instance, the rapid pace of technological evolution may necessitate the adoption of new tools or frameworks, introducing unforeseen expenses. Bugs, security vulnerabilities, or unexpected user requirements can also drive-up costs as development progresses. Additionally, as the product scales and the user base grows, costs related to cloud infrastructure, customer support systems, or other backend enhancements can rise significantly.

Moreover, the challenges are not limited to the technology side. Building and managing a team, particularly when relying on part-time contributors or volunteers, can be unpredictable, leading to delays or unplanned expenses. Even seemingly minor costs, such as meeting users for feedback or conducting user research, can become substantial when logistics, travel, or accommodation are factored in. These unpredictable elements highlight the importance of using analogous estimating as a starting point while remaining flexible and prepared to adjust as the MVP progresses. By acknowledging these challenges and incorporating contingencies, entrepreneurs can factor in cost while building a business model.

To estimate the MVP cost, Tara began by calculating average monthly costs for each key system based on available options in *India*:

Key system	Estimated cost (average per month)
Analytics system	₹15,000
Content management system (CMS)	₹8,000
Customer relationship management (CRM)	₹10,000
Inventory management system (IMS)	₹12,000
Logistics and shipping support (based on estimated volumes)	₹5,000
Marketing platform	₹10,000
Order management system (OMS)	₹7,000
Payment gateway (based on estimated volumes)	₹3,000
Social media integration	₹5,000
Support helpdesk management	₹7,000

Table 8.1: Tara's systems cost estimation

Note: These figures are illustrative and do not represent actual market prices. Entrepreneurs should conduct their own market research for accurate cost estimation.

Tara met Prabjot in a startup mixer and came to know she had recently built something like an artisan-facing app and a customer-facing app for another business case. Later, over tea at a local shop, Tara spent a few hours diving deeper into the development costs involved.

She used insights from this conversation to apply the analogous estimating method for her own project. By comparing her app requirements with Prabjot's recently completed applications, Tara was able to estimate costs based on feature scope, technical complexity, and team structure.

Prabjot shared that each app took about 4-5 months to develop with a mid-sized development team, which gave Tara a realistic understanding of timelines. Prabjot's team included a UI/ UX designer, 3-4 developers, and a QA engineer, which Tara noted for her planning. Custom integrations, scalability requirements, and ongoing maintenance were significant contributors to the overall cost.

Here is how she summarized the costs:

- **Artisan-facing app**:

  - **Comparable features**: Prabjot's app included functionalities like profile creation, product uploads, inventory tracking, and communication with buyers, many of which aligned with Tara's artisan-facing app.

  - **Adjustments for differences**: Tara's app required additional features like storytelling, video uploads, and multi-language support, which slightly increased the complexity.

  - **Estimated cost**: Prabjot mentioned her app costs approximately ₹12,00,000. Considering the additional features Tara needed, she adjusted the estimate to ₹14,00,000 for the artisan-facing app.

- **Customer-facing app**:

  - **Comparable features**: Prabjot's app focused on user-friendly browsing, order management, secure payments, and feedback mechanisms, which closely matched Tara's vision for the customer-facing app.

  - **Adjustments for differences**: Tara's app required advanced filters for product discovery and integration with an artisan storytelling feature, adding to the development cost.

  - **Estimated cost**: Prabjot revealed her app cost around ₹15,00,000. After factoring in Tara's additional needs, she estimated the cost to be around ₹17,00,000.

For each phase, based on the activities that may cost additional, Tara organized the activities for each phase of MVP development along with estimated costs:

Phase		Estimated cost (average per month)
Artisan onboarding and training	Training artisans on app usage and onboarding process	₹25,000
Product listing on e-commerce platform	Listing products on the platform and integrating with IMS	₹20,000
Product marketing and promotion	Running marketing campaigns and customer outreach	₹50,000
Customer decision-making	Providing detailed product information to assist decision-making	₹20,000
Order placement and payment	Processing orders and facilitating payments securely	₹60,000
Product packaging	Preparing products for shipment	₹15,000
Shipping and delivery	Coordinating delivery logistics and shipping	₹45,000

Phase		Estimated cost (average per month)
Customer support (when needed)	Addressing customer inquiries and complaints	₹35,000
Payment to artisan	Processing artisan payments securely	₹15,000
Replenishment and inventory management	Managing inventory levels and restocking	₹25,000
Post-purchase engagement	Engaging with customers post-purchase through promotions or updates	₹40,000

Table 8.2: Tara's activities cost estimation

Note: These figures are illustrative and do not represent actual market prices. Entrepreneurs should conduct their own market research for accurate cost estimation.

Finally, by consolidating all the estimates, Tara now has a comprehensive view of the total costs, broken down by phase and component. This detailed breakdown serves as a critical input for modeling the business effectively, enabling her to make informed decisions and plan strategically for sustainable growth:

Components	Estimated cost (average per month)
Third party product cost	₹82,000
Various activities cost	₹3,50,000
Custom software development cost	₹5,17,000
Total	₹9,49,000

Table 8.3: Tara's overall cost estimation

Note: These figures are illustrative and do not represent actual market prices. Entrepreneurs should conduct their own market research for accurate cost estimation.

Product pricing

Pricing strategies play a pivotal role in shaping an MVP's revenue model, as they are deeply influenced by market demand, competitive dynamics, and customer expectations. While entrepreneurs hold significant influence over the pricing strategy to be adopted, they rarely have the luxury of deciding it independently. External factors such as customer perception of value, industry benchmarks, and cost structures often shape the ultimate pricing approach.

The success of any pricing strategy hinges on a deep understanding of key factors: how customers perceive the value of the product, the competitive landscape, the unit being sold, and the financial goals of the MVP. For this reason, entrepreneurs must develop a solid grasp of foundational concepts like cost, margin, and markup to ensure their pricing approach aligns with both market realities and business objectives.

Understanding margin and markup

To recap, cost represents the expenses incurred in manufacturing, sourcing, or creating the product. It includes direct expenses like materials, labor, and supplier fees, as well as losses that may occur during production. However, overhead and operational expenses—such as marketing and maintenance—are typically excluded from the direct cost calculation but are crucial for understanding the full financial picture. A detailed understanding of costs is crucial because it serves as the foundation for pricing decisions. This concept was covered extensively in the earlier section, *Product costing*, which emphasized the importance of identifying and allocating costs accurately during MVP development. Grasping the distinction between cost, margin, and markup empowers entrepreneurs to price their MVP competitively while ensuring profitability.

Margin

Gross margin is a critical metric that reflects the amount a business earns after subtracting the manufacturing costs from the selling price. It provides insights into profitability and helps assess whether the pricing model is sustainable. Gross margin is calculated using the formula:

Gross margin = (Selling price - Cost price) / Selling price

For example, if the selling price of a product is ₹1,000 and the cost price is ₹600, the gross margin would be 40%:

(₹1,000 - ₹600) / ₹1,000 = 0.4 (40%)

Understanding gross margin is essential for ensuring that the pricing strategy meets the business's profitability goals, while also remaining competitive in the market. For early-stage MVPs, maintaining a healthy gross margin is particularly important, as it allows room for reinvestment in product development, marketing, and customer support.

Markup

Markup refers to the additional amount charged over the product's cost to determine its selling price. Unlike gross margin, which focuses on profitability relative to revenue, markup directly indicates how much more the selling price is than the production cost. Markup is calculated using the formula:

Markup = (Selling price - Cost price) / Cost price

For example, if the cost price of a product is ₹600 and the selling price is ₹1,000, the markup would be approximately 66.7%:

$$(₹1,000 - ₹600) / ₹600 = 0.667\ (66.7\%)$$

Markup is particularly useful when assessing how much flexibility the entrepreneur has in pricing to cover other operational costs or to compete effectively in the market.

By understanding costs, entrepreneurs can set a baseline for pricing; by calculating margins, they can evaluate profitability; and by determining markup, they can gauge pricing flexibility. It is important to note that while markup and margin are related, they are not interchangeable; using the wrong metric can lead to mispriced products and flawed profitability assumptions.

Pricing techniques

Entrepreneurs can choose from various pricing techniques, each tailored to different objectives, such as maximizing profit, penetrating markets, or aligning with customer value. Following are some common product pricing techniques that entrepreneurs can explore:

- **Cost-plus pricing**: Cost-plus pricing is one of the simplest and most widely used strategies. The selling price is determined by adding a margin, either a fixed amount or a percentage, to the product's cost. This ensures that all costs are covered, and the business generates a profit. Typically, the cost considered includes operating expenses, which encompass day-to-day operational costs as well as product development expenses. The primary goal of this approach is to recover running costs while maintaining a margin to reinvest in growth, research, or innovation.

- **Competitive pricing**: Competitive pricing involves setting prices based on competitors' pricing strategies. This approach is particularly effective in markets with homogenous products or services where differentiation is minimal. Companies use this strategy to either match competitors' prices to stay relevant or undercut them to dislodge competition and gain market share. The aim is to dominate a market by leveraging pricing as a competitive advantage.

- **Penetration pricing**: Penetration pricing is a strategy where businesses set a low initial price to quickly attract customers and gain market share. Once a loyal customer base is established, the price is gradually increased. This strategy is commonly used by startups, especially those offering free or heavily discounted versions of their products, to build traction. The goal is to create a foothold in the market, often at the expense of short-term profitability.

- **Skimming pricing**: Skimming pricing takes the opposite approach to penetration pricing, targeting early adopters by setting a high initial price. This strategy maximizes revenue from customers who are less price-sensitive and willing to pay a premium for new or innovative products. Over time, as the market matures or competition increases, prices are lowered. A variation of this strategy is high-low pricing, where prices start high and are reduced as novelty fades. Apple is a well-known practitioner of this approach[1].

- **Value-based pricing**: Value-based pricing is determined by the perceived value of a product or service to the customer rather than the cost of production or market rates. This strategy is particularly effective for unique or innovative offerings with a high perceived value. While not commonly used for software MVPs due to the difficulty of gauging perceived value early on, this approach is ideal for industries where emotional or experiential factors significantly influence purchasing decisions.

- **Dynamic pricing**: Dynamic pricing adjusts prices based on market demand, time, seasonality, or customer behavior. It is commonly seen in industries like airline ticketing, hotel bookings, ride-hailing services, and e-commerce. While this strategy is less common for software MVPs, it can be effective in specific scenarios, such as SaaS platforms with tiered usage plans or seasonal promotions.

- **Premium pricing**: Premium pricing positions a product as exclusive or luxurious by setting prices higher than competitors. The aim is to create a perception of superior quality, exclusivity, or status. While this strategy can be effective for niche markets or high-end products, it requires careful alignment with the product's branding and target audience. Premium pricing is not universally applicable and works best in markets that value quality and exclusivity over cost savings.

- **Psychological pricing**: Psychological pricing is a strategy that leverages human psychology to influence purchasing decisions and drive sales. One of the most common techniques in this strategy is the 9-digit effect, where prices are set just below a round number, such as ₹499 instead of ₹500 or $9.99 instead of $10. This small difference creates a perception of value, making the price appear significantly lower than it actually is. Another effective tactic includes creating urgency or scarcity through limited time offers, flash sales, or deals like buy one, get one free, which encourages customers to act quickly, believing they are getting an exceptional bargain.

A notable January 2008 study by authors *Manoj Thomas* and *Vicki Morwitz*[2] explored the psychological mechanisms behind consumer responses to prices. Their research highlighted three key mental shortcuts, or heuristics, that shape how customers perceive and evaluate prices:

- **Left-digit anchoring effect**: Consumers tend to overestimate the difference between prices like $4.00 and $2.99, perceiving it as more significant than the difference between $4.01 and $3.00. This is because of the left-most digit changes, anchoring their perception of the price change.

- **Precision effect**: Consumers interpret prices with more digits as being smaller. For instance, a price like $391,534 might feel lower than $390,000, despite it being higher.

---

1 **https://www.paddle.com/blog/price-skimming**. Accessed 26 Jan, 2025.
2 Thomas, Manoj & Morwitz, Vicki. (2008). Heuristics in Numerical Cognition: Implications for Pricing. Handbook of Pricing Research in Marketing. 10.4337/9781848447448.00015.

This occurs because the longer number feels more specific, which can create an illusion of a bargain.

- **Ease of computation effect**: Consumers judge price differences based on how simple they are to calculate. For example, the difference between $5.00 and $4.00 is perceived as larger than the difference between $4.97 and $3.96 because the former is easier to compute mentally.

These findings demonstrate that price perception is not always rooted in logical thinking but is influenced by instinctive and cognitive biases. Entrepreneurs can use these insights to design pricing strategies that resonate with their target audience's subconscious decision-making process.

Pricing models

Entrepreneurs can choose from a variety of pricing models depending on the nature of their MVP—whether it is an enterprise product, a consumer offering, or a mobile app. The following are several common pricing models along with recommendations for their use:

- **Perpetual licensing**: This traditional model involves customers paying a significant upfront fee to use the software indefinitely. It is well-suited for niche software products in slow-evolving industries where customers can derive long-term value from the product without frequent updates. This approach works particularly well for specialized tools that are stable and used consistently over several years.

- **Subscription licensing**: In a subscription model, customers pay a recurring fee, monthly or annually, to access the software. This fee often includes updates and customer support, making it ideal for businesses that frequently enhance and improve their software. This model fosters customer loyalty, offers predictable recurring revenue, and is particularly effective in industries where regular updates are a competitive advantage.

- **Usage-based pricing**: Also known as pay-as-you-go, this model ties the pricing to the customer's usage level. It is most effective for software where value correlates directly with usage, such as cloud computing services, data storage platforms, or API-based products. This model allows customers to scale their spending according to their needs, which can be appealing for startups and cost-conscious businesses.

- **Tiered pricing**: This strategy offers multiple pricing tiers, each with a different level of functionality, usage limits, or features. It is a versatile model that caters to a diverse customer base with varying needs and budgets. For example, a basic tier may attract smaller businesses, while an advanced tier targets enterprises needing more comprehensive solutions.

- **Bundled pricing**: In this model, multiple products or services are packaged together and sold at a discounted price compared to buying each item individually. It is commonly used for software suites where complementary tools or features can be bundled to create added value for the customer while encouraging higher overall spending.

- **Price discrimination**: This involves setting different prices for different customer segments based on factors like willingness to pay, location, or purchasing power. While rarely used for software products, this model could be applied in specialized scenarios, such as offering discounted pricing for educational or non-profit organizations.

- **Freemium**: The freemium model provides basic features for free while charging for premium features, advanced functionality, or additional services. It is particularly effective for consumer-focused software, such as productivity tools or streaming services, where the goal is to attract a large user base and convert a percentage of free users into paying customers. However, profitability relies on a strong conversion rate to the premium tier.

- **One-time purchase**: In this model, customers pay a one-time fee to download and use the software indefinitely. It is commonly used for high-value apps or professional tools, such as graphic design software or video editing programs, where customers are willing to pay upfront for the perceived long-term value.

- **In-app purchases**: This model offers the app for free but charges users for additional features, digital goods, or services within the app. It works especially well for gaming apps or apps that offer optional enhancements, such as extra lives in a game or premium filters in a photo-editing app.

- **Paid apps**: Users pay a one-time fee to download and use the app. Although this model has become less common due to the popularity of free apps, it remains effective for apps with unique features or a strong brand presence. For example, a niche productivity tool with robust features may justify a paid app model.

Each of these models has its strengths and limitations, and entrepreneurs should carefully consider their product's value proposition, target audience, and market dynamics when selecting the most suitable pricing strategy.

Pricing tables

We have all come across pricing tables, even if we did not realize it at the time. Let us begin with an example shown in the following figure:

Business Bundle	Pro Bundle	Starter Single
✔ Windows	✔ Windows	○ Windows
✔ MacOS	✔ MacOS	◉ **MacOS**
✔ Linux (*many distros* ⓘ)	✔ Linux (*many distros* ⓘ)	○ Linux (*1 distro*)
✔ Raspberry Pi	—	○ Raspberry Pi
✔ Live ISO	—	—
✔ Virtual Appliance (VNF)	—	—
✔ Docker container	—	—
✔ Example Streams ⓘ	✔ Example Streams ⓘ	—
✔ Free upgrades	✔ Free upgrades	—
⚎ Priority support	✉ Email support	🖥 Community support
$641 **$289**[+]/user/yr	$392 **$169**[+]/user/yr	**$49**[+]/user
Buy	Buy	Buy

[+] *VAT/GST extra, if applicable*

Capterra ★★★★★ 4.8

Figure 8.1: *A sample pricing table*
Source: *https://ostinato.org/pricing/#tiers*

Entrepreneurs looking to describe their MVP succinctly can use the following essential details to communicate their product's value effectively:

- **Key features**: Highlight the core features that make the product useful and valuable to customers.
- **Additional features**: Mention features that allow the product to perform under specific circumstances or scale as customer needs grow.
- **Pricing**: Specify how the product is priced, whether based on usage, audience, or scale, to give clarity on affordability and value.
- **Purchase process**: Clearly outline the simplest and most intuitive way for potential customers to buy the product.

Interestingly, this format mirrors the structure of a pricing table, which serves as both a functional tool and a persuasive pitch for potential customers.

A pricing table is a concise visual representation of a product's pricing plans and the features available at each level. It helps customers easily compare and contrast options, offering a straightforward way to assess value. In essence, a pricing table doubles as a one-page product pitch, juxtaposing key features with their corresponding price points, making it immediately clear what customers will receive for their investment.

The structure of a pricing table ensures that product features are clearly marked across different pricing tiers, with additional features for higher-tier plans prominently called out. This not only aids in decision-making but also highlights the product's scalability and adaptability, reinforcing its appeal to a broader audience. By combining clarity and persuasion, a well-designed pricing table can be a powerful tool to convey the essence of an MVP while guiding customers through the decision-making process.

Deciding on pricing

Testing the price of an MVP is critical to ensure it aligns with customer expectations and maximizes revenue potential. Entrepreneurs can leverage any of these methods.

A/B testing

A/B testing is a valuable tool for experimenting with pricing strategies in controlled environments, such as digital platforms, where customer interactions are limited and price comparisons are unlikely. This method involves offering different price points (A and B) to two randomly selected customer segments and then comparing their performance based on metrics such as conversion rates, revenue, or customer acquisition costs. A/B testing provides real-world feedback on customers' willingness to pay and helps entrepreneurs identify the price point that maximizes revenue.

However, this method does have its challenges. If customers discover price discrepancies, it could lead to dissatisfaction or a perception of unfairness. Therefore, A/B testing is most effective for testing small pricing changes or exploring new price points discreetly. To minimize risks, entrepreneurs should ensure that test groups are sufficiently distinct and that results are monitored closely.

Van Westendorp Price Sensitivity Meter

The Van Westendorp Price Sensitivity Meter is a widely used technique to understand customer perceptions of value during the early stages of pricing research or when launching a new product or service. It involves surveying potential customers with four key questions[3]:

- *At what price would you consider the product too expensive?*
- *At what price would you consider the product too cheap?*
- *At what price would you consider the product a good deal?*
- *At what price would you consider the product expensive but still acceptable?*

The responses are analyzed to identify a pricing range that aligns with customer perceptions. This method provides a quick, low-cost way to establish upper and lower price boundaries and pinpoint the sweet spot where customers perceive the price as fair and valuable. While

---

3 **https://www.forbes.com/sites/rebeccasadwick/2020/06/22/how-to-price-products/**. Accessed 26 Jan, 2025.

this approach offers foundational insights into pricing strategy, entrepreneurs should follow up with additional validation methods to refine their pricing further.

Conjoint analysis

Conjoint analysis is ideal for testing pricing in combination with other product features or attributes, especially when the product or service has multiple differentiators, such as quality, delivery speed, or add-on features. In this method, entrepreneurs present customers with various product configurations at different price points and analyze their choices to determine the perceived value of specific features and the level of price sensitivity.

This approach provides a nuanced understanding of how customers prioritize features and how price interacts with those preferences. It is particularly effective in competitive markets, helping entrepreneurs optimize pricing while differentiating their offerings. However, conjoint analysis is complex to design and requires significant time and effort to conduct. Entrepreneurs should ensure they have access to robust analytical tools or professional expertise to interpret the results effectively.

Willingness-to-pay surveys

Willingness-to-pay (WTP) surveys are a straightforward approach to understanding customer pricing expectations, particularly during early product development or for niche markets. In this method, customers are directly asked how much they would be willing to pay for a product or service. This approach is cost-effective, quick to implement, and provides exploratory insights into pricing boundaries.

While WTP surveys help establish initial price hypotheses, they are based on hypothetical scenarios rather than actual purchasing behavior. Entrepreneurs should treat the findings as a starting point and complement this method with real-world validation, such as A/B testing or market experiments, to ensure the pricing strategy resonates with the target audience.

Let us summarize with the help of the following table:

Method	Best used for	Pros	Cons
A/B testing	Small pricing changes in isolated environments	Real-world data, quick feedback	High traffic needed, customer dissatisfaction risk
Van Westendorp	Exploring price perception	Simple, cost-effective	Hypothetical answers, lacks competitive insights
Conjoint analysis	Multi-feature product pricing	In-depth insights, considers features	Complex, expensive
WTP	Hypothetical pricing feedback	Fast, cost-effective	Biased, may not reflect real behavior

Table 8.4: Comparison of key pricing testing methods

Tara chose a pricing approach for **IndicOcean.com** that balances the unique value of artisan-made products with competitive positioning, ensuring it resonates with her target customers. Her strategy reflects insights gained from various pricing techniques, models, and testing methods.

Recognizing the cultural and handcrafted value of the products, Tara adopted value-based pricing to set prices that align with customers' willingness to pay for authenticity, quality, and the stories behind each item. To remain competitive, she incorporated elements of Competitive Pricing, benchmarking against platforms like *Etsy* and *Jaypore* to position **IndicOcean.com** effectively within the market.

Tara determined a minimum 30% markup on each product to cover essential costs, including platform maintenance, marketing, and logistics. For example, a product with a total cost (encompassing production, packaging, and shipping) of ₹500 would be priced at ₹650, ensuring sustainability while remaining affordable for customers.

To validate her pricing strategy, Tara decided to conduct WTP surveys targeting potential customers who fit IndicOcean.com's primary persona, *Digital Divya*. These surveys aimed to gauge what customers consider too expensive, too cheap, or just right for various product categories. Distributed through email campaigns and social media channels, these surveys would provide actionable insights into customer perceptions and help refine pricing for maximum impact.

Business Model Canvas

The **Business Model Canvas** (**BMC**) is a strategic management tool and a lean startup template designed to help entrepreneurs and businesses conceptualize, develop, and refine their business models. It serves as a visual framework, that maps out the key components of an organization's value proposition, infrastructure, customer segments, and financial structure. This accessible and intuitive template enables teams to document and analyze their business models effectively, making it a popular choice for startups, established corporations, and academic institutions alike.

The BMC was introduced by *Alexander Osterwalder*[4], founder of *Strategyzer*, and has since become a foundational tool in business strategy and innovation. Its widespread adoption can be attributed to its simplicity and ability to distill complex business ideas into a single, cohesive framework. Each of the nine BMC building blocks provides a snapshot of a business's operations, helping teams identify assumptions that need testing during the MVP phase.

Following is a one-page visualization of the canvas:

---

4 **https://www.strategyzer.com/library/the-business-model-canvas**. Accessed 26 Jan, 2025.

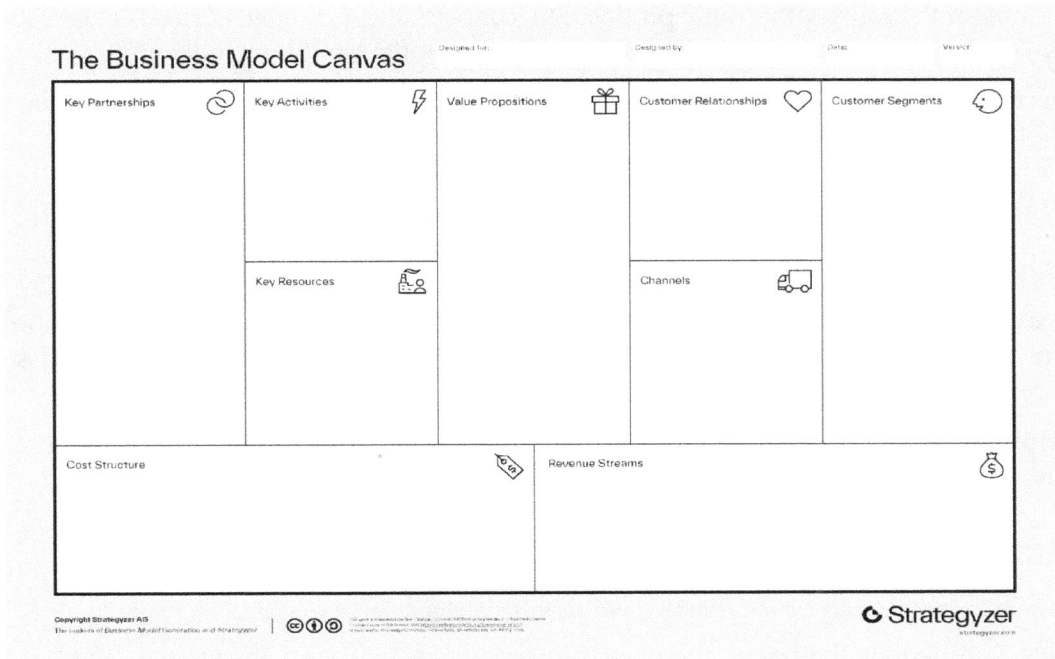

Figure 8.2: Business Model Canvas by Strategyzer

The right-hand side focuses on external, customer-facing elements:

- **Customer segments**: Identifying the different groups of people or organizations the business aims to serve.
- **Channels**: Describing how the business delivers its value proposition to its customer segments.
- **Customer relationships**: Outlining how the business interacts with and engages its customers.
- **Revenue streams**: Highlighting how the business earns money from its value propositions.

The left-hand side addresses internal, operational aspects:

- **Key activities**: Pinpointing the most critical tasks the business must perform to deliver value.
- **Key resources**: Identifying the assets required to make the business model work.
- **Key partnerships**: Highlighting the external companies, suppliers, or partners that help execute the business.
- **Cost structure**: Mapping out the major costs involved in operating the business model.

The center of the canvas, the value proposition, connects the customer-facing and operational sides, serving as the bridge between what the business offers and how it delivers it.

Let us explore the key sections of the Business Model Canvas and the suggested sequence for filling them out, providing clarity and focus to each element.

Value propositions

What value do we deliver to the customer? Which customer problems are we solving?

This section highlights the unique selling propositions, benefits, and reasons why customers would choose the product or service. Entrepreneurs should focus on a very limited set of features that make the product stand out.

Example: If the product is a platform for artisan-made goods, the value proposition could include authenticity, quality craftsmanship, and cultural significance.

Customer segments

For whom are we creating value? Who are our most important customers?

This section defines the target audience, user personas, and market segments the business serves. Entrepreneurs can include:

- Primary and secondary target audiences, such as niche customer groups or broader markets.
- User personas based on interviews, surveys, or market data, which help represent the needs, goals, and behaviors of specific customer types.
- Results from market research that segment users by demographics, preferences, or buying behavior.

Example: The platform for artisan goods may target culturally conscious shoppers, urban professionals, or gift-buyers seeking unique, handcrafted items.

Channels

Through which channels do our customer segments want to be reached?

This section outlines the methods and platforms through which the product or service reaches its customers. The key considerations include:

- Ideal platforms for distribution, such as e-commerce websites, mobile apps, or physical stores.
- Distribution partnerships, such as collaborations with influencers or retail stores.
- A mix of direct and indirect sales channels.

- Online versus offline sales strategies to meet customer preferences.

Example: The artisan platform might prioritize an e-commerce website and social media campaigns to reach urban millennials and tech-savvy shoppers.

Customer relationships

What type of relationship does each customer segment expect us to establish with them?

This section describes how the business will interact with its customers across the entire lifecycle, from discovery to loyalty. The key considerations include:

- Post-sale support plans, such as chatbots or customer care teams, for addressing inquiries.
- Feedback mechanisms, like regular surveys or reviews, to gather customer insights and improve offerings.
- Community engagement strategies, such as creating user forums, social media groups, or events, to foster connection.
- Loyalty programs or incentives to encourage repeat purchases and long-term relationships.

Example: For the artisan platform, customer relationships might involve personalized thank-you notes from artisans, community-building initiatives, or a loyalty rewards program that incentivizes repeat purchases.

Revenue streams

For what value are customers willing to pay? What are they currently paying, and how are they paying?

This section highlights the outcomes of product pricing analysis. It includes:

- Pricing strategies for the product (e.g., freemium, subscription, pay-per-use).
- Potential upsells or cross-sells to increase revenue per customer.
- Subscription models versus one-time payments, based on the product's nature and customer preferences.
- Additional revenue opportunities, such as affiliate programs or licensing intellectual property.

Example: If offering a SaaS platform, entrepreneurs might explore monthly subscriptions with tiered pricing based on features or usage, alongside premium add-ons for advanced users.

Key resources

What key resources do our value propositions, distribution channels, customer relationships, and revenue streams require?

This section focuses on the essential assets needed to make the business model work, such as:

- Technologies and platforms necessary for product development and delivery.
- Intellectual property, such as proprietary algorithms, trademarks, or patents.
- Personnel, including developers, designers, and support teams.
- Financial resources for scaling operations, launching campaigns, or entering new markets.

Example: An e-commerce platform may require a robust inventory management system, a high-performing website, and skilled customer support teams.

Key activities

What key activities are essential for delivering our value propositions, maintaining distribution channels, fostering customer relationships, and generating revenue streams?

This section covers the most critical actions that drive the business forward, such as:

- Product development and iteration to keep the offering competitive.
- Go-to-market strategies to launch and scale the product effectively.
- Building and nurturing partnerships to expand reach and capability.
- User acquisition strategies, including marketing campaigns and referral programs.

Example: For a marketplace, key activities might involve onboarding sellers, optimizing the user experience, and running targeted ad campaigns.

Key partnerships

Who are our key partners and suppliers? What resources or activities are provided by partners?

This section identifies the external organizations, resources, or activities leveraged to achieve business objectives. It includes:

- Tech partners for integrations or custom development.
- Distribution or channel partners to extend market reach.
- Co-branding collaborations with complementary brands or influencers.
- Vendors for logistics, raw materials, or third-party services are essential to operations.

Example: An artisan marketplace could partner with local logistics providers to ensure timely deliveries and collaborate with NGOs to onboard rural artisans.

Cost structure

What are the most significant costs in our business model? Which resources and activities are the most expensive?

This section focuses on analyzing and understanding the costs associated with running the business. It includes:

- Expenses related to product development, maintenance, and support.
- Marketing and promotion costs, including digital ad spend or influencer partnerships.
- User acquisition expenses, such as referral programs or introductory discounts.
- Third-party service costs for tools, platforms, or outsourced activities.

Example: A SaaS platform's cost structure might prioritize server costs, developer salaries, and customer support tools.

By addressing these elements systematically, entrepreneurs can create a comprehensive and actionable Business Model Canvas. This ensures a balanced view of customer-facing elements and internal operations, enabling them to build and scale a sustainable business.

Unit economics

Unit economics refers to the direct revenues and costs associated with a single unit of a product or service. For startups and entrepreneurs, understanding unit economics is essential for validating whether their business model can be profitable and sustainable in the long term. It provides insights into the financial performance of a business at a granular level and is a critical step in determining the viability of scaling the business.

Two primary metrics in unit economics are **customer acquisition cost** (**CAC**) and customer **lifetime value** (**LTV**). Together, these metrics help entrepreneurs assess profitability and measure how effectively their business is generating value from customers.

Customer acquisition cost

CAC is the cost incurred to acquire a single paying customer. This metric includes all expenses related to sales and marketing, such as advertising, promotions, salaries for sales teams, and tools used for customer acquisition.

CAC = Total sales and marketing expenses / Number of new customers acquired

For example, if a startup spends ₹100,000 on marketing campaigns and acquires 50 new customers, the CAC is:

CAC = ₹1,00,000 / 50 = ₹2,000

Understanding CAC helps entrepreneurs ensure they are not overspending to acquire customers, especially in the early stages of MVP validation.

Customer LTV

LTV represents the total revenue a business expects to generate from a single customer over the course of their relationship with the business. This metric accounts for the customer's purchasing behavior, the average transaction value, and how long they are likely to remain a customer.

$$LTV = Average\ purchase\ Value \times Purchase\ frequency \times Customer\ lifespan$$

For instance, if a customer spends ₹1,000 per transaction, makes 10 purchases a year, and remains a customer for 3 years, the LTV is:

$$LTV = ₹1,000 \times 10 \times 3 = ₹30,000$$

By comparing LTV to CAC, entrepreneurs can determine whether acquiring customers is profitable. Ideally, the LTV to CAC ratio should be at least 3:1, meaning that for every ₹1 spent on acquiring a customer, the business generates ₹3 in lifetime revenue.

Go-to-market

A **go-to-market** (**GTM**) strategy is a structured action plan that outlines how a business will introduce its MVP to customers. For an entrepreneur, the GTM strategy is a pivotal step that bridges the gap between product development and market entry. It addresses how the MVP will be positioned, communicated, distributed, and sold to ensure successful adoption and maximize market impact. A robust GTM strategy not only accelerates customer acquisition but also helps create a strong foundation for scaling the product.

A well-executed GTM strategy requires clarity on multiple fronts to ensure consistent and compelling messaging, as well as a seamless customer experience. The following are the key components that entrepreneurs must focus on:

- **Target market**: Identifying the precise market segment for the MVP is fundamental. This involves defining an ideal customer profile and gaining a deep understanding of their needs, preferences, and pain points. Entrepreneurs must conduct detailed market research, such as customer interviews, surveys, and competitor analysis, to identify primary and secondary target audiences. A nuanced understanding of the customer base allows entrepreneurs to tailor their positioning, pricing, and outreach efforts effectively, ensuring a strong connection between the product and its intended users. This is covered in *Chapter 2, Market Analysis and Validation*.

- **Positioning**: Positioning involves crafting a compelling narrative that highlights the unique value proposition of the MVP relative to competitors. Entrepreneurs should revisit competitive analysis to identify market gaps and opportunities. By emphasizing the MVP's distinct features and benefits, the team can create messaging that resonates with customers and sets the product apart. Additionally, internal alignment, such as conducting sales training and providing marketing teams with battlecards, ensures consistency in communicating the MVP's strengths across all customer touchpoints. This, too, is covered in *Chapter 2, Market Analysis and Validation*.

- **Market fit**: Evaluating market fit is crucial to measure whether the MVP aligns with customer needs and expectations. Entrepreneurs must establish **key performance indicators** (**KPIs**) and track metrics like customer acquisition rates, churn, and retention. Regular assessments against predefined success thresholds ensure the MVP remains relevant. If performance consistently falls short, pivoting or redesigning the MVP may be necessary. Setting measurable benchmarks allows for informed decision-making and continuous improvement, ensuring the product evolves alongside market dynamics. This is covered in *Chapter 5, Problem-solution Fit*.

- **Pricing**: Pricing is one of the most critical levers in any GTM strategy. Entrepreneurs must balance competitive pricing, customer value perception, and profitability. The pricing model—whether subscription-based, value-driven, or freemium—should align with the target market's preferences and the MVP's cost structure. A well-defined pricing strategy also enables clear communication across teams, helping align sales, marketing, and customer success efforts around shared goals. This is covered earlier in this chapter as part of the section, *Product pricing*.

- **Bundling**: Bundling allows businesses to package the MVP with complementary products or services to enhance perceived value. Entrepreneurs can also include the MVP in existing offerings to introduce it to a specific customer segment. Bundling creates opportunities to cross-sell and upsell while providing customers with more comprehensive solutions that address their needs.

- **Distribution channels**: Strategically choosing distribution channels ensures the MVP reaches its target audience efficiently. Channels may include direct sales, partnerships with resellers, e-commerce platforms, or a combination thereof. To optimize customer reach, businesses must evaluate the advantages of each channel and ensure they have robust systems for maintaining availability and a frictionless purchasing experience. This is covered earlier in this chapter as part of the section, *Business model validation*.

- **Launch planning**: The launch plan is a blueprint for releasing the MVP and creating initial market traction. Entrepreneurs must establish timelines, plan marketing campaigns, and introduce promotional offers. Launch planning includes cross-departmental coordination to address tasks such as preparing FAQs, known issue documentation, and ensuring the support team is equipped to handle inquiries. By addressing pre-launch and post-launch activities comprehensively, businesses can ensure a smooth release and maximize impact.

- **Sales enablement**: Equipping the sales team with the necessary tools and knowledge is crucial for GTM success. Sales collateral, such as presentations, scripts, and case studies, should clearly communicate the MVP's features and benefits. Training programs ensure that the sales team understands the product thoroughly and can handle objections effectively. By addressing ongoing sales team needs, businesses can foster a confident, informed sales force that drives adoption.

- **Marketing and promotion**: Marketing efforts must align with the MVP's value proposition and target market. Campaigns across digital and offline channels should aim to capture leads and generate awareness. Entrepreneurs must identify social media platforms frequented by their audience and actively engage with potential customers through comments, shares, and community building. Additionally, creating a centralized repository of marketing assets ensures team members have access to up-to-date information.

- **Internal messaging**: Internal messaging ensures all teams share a unified understanding of the MVP's purpose and value proposition. By cultivating alignment across departments, businesses can prevent miscommunication and maintain consistent external messaging. A cohesive internal narrative fosters collaboration, ensuring that teams work together effectively toward shared objectives.

Due to a well-crafted GTM strategy, with a clear, coordinated approach, entrepreneurs can confidently take their MVP to market and maximize its potential impact.

Product launch

Launching a new MVP requires meticulous planning and execution. It is not just about making the product available but ensuring that every aspect of the launch, from customer engagement to internal preparation, is aligned for maximum impact. Entrepreneurs launching their MVPs can draw from tried-and-tested strategies to navigate this crucial phase successfully.

Preparing for a product launch

Bringing a new product into the market is an exciting milestone, but it also demands careful orchestration across strategy, operations, and marketing. A successful launch does not begin with the first advertisement or social media post—it begins with early preparation.

- **Soft vs. full-scale launch**: Entrepreneurs must decide between a soft launch, where a limited audience previews the product, or a full-scale launch, aimed at making a major market impact. A soft launch allows for testing and iteration based on real-world feedback, while a full-scale launch seeks immediate traction and visibility.

- **Budgeting and funnel optimization**: An effective launch requires a well-defined budget to cover marketing, distribution, and potential partnerships. Entrepreneurs should also optimize the launch funnel by incorporating upsells, bundles, or cross-promotions with other products to maximize revenue.

- **Content strategy**: Creating compelling content is critical to showcasing the product's value. Content like blogs, social media posts, and videos should address customer pain points, highlight benefits, and differentiate the product from competitors.

- **Audience segmentation and buying journey**: Clearly define the target audience and their specific needs. Understanding the customer's journey, pain points, information sources, and influencers allows entrepreneurs to craft tailored marketing strategies that resonate with their audience.

Key launch tactics

The tactics employed in the weeks leading up to the launch can make a significant difference in how the product is received and how quickly traction is built. Here are some common activities to precede a launch:

- **Pre-orders and influencer partnerships**: Offering pre-order options can help spread demand and generate early revenue. Collaborations with influencers can amplify visibility and credibility, driving significant customer interest.

- **Internal and partner preparation**: Internal teams and external partners, such as distributors, need to be aligned with the launch strategy. Training sessions, clear communication, and collaborative planning ensure seamless execution.

- **Setting the launch date and building anticipation**: Selecting the right launch date ensures maximum attention and minimal competition. Pre-launch activities, such as teasers, early access offers, and dedicated landing pages, help build excitement among potential customers.

Leveraging channels and platforms

A well-built product will only succeed if it reaches the right people at the right time through the right mediums. Consider the following strategies to ensure visibility, accessibility, and community engagement:

- **Distribution channels**: Entrepreneurs should identify the most effective channels for their product, including direct sales, e-commerce platforms, or partnerships. A well-maintained and frictionless distribution system ensures customers can access the product easily.

- **Social media and community platforms**: Maximizing the MVP's online presence is essential. Social media campaigns and platforms like Product Hunt can generate buzz and gather feedback from tech-savvy users.

Post-launch strategies

The journey does not end at launch; what comes next is equally important. Consider the following to nurture a product in its early days to set it up for long-term success:

- **Engaging early adopters and feedback collection**: Early adopters can provide valuable feedback for last-minute refinements and help generate word-of-mouth marketing.

Capturing leads and establishing feedback loops ensures continuous improvement and sustained interest.

- **Crisis management planning**: Entrepreneurs must prepare for potential setbacks, such as negative reviews or technical issues, with a robust crisis management plan. Addressing problems proactively can mitigate damage to the brand's reputation.

Collaterals for product launch

Effective product launch collaterals ensure that all stakeholders, internal teams, partners, and customers are well-informed. These include:

- **User manuals**: Comprehensive guides with streamlined user flows and troubleshooting steps.

- **FAQs**: Addressing common queries helps reduce support requests.

- **Sales battlecards**: Equipping sales teams with competitor analysis and talking points for customer meetings.

- **Press releases**: Capturing media and public attention with clear, concise announcements.

- **Partner/reseller guides**: Providing partners with resources to market and sell the product effectively.

Launching an MVP successfully requires entrepreneurs to be well-prepared. By focusing on key strategies—targeting the right audience, crafting compelling content, aligning internal and external teams, and leveraging the right distribution channels—entrepreneurs can maximize their MVP's potential.

Tara plans to host a live online event where artisans will demonstrate their craftsmanship, share their stories, and interact with the audience. This showcase will highlight the authenticity and cultural richness of IndicOcean.com's offerings.

Tara has organized an exclusive discount for the first 100 customers to create excitement and encourage early purchases. She will also announce a social media giveaway featuring curated artisan bundles to increase engagement and broaden the platform's reach.

To create buzz around the launch, Tara has planned a series of posts, stories, and reels to be shared across *Instagram*, *Facebook*, and *Pinterest*. These will feature vibrant visuals and use branded hashtags like *#ShopArtisan* and *#IndicOceanLaunch* to build awareness and engagement.

Tara will send targeted emails to IndicOcean.com's subscriber list, emphasizing the platform's unique features and introductory offers. These emails are designed to draw attention to the value proposition and create urgency around the launch.

Tara has allocated resources for *Google* and *Facebook* ad campaigns aimed at the platform's target customer segments. These ads will focus on highlighting IndicOcean.com's unique selling points, such as authentic artisan products and cultural storytelling.

Tara has ensured the platform undergoes thorough load testing to handle the anticipated traffic spikes on launch day, minimizing any risk of downtime or performance issues.

Tara has prepared the support team with comprehensive FAQs, escalation matrices, and troubleshooting guides to ensure customer inquiries are addressed efficiently and professionally during the launch period.

This structured and detailed launch phase reflects Tara's commitment to positioning IndicOcean.com as a unique and compelling destination for artisan-crafted goods.

Digital advertising

Digital advertising is a rapidly evolving domain that offers unparalleled opportunities for entrepreneurs to launch an MVP. By leveraging various digital ad formats, platforms, and strategies, entrepreneurs can effectively reach their target audience, create brand awareness, and drive conversions. This guide provides a comprehensive overview of digital advertising essentials tailored for MVP launches.

Basics of digital advertising

Digital advertising encompasses various formats and strategies designed to promote products online. It includes display ads, video ads, search ads, native ads, and in-app ads. Each type has unique characteristics, catering to specific goals like awareness, engagement, or conversions.

Ad types

The following are the types of ads:

- **Display ads**: Visual banners that appear on websites or apps.
- **Video ads**: Found on platforms like *YouTube*, offering dynamic and engaging storytelling opportunities.
- **Search ads**: Text-based ads displayed in search engine results when specific keywords are queried.
- **Native ads**: Seamlessly integrated with the content of websites or apps, making them less intrusive.
- **Interstitial ads**: Full-screen ads that cover the interface, ideal for capturing attention during app transitions.
- **Rich media ads**: Interactive ads with elements like video and audio for enhanced engagement.

- **Click-through URL: Click-through URL (CTURLs)** are hyperlinks that guide users to a specific landing page after clicking an ad. Entrepreneurs should use well-structured CTURLs with parameters (e.g., campaign source, medium, and ID) to track user activity and optimize campaigns effectively.

- **Landing pages**: Landing pages play a pivotal role in driving conversions and must be optimized for effectiveness. They should load quickly to minimize bounce rates, ensuring that users do not abandon the page due to delays. Responsiveness is equally important, as the landing page must seamlessly adapt to desktops, tablets, and smartphones for a consistent user experience across devices. Finally, a well-designed landing page should be action-oriented, featuring a clear and compelling **call-to-action (CTA)** that encourages users to take the desired next step, such as signing up, making a purchase, or exploring further.

- **Tracking pixels**: Tracking pixels are 1x1 transparent images embedded in web pages to track user behavior, such as purchases or sign-ups. They provide valuable data on campaign performance and user actions.

Pricing models

The following are the common pricing models:

- **Cost per mille (CPM)**: Cost per 1,000 displays of the digital ad.
- **Cost per click (CPC)**: Payment for each click.
- **Cost per lead (CPL)**: Cost per acquired lead, typically a user filling up a form on the landing page.
- **Cost per action (CPA)**: Cost for specific actions like purchases.

Audience targeting and ad formats

Running effective digital campaigns is not just about creating ads; it is about making sure those ads reach the right people, in the right place, at the right time. Entrepreneurs must pair smart targeting strategies with the right ad formats to maximize their return on ad spend.

Audience targeting

Understanding the audience is pivotal for campaign success. Targeting methods include:

- **Demographics**: Age, gender, location, etc.
- **Retargeting**: Engaging users who previously interacted with the brand.
- **Lookalike audiences**: Targeting users similar to existing customers.

Display ads

Display ads combine creativity with data-driven strategies. Standard ad sizes, such as medium rectangle (300 pixel by 250 pixel) and leaderboard (728 pixel by 90 pixel), ensure compatibility across platforms. Entrepreneurs should focus on compelling headlines, visuals, and CTAs to maximize impact.

Video ads

Video ads are highly engaging and offer a powerful storytelling medium. The key elements include:

- **Video content**: The main message.
- **Audio**: Enhancing the ad's impact.
- **CTA**: Encouraging desired actions. Formats like pre-roll, mid-roll, and post-roll cater to different stages of user engagement.

Search ads

Search ads, driven by keywords, are precise and timely. The entrepreneurs should:

- Use keyword research tools like Google Keyword Planner.
- Focus on long-tail keywords for better conversion rates.
- Optimize ads for relevance to improve quality scores and reduce costs.

Native ads

Native ads blend seamlessly with content, providing a non-disruptive user experience. Common types include in-feed ads, search and promoted listings, and content recommendations. By aligning with the platform's tone and style, native ads can drive higher engagement rates.

In-app advertising

As users spend more time on apps, in-app advertising has gained prominence. The popular formats include:

- **Standard banner ads**: Simple, static, or animated ads at the top or bottom of the app interface.
- **Interstitial ads**: Full-screen ads placed between app transitions.
- **Rewarded ads**: Offering users in-app rewards in exchange for viewing ads.
- **Expandable ads**: Starting as a banner and expanding when interacted with.

When planning in-app ads, it is essential to prioritize a responsive design that adapts seamlessly to varying screen sizes, ensuring a consistent experience across devices. Extensive testing of ads on multiple devices is crucial to identify and resolve any inconsistencies or issues. Equally important is striking a balance between monetization and maintaining a positive user experience, as overly intrusive or poorly designed ads can lead to user dissatisfaction and app abandonment.

Ad serving and publishing

Digital advertising is all about precision, automation, and performance. For entrepreneurs, understanding how ads are served, published, and optimized is key to unlocking cost-effective customer acquisition.

Ad serving

Ad servers manage ad placement and user targeting in real-time. Key capabilities include:

- **Targeting**: Based on user behavior, location, and demographics.
- **Retargeting**: Engaging users who previously interacted with ads.
- **Real-time reporting**: Monitoring campaign performance.

Ad publishing

Websites or apps display ads using:

- **Direct ad code**: Specific advertiser partnerships.
- **Ad server tags**: Dynamic ad selection.
- **Ad network code**: Aggregating ads from multiple advertisers.

Entrepreneurs can choose from various pricing models, such as CPM, CPC, and CPA, to monetize their ad spaces effectively.

Programmatic advertising

Programmatic advertising automates the buying and selling of ad space, enabling precise audience targeting. It involves:

- **Demand side platforms (DSPs)**: Automating ad purchases across exchanges.
- **Data management platforms (DMPs)**: Collecting and analyzing audience data for targeted campaigns.

This approach enhances ROI by delivering relevant ads to the right audience at the right time.

Digital agencies and rating companies

As an MVP enters the market, visibility and credibility become key drivers of traction. Entrepreneurs can take of help of digital marketing companies not only to promote effectively but also to measure performance with precision.

Digital agencies

Digital agencies act as strategic partners, helping startups craft and execute high-impact online marketing campaigns. These agencies bring deep expertise in areas like media planning, content creation, social media engagement, and SEO optimization. For entrepreneurs lacking in-house marketing capabilities, collaborating with a digital agency ensures access to talent, tools, and creative direction without the overhead of building a full-fledged team.

Digital rating companies

Digital rating companies analyze campaign performance, website traffic, and audience behavior. Their insights enable entrepreneurs to refine strategies and optimize ad spending.

Digital advertising offers a powerful toolkit for entrepreneurs launching an MVP. By understanding ad formats, leveraging audience targeting, and adopting the right pricing models, entrepreneurs can create impactful campaigns that drive awareness, engagement, and conversions. With the right blend of creativity, strategy, and analytics, a well-executed digital advertising plan can propel an MVP toward market success.

Tara's pricing model for her ads included a combination of CPC for search ads and CPM for display ads, ensuring she could track engagement while controlling costs. Her native ads and in-app ads further complemented her strategy, blending seamlessly with platforms and reaching her target audience without being intrusive.

Actions for the entrepreneur

1. Build a cost model for the MVP.
2. Determine the pricing model for the MVP based on user testing insights.
3. Develop a Business Model Canvas to outline the business strategy.
4. Define the **go-to-market** (**GTM**) strategy for the MVP.

Conclusion

Validating a business model is one of the most critical steps for any entrepreneur launching an MVP. It transforms an idea into a structured, scalable strategy that aligns with market needs and ensures sustainable growth. A well-validated business model provides clarity on how value is created, delivered, and captured, forming the backbone of a successful product launch and long-term business strategy.

Throughout this chapter, we explored essential concepts like product costing, pricing strategies, revenue streams, and customer segmentation, each serving as a building block for business model validation. Entrepreneurs were introduced to practical frameworks such as the Business Model Canvas, which offers a structured approach to mapping out and analyzing key components like value propositions, customer relationships, and cost structures. These tools empower entrepreneurs to articulate their vision effectively and ensure all aspects of their business are interconnected and aligned.

The chapter also emphasized the importance of pricing and revenue strategies. Techniques like cost-plus pricing, value-based pricing, and psychological pricing allow entrepreneurs to align their pricing models with customer expectations and market dynamics. Coupled with the exploration of revenue streams like subscription models, freemium offerings, and tiered pricing, these insights enable entrepreneurs to build a financial structure that balances profitability with customer acquisition and retention.

Validation is not a one-time activity; it is an iterative process that requires entrepreneurs to test, learn, and adapt continuously. Techniques such as A/B testing, conjoint analysis, and customer interviews provide actionable data that help refine the business model. By understanding metrics like CAC and customer LTV, entrepreneurs can evaluate the financial viability of their strategies and make informed decisions about scaling their business. These insights also help identify potential challenges early, enabling entrepreneurs to pivot or optimize as needed.

Moreover, the chapter highlighted the role of GTM strategies in bridging the gap between product development and market entry. A clear and actionable GTM plan ensures that the product reaches the right audience, with the right message, through the right channels. Components such as positioning, bundling, distribution, and launch planning were discussed to help entrepreneurs maximize market impact and accelerate customer adoption.

Business model validation is more than just a technical exercise; it is a disciplined approach that fosters resilience, adaptability, and customer-centricity.

In the next chapter, the entrepreneur will learn the development process of an MVP.

Join our Discord space

Join our Discord workspace for latest updates, offers, tech happenings around the world, new releases, and sessions with the authors:

https://discord.bpbonline.com

CHAPTER 9
Iterative MVP Development

Introduction

Building an MVP is not a one-time effort; it is a dynamic process that evolves with every iteration. The goal is to develop a product that addresses core customer needs while adapting to market feedback, all while maintaining efficiency and resource optimization. For entrepreneurs, especially those venturing into software development for the first time, embracing iterative development is key to navigating the complexities of building an MVP. This approach not only minimizes risks but also ensures the product aligns with evolving customer expectations and market realities.

At the heart of iterative MVP development lies Agile methodology, a framework that emphasizes adaptability, incremental progress, and continuous learning. Agile provides the structure for iterative development cycles, enabling teams to deliver value in small increments and adapt quickly to changes. This empowers entrepreneurs to develop MVPs that are efficient, customer-centric, and scalable.

The success of iterative MVP development depends heavily on the team executing it. Key roles such as the product owner, scrum master, UX/UI designers, QA testers, and customer success managers play vital parts in ensuring collaboration, clarity, and execution. Each team member brings a unique perspective and expertise to the table, contributing to the creation of a product that not only works but also delivers exceptional value to users.

Another critical aspect of MVP development is deciding whether to outsource or insource the work. Factors such as expertise, cost, scalability, and risk must be carefully evaluated to determine the most effective approach. While outsourcing offers access to specialized skills and flexibility, insourcing ensures greater control and alignment with the entrepreneur's vision. Making this decision strategically is essential for optimizing resource allocation and maintaining momentum.

Structure

In this chapter, we will cover the following topics:

- Software development
- Team development

Objectives

By the end of this chapter, entrepreneurs will gain a comprehensive understanding of how to approach MVP development iteratively, leveraging Agile methodologies to ensure continuous improvement and adaptability. They will learn how to structure development processes that are both efficient and responsive to user feedback, fostering a product that aligns closely with customer needs and market demands.

Entrepreneurs will explore key frameworks such as the scrum framework, equipping them with practical tools to manage their MVP development cycles effectively. They will also understand the critical roles within a development team, including the product owner, scrum master, UX/UI designers, QA testers, and customer success managers, and how these roles collaborate to drive success.

The chapter will also provide insights into making strategic decisions between outsourcing and insourcing MVP development. Entrepreneurs will learn to conduct a cost-benefit analysis, assess risks, define vendor selection criteria, and negotiate contracts effectively, enabling them to optimize resource allocation and execution.

Through these topics, entrepreneurs will be empowered to guide a well-functioning MVP development process that minimizes waste, reduces risk, and accelerates time to market—all while ensuring a strong alignment between the vision and what customers value today.

Software development life cycle

The **software development life cycle** (**SDLC**) is a structured process that guides the development of software from an initial idea to a finished product. Think of it as a roadmap that ensures your MVP is built efficiently, meets user needs, and is delivered on time and within budget. While technical teams handle the intricate details, understanding the big picture of SDLC helps you, as an entrepreneur, communicate effectively with your team and stay in control of your MVP's progress.

Waterfall model

The Waterfall model is a traditional software development methodology that follows a linear, step-by-step process. Each phase must be completed before moving on to the next, and there's minimal room for revisiting or revising previous steps. While this approach is highly structured and works well for projects with clearly defined requirements, it can be rigid and costly when changes are needed.

The Waterfall model is typically broken into the following key stages:

- **Planning**: This is where it all begins. The focus is on understanding the problem your MVP is solving, defining objectives, and setting the scope of the product. Here, you collaborate with your team to outline what features are essential for your MVP and prioritize them based on customer needs and business goals.

- **Requirements gathering**: In this stage, the development team gathers detailed information about what your MVP should do. For a non-technical entrepreneur, your role is to articulate the value you want to deliver to customers, highlight pain points you are solving, and provide insights into the target audience. These discussions translate into technical requirements for developers.

- **Design**: Once the requirements are clear, the team creates a blueprint for your MVP. This includes wireframes for the **user interface** (**UI**) and plans for how the system will work behind the scenes. While technical teams focus on design details, you can participate by reviewing wireframes and ensuring the product aligns with your vision.

- **Development**: This is where your MVP starts taking shape. Developers write the code, create the features, and integrate any necessary tools or services. While this stage is primarily technical, your role involves staying informed about progress, clarifying doubts from the team, and ensuring alignment with your product goals.

- **Testing**: Before the MVP is launched, it is thoroughly tested to ensure it functions as intended. The team identifies bugs, evaluates usability, and ensures the product delivers a smooth user experience. As an entrepreneur, you can participate in **user acceptance testing** (**UAT**), where you provide feedback on whether the MVP meets your expectations.

- **Deployment**: This is the big moment, your MVP is launched and made available to users. The deployment process involves ensuring that the product is set up in its intended environment, whether that is an app store, website, or other platform. Your focus here is on ensuring that the launch goes smoothly and aligns with your marketing and go-to-market strategy.

- **Maintenance and iteration**: Post-launch, the work does not stop. Based on user feedback and market data, your MVP may need updates, bug fixes, or new features. This iterative process ensures your product evolves to meet customer needs and stays relevant in the market.

Iterative approach

In contrast, it is a flexible development methodology that focuses on creating, testing, and refining a product through multiple cycles or iterations. This approach stands in contrast to linear models like the Waterfall model, as it emphasizes adaptability, continuous feedback, and gradual improvement. It is a conceptual abstraction that encompasses methodologies like Agile and design thinking (covered in *Chapter 4, Ideation and Solution Generation*), all of which share the core principle of iteration.

The iterative approach is typically broken into the following key stages:

1. **Define goals**: Each cycle begins with clear objectives, such as developing a feature, addressing user pain points, or testing a hypothesis. This is covered in *Chapter 2, Market Analysis and Validation*.

2. **Build incrementally**: Teams work on a small, defined portion of the product rather than attempting to complete everything upfront.

3. **Test and gather feedback**: The output of each iteration is tested with real users, stakeholders, or the internal team to gather actionable insights.

4. **Analyze and refine**: Feedback is analyzed to identify areas of improvement, guiding the focus of the next iteration.

5. **Repeat the cycle**: The process repeats until the product meets its goals or aligns with market needs.

Thus, work is divided into manageable cycles or iterations, with each iteration producing an output that provides value to the customer in some way. This output is then refined based on feedback. Throughout the process, input from stakeholders, customers, and team members is continuously integrated to ensure the MVP aligns with user needs and market expectations, grounded in real-world evidence rather than solely relying on the entrepreneur's vision or assumptions.

Instead of striving for perfection in a single attempt, the MVP is improved incrementally. This involves addressing issues, making targeted adjustments based on new insights, and incorporating enhancements in each iteration. By prioritizing the most valuable aspects of the MVP early on, this approach ensures that even the initial versions deliver tangible value to users, laying a strong foundation for further refinement and growth.

Comparing iterative approach to Waterfall model

The choice between an iterative and a Waterfall approach significantly shapes how a product evolves—from how feedback is handled to how quickly value is delivered. Understanding the core differences across key aspects helps entrepreneurs choose the right methodology for their MVP journey.

Aspect	Iterative approach	Waterfall model
Flexibility	Adaptable to change; embraces evolving requirements throughout the development process.	Fixed plan and so changes are difficult and costly once the project begins.
Feedback integration	Continuous feedback from stakeholders, customers, and team members is incorporated during each cycle, ensuring alignment with real-world needs.	Feedback is typically gathered only after the final product is delivered, limiting the opportunity to make timely adjustments.
Risk management	Reduces risk by allowing early testing, validation, and course corrections during each iteration.	Risks are compounded as issues are often identified late in the process, making mitigation more challenging and costly.
Timeline	Deliverables are produced in shorter, manageable cycles (iterations), ensuring quicker outputs and ongoing progress.	The entire product is delivered only at the end of the development cycle, potentially delaying value realization.
Customer-centricity	Focused on delivering incremental value to customers with each iteration, using feedback to improve user satisfaction.	Customer input is usually limited to the initial requirement phase, potentially leading to a final product misaligned with user needs.
Ambiguity and uncertainty	Continuous feedback allows the incorporation of learnings, emerging clarity, and stakeholder input, adapting to changing conditions and insights.	The rigidity of structure and the need for predictability make it difficult to handle ambiguity, with changes often being expensive and hard to gain buy-in for.
Documentation	Prioritizes lightweight documentation that evolves with the project, focusing on real-time collaboration.	Relies heavily on comprehensive upfront documentation, which may become outdated as requirements or conditions change.
Goal alignment	Encourages continuous alignment with user needs and business goals by adapting based on feedback and changing priorities.	Assumes all requirements are known upfront, risking misalignment if initial assumptions prove incorrect.

Table 9.1: Comparing iterative and Waterfall

The iterative approach is particularly well-suited for entrepreneurs building an MVP. It allows for quick testing of assumptions, enables the validation of business hypotheses, and reduces the risk of over-investing in unproven ideas. By refining the MVP incrementally, entrepreneurs can adapt their solutions to better meet user needs and market demands, ensuring a stronger fit and a faster path to success.

Scrum

Agile methodologies are frameworks that emphasize iterative development, collaboration, and adaptability. Scrum, Kanban, lean, **extreme programming** (**XP**), and so on. However, scrum is what an entrepreneur is likely to encounter when working with software development teams.

Scrum is a lightweight framework that enables teams to tackle complex projects by breaking them into smaller, iterative cycles called sprints. Each sprint, typically lasting 1–4 weeks, focuses on delivering a usable increment of the product. Each sprint is a time-boxed period where the team works on a specific set of tasks or features. At the end of each sprint, the team delivers a working increment of the MVP that can be reviewed and tested.

Roles in scrum

These roles in scrum define the responsibilities and collaboration dynamics within the team, ensuring clarity and efficiency in delivering the MVP.

Product owner

The **product owner** (**PO**) plays a crucial role in scrum, acting as the bridge between business objectives and the development team. Representing the entrepreneur, business stakeholder, or customer, the PO is responsible for defining and championing the product vision while ensuring that development efforts align with business goals. By making strategic decisions about what gets built and in what order, the PO ensures that the team focuses on delivering maximum value to users and stakeholders.

A key responsibility of the PO is managing and prioritizing the product backlog. This involves translating business needs into well-defined user stories, refining requirements, and continuously re-evaluating priorities based on market feedback, customer insights, and changing business needs. The PO also works closely with the development team to clarify requirements, address questions, and provide direction throughout the sprint. While they do not dictate how to implement solutions, they must clearly communicate what needs to be built and why it matters.

To be effective, a PO should embody a mix of leadership, decisiveness, and customer-centric thinking. They must be accessible to the team, ready to make quick decisions, and open to feedback from both customers and developers. Strong collaboration skills are essential, as they frequently interact with stakeholders, engineers, designers, and scrum masters to ensure alignment across all levels. Additionally, the PO must be adaptable—willing to pivot when necessary, based on data, user behavior, or new business opportunities.

The key outcomes of an effective PO include a clear and well-maintained product backlog, a development roadmap aligned with business priorities, and a product that continuously evolves to meet customer needs. When done well, this role ensures that every sprint contributes meaningfully to the broader product vision, ultimately leading to a successful MVP and a scalable, market-ready solution.

Scrum master

The scrum master plays a vital role in ensuring that scrum principles and Agile practices are followed, creating an environment where the development team can operate at its best. Acting as a facilitator rather than a manager, the scrum master focuses on enabling collaboration, removing impediments, and fostering a culture of continuous improvement. Their primary responsibility is to ensure smooth execution of the scrum process, guiding the team through ceremonies such as sprint planning, daily standups, sprint reviews, and retrospectives.

A key aspect of the scrum master's role is shielding the team from distractions and external interruptions, allowing developers to focus on delivering high-quality work. They proactively identify and remove obstacles that could slow down progress, whether they are technical blockers, process inefficiencies, or organizational challenges. By closely monitoring team dynamics, they help resolve conflicts, encourage open communication, and ensure that collaboration remains productive and positive.

To be effective, a scrum master should embody servant leadership, adaptability, and a coaching mindset.

Servant leadership is a leadership approach that prioritizes the growth, well-being, and success of the team, empowering them to self-organize and perform at their best.

The coaching mindset is a mindset that focuses on guiding, mentoring, and enabling the team to find solutions, improve continuously, and develop their skills rather than providing direct answers or commands.

Instead of micromanaging, they empower the team to self-organize, guiding them toward solutions rather than dictating decisions. They should encourage a culture of trust and accountability, ensuring that team members feel safe to share ideas, raise concerns, and experiment with new approaches. Strong facilitation skills are essential, as they must ensure that Scrum ceremonies are efficient, engaging, and result-oriented. Additionally, they should continuously seek opportunities to optimize workflows, improve team velocity, and foster a mindset of learning and innovation.

The key outcomes of an effective scrum master include a high-performing, self-organizing team that consistently delivers value, a culture of transparency and continuous improvement, and a seamless development process where roadblocks are swiftly addressed. When done well, this role ensures that the team remains aligned with Agile principles, making incremental progress toward building a successful MVP and a scalable product.

Developers

Developers play a pivotal role in MVP development, transforming ideas and requirements into a working product. As core members of the development team, they are responsible for writing high-quality, maintainable code that aligns with the product owner's vision and business objectives. By collaborating closely with UI designers, QA testers, and other team members, developers ensure that each sprint delivers tangible, functional increments of the MVP.

A key responsibility of developers is breaking down user stories into technical tasks, estimating effort, and implementing features efficiently. Their work goes beyond just coding—they participate in backlog refinement, contribute to architectural discussions, and proactively address technical challenges. They also conduct code reviews, optimize system performance, and integrate third-party services where necessary. Strong problem-solving skills and a commitment to continuous improvement help developers build a market-aligned MVP.

To be effective, developers should embrace a mindset of collaboration, ownership, and adaptability. They must be open to feedback, willing to work iteratively, and capable of troubleshooting issues with minimal guidance. A strong sense of responsibility ensures that they not only complete their assigned tasks but also consider the broader impact on the overall MVP. Developers should foster a culture of knowledge sharing by mentoring teammates, documenting best practices, and staying updated on industry trends and technologies.

The key outcomes of an effective development team include well-structured, efficient, and secure code, timely delivery of MVP increments, and an MVP that meets both functional and technical expectations. When done well, developers drive innovation, enhance user experience, and ensure the long-term scalability of the MVP.

UI designers

UI designers play a crucial role in shaping the look and feel of the MVP, ensuring that users can navigate it effortlessly while enjoying a seamless experience. They are responsible for designing intuitive, aesthetically pleasing, and accessible interfaces that align with business goals and user needs. By collaborating with product owners, developers, and QA testers, they translate concepts into visual designs, wireframes, and interactive prototypes that bring the MVP to life. We cover wireframes and prototypes in *Chapter 7, Building Successful MVP.*

A key responsibility of UI designers is creating and refining the MVP's design system, ensuring consistency in branding, typography, colors, and layout. They conduct user research and usability testing to validate design decisions and refine interfaces based on feedback. Additionally, they work closely with developers to ensure design feasibility, providing assets, documentation, and guidance to maintain design integrity throughout implementation. Their ability to balance creativity with usability is essential in delivering a compelling user experience.

To be effective, UI designers should cultivate a user-first mindset, strong attention to detail, and adaptability. They must be open to iterative improvements, using data-driven insights to refine designs over time. Clear communication and a collaborative approach help bridge the gap between design and development, ensuring that technical constraints and user expectations are both met. They should also stay updated on UI/UX trends, accessibility standards, and emerging design tools to continuously enhance their craft.

The key outcomes of an effective UI designer include a visually cohesive and user-friendly interface, improved usability and engagement, and an MVP that aligns with both the entrepreneur's objectives and user needs. When done well, their work elevates the MVP's appeal, making it more accessible, engaging, and enjoyable for users.

QA testers

QA testers play a vital role in maintaining the quality, stability, and reliability of the MVP. As dedicated quality advocates, they are responsible for identifying defects, verifying functionality, and ensuring that the MVP meets both technical and business requirements. Working closely with developers, product owners, and UI designers, QA testers help ensure that every sprint delivers an MVP that functions as expected and meets user expectations.

A key responsibility of QA testers is creating and executing test cases, covering functional, usability, and performance testing. They perform manual and automated testing, identify and report defects, and validate fixes before deployment. Beyond detecting bugs, they ensure compliance with industry standards, assess security vulnerabilities, and improve test coverage over time. By proactively identifying potential risks and edge cases, they help prevent issues from reaching users.

To be effective, QA testers should embrace a detail-oriented, analytical, and problem-solving mindset. They must have a strong understanding of testing methodologies, automation tools, and Agile best practices to optimize the testing process. Effective communication is essential, as they must collaborate with developers to debug issues and provide clear, actionable feedback. Adaptability is also key, as they must continuously refine testing strategies based on evolving product requirements and real-world usage data.

The key outcomes of an effective QA team include a bug-free, stable, and high-performing MVP, an efficient testing process that prevents delays, and a seamless user experience that builds trust with customers. When done well, their work ensures that every release meets quality standards, reducing technical debt and minimizing costly post-launch issues.

However, an entrepreneur may not encounter someone with these titles when they work with a software development team. A role defines the responsibilities and expectations within a team or project, while a job title is the formal designation that represents an individual's position in an organization. One way to understand the distinction is, one person might perform multiple roles despite having a single job title.

Artifacts in scrum

The following artifacts provide transparency, track progress, and ensure alignment with the MVP's development goals.

Product backlog

The product backlog is a dynamic, prioritized list of product capabilities, broken down into features, tasks, and improvements that shape the MVP. It serves as the single source of truth for what needs to be built, ensuring alignment with the product vision and business goals.

While the backlog often starts as a structured list based on the initial concept, it is not static. It continuously evolves throughout the development process. As the entrepreneur and the team gain new insights from market trends, user research, early adopters' feedback, and business needs, new ideas emerge, priorities shift, and the backlog is refined.

A well-maintained product backlog enables teams to focus on delivering high-value features first, adapt to changing customer needs and market conditions, and maintain clarity on upcoming work and long-term priorities.

For a deeper understanding of how to structure and prioritize your product backlog effectively, refer to *Chapter 3, Opportunity Prioritization*, and *Chapter 7, Building Successful MVP*.

Sprint backlog

The sprint backlog is a focused, time-bound subset of the product backlog that the team commits to completing within a sprint (typically 1–4 weeks). It represents the work-in-progress for that sprint and consists of selected features, translated into user stories, along with associated tasks.

During the sprint, the team also carries out the detailed technical and design work needed for implementation. The sprint backlog is owned and managed by the development team, ensuring that only realistic and achievable work is planned within the sprint timeframe.

Since Agile embraces adaptability, teams continuously reassess and refine the sprint backlog to address unexpected challenges while staying aligned with the sprint goal.

By breaking down work into smaller, incremental tasks, the sprint backlog ensures that work is manageable and transparent, teams deliver value consistently within each sprint, and stakeholders can see tangible progress and provide timely feedback.

Epic

An epic is a high-level feature or initiative that represents a large body of work too big to complete in a single sprint. Epics often span multiple sprints and are later broken down into smaller, actionable user stories to facilitate progress and delivery. Epics provide a strategic view of broader objectives and are essential for aligning the team with long-term goals. Typically, an item from a product backlog maps to an epic.

Example: *Enable users to discover and purchase handmade artisan products through a mobile app.*

Story

A user story is a small, well-defined unit of work that describes a specific functionality from the end-user's perspective. It serves as a building block within an epic and is small enough to be completed within a sprint. A standard user story format follows the structure:

As a [user type], I want to [action or feature], so that I can [benefit or reason].

User story focuses on the needs of the end-user, can be completed within a sprint, and delivers a tangible benefit to the user.

Example: *As a user, I want to search for handmade products by category, so that I can quickly find items that match my interests.*

Ceremonies in scrum

The following are structured meetings designed to facilitate collaboration, transparency, and continuous improvement throughout the scrum process.

Sprint planning

The purpose of sprint planning is to define what the team can achieve during the sprint and establish a clear plan for how they will accomplish it. This ceremony sets the foundation for a successful sprint by ensuring alignment between priorities, capacity, and execution.

During sprint planning, the product owner presents the highest-priority backlog items, providing context and rationale for their selection. The team then collaborates to define a clear sprint objective, ensuring that the chosen work aligns with both business goals and technical feasibility. Based on the team's capacity and priorities, selected items are moved from the product backlog to the sprint backlog.

Once the scope is determined, developers break down the selected user stories into actionable tasks, estimating the effort required for each. If the total estimated effort exceeds the available sprint duration, the team conducts another round of prioritization to refine the scope. This iterative approach ensures that the workload remains realistic and achievable within the sprint timeframe.

Before concluding sprint planning, the team collectively reviews the plan, clarifies any uncertainties, and commits to delivering the agreed-upon work.

The outcome of this ceremony is a well-defined sprint backlog with actionable tasks and a shared sprint goal, providing a clear direction for the team's work over the coming sprint.

Daily standups

The purpose of daily standup is to facilitate the team synchronizing on progress, discussing upcoming plans, and surfacing any roadblocks that may be hindering progress. This ceremony, a short, focused meeting, fosters transparency, accountability, and quick issue resolution, ensuring that everyone stays aligned toward achieving the sprint goal.

During the daily standup, each team member provides a brief update by answering three key questions:

- *What did I work on yesterday?*
- *What will I work on today?*
- *Are there any blockers preventing my progress?*

These structured updates help the team stay informed and provide an opportunity to identify potential roadblocks early. While the scrum master typically facilitates the meeting, the development team actively participates, and the product owner may join when necessary to offer additional context or guidance.

To maintain efficiency, the daily standup should be concise and to the point, typically lasting no more than 15 minutes. It is important to avoid deep-dive problem-solving during the meeting; instead, any discussions requiring further exploration should be taken offline with the relevant stakeholders.

The outcome of this ceremony is team alignment and fosters a culture of collaboration and transparency.

Sprint review

The purpose of the sprint review is to showcase the completed work to stakeholders, gather valuable feedback, and validate progress against the sprint goal. This ceremony provides an opportunity for transparency and collaboration, ensuring that the team's work aligns with business objectives and customer needs. By demonstrating working software rather than static presentations, the team facilitates meaningful discussions and insights that shape future development.

During the sprint review, the scrum team presents the features and functionality completed during the sprint. Stakeholders, including customers, business owners, and leadership, participate by reviewing the work and providing input. This feedback loop is essential for refining future priorities and ensuring that the product evolves in the right direction. The team also assesses whether the sprint goal was achieved and discusses any challenges encountered along the way.

To maximize the effectiveness of the sprint review, the focus should remain on real, working software rather than slides or prototypes. Encouraging open, collaborative discussions allows stakeholders to share insights that can directly impact future iterations. Any unfinished work is identified, and the next steps are determined to ensure continuity in development.

The outcome of this ceremony is stakeholder validation and potential refinements to the product backlog based on the feedback received. This iterative approach ensures that each sprint contributes meaningful progress toward delivering a valuable product.

Sprint retrospective

The purpose of the sprint retrospective is to provide the team with a dedicated space to reflect on their recent sprint, discussing what went well, what did not, and how they can improve in future iterations. This ceremony fosters continuous improvement by encouraging honest conversations about successes, challenges, and opportunities for growth. By taking time to analyze past performance, teams can refine their processes, enhance collaboration, and ultimately deliver more value.

The scrum master facilitates the retrospective, guiding the development team and, optionally, the product owner, through a structured discussion. The team begins by celebrating wins and acknowledging effective practices that contributed to the sprint's success. Next, they identify areas where they faced difficulties, whether technical, procedural, or related to teamwork. The discussion then shifts to actionable improvements, where the team proposes concrete steps to address these challenges and enhance the workflow in the next sprint.

To create an environment that encourages open, constructive feedback, many retrospectives begin with reading the prime directive:

Regardless of what we discover, we must understand and truly believe that everyone did the best job they could, given what was known at the time, their skills and abilities, the resources available, and the situation at hand.[1]

This principle sets the tone for a blame-free discussion, ensuring that retrospectives remain focused on learning and team growth rather than assigning fault.

An effective sprint retrospective emphasizes actionable improvements over abstract discussions. Tracking previous retrospective action items helps ensure follow-through on commitments and fosters accountability. By maintaining a culture of continuous learning, the team builds trust, transparency, and a shared commitment to improvement.

The outcome of this ceremony is a set of well-defined, actionable improvements that the team will implement in the next sprint. These iterative refinements help the team optimize their processes, improve efficiency, and create a more effective and collaborative working environment.

Backlog refinement

The purpose of backlog refinement is to ensure that the product backlog remains up to date, well-organized, and ready for sprint planning. This ongoing process helps the team clarify, estimate, and prioritize upcoming work, making it easier to select and commit to items during the sprint. By refining backlog items in advance, teams avoid last-minute uncertainty and ensure a smoother, more efficient planning process.

The product owner leads the backlog refinement, with active participation from the scrum master and development team. Together, they review and clarify user stories and requirements, ensuring that each item is well-defined and actionable. The team also refines or updates acceptance criteria, setting clear expectations for what needs to be achieved. Additionally, they estimate the effort required for upcoming backlog items, helping gauge the complexity and workload associated with each task. Prioritization plays a crucial role in this process, as features must be ranked based on business value, market needs, and customer feedback.

Regular backlog refinement sessions prevent sprint planning from becoming overwhelming and allow the team to stay proactive rather than reactive. By continuously refining the backlog, the team ensures that only the most valuable, feasible, and well-understood items make it into upcoming sprints.

The outcome of this ceremony is a well-organized product backlog that is closely aligned with product-market fit and fully prepared for sprint planning. This ensures that the development team can focus on delivering high-impact features without unnecessary delays or ambiguities.

1 Kerth, Norman. Project Retrospectives: A Handbook for Team Reviews. United Kingdom, Pearson Education, 2013.

The following figure illustrates the iterative scrum workflow for MVP development. It highlights the cyclical nature of backlog refinement and continuous improvement through sprint retrospectives:

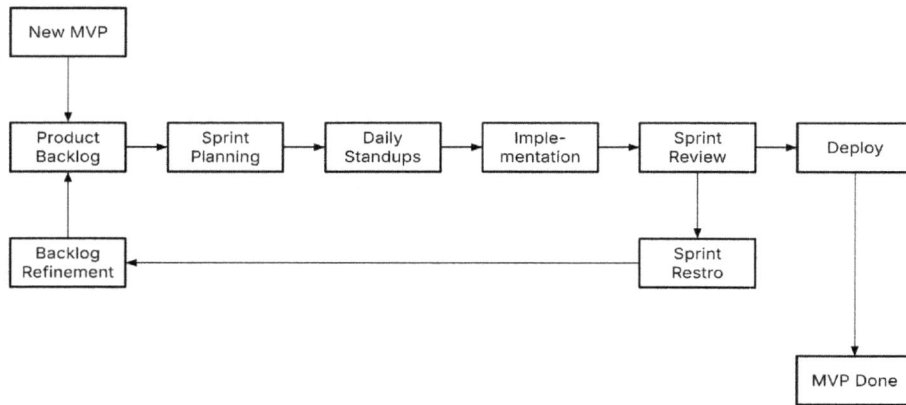

Figure 9.1: Scrum flow

Entrepreneurs' participation

Entrepreneurs' active involvement in key Scrum activities to provide vision, prioritize needs, and ensure the MVP aligns with business goals and user expectations. The following things need to be kept in mind:

- **Define priorities**: Work closely with the product owner to communicate business goals and prioritize backlog items that align with customer needs.

- **Engage in reviews**: Attend sprint reviews to provide feedback on the MVP's progress and align future iterations with the business vision.

- **Encourage collaboration**: Support open communication among team members to foster innovation and problem-solving.

- **Stay open to change**: Embrace the iterative nature of scrum and adapt plans based on user feedback and market dynamics.

Scrum's structure—centered around roles, ceremonies, and artifacts—ensures alignment and accountability, enabling incremental progress while delivering value early and often. However, its effectiveness relies on disciplined execution and team commitment. Common pitfalls to watch out for include poorly defined backlogs, excessive focus on delivering over learning, and neglecting retros, which are critical for continuous learning and improvement.

Tara takes the help of Scully, who has years of experience as a scrum master in an MNC. He now wants to explore the world of startups. They knew each other from college days, and Scully decided to help Tara for a few months as he took a sabbatical from his job.

Based on the JTBD analysis (*Chapter 7, Building Successful MVP*) and his knowledge of what essential features a mobile app should have, he creates the following product development backlog.

Here is the product development backlog for the customer-facing app for the purpose of scrum development:

1. When browsing for unique handmade products, the customer wants to easily search and filter by category, price, or artisan, so they can find items that suit their preferences quickly.

2. When considering a purchase, the customer wants to see artisan stories, so they can feel confident that the product is genuine and handmade.

3. When a customer decides to buy a product, they want a smooth and secure checkout process, so they can complete their purchase without hassle.

4. When waiting for their purchase to arrive, the customer wants to track their order in real-time, so they can know its status and estimated delivery date.

5. Once the customer has received their order, they want to leave a review or rating, so that they can share their experience and help other buyers.

6. When a customer finds something they love, they want to share it with friends or on social media, so they can get opinions or spread awareness about artisan-made products.

7. When deciding to buy, a customer wants to see clear pricing, including taxes and delivery charges, so they can avoid surprises at checkout.

8. When a customer faces an issue, they want quick access to customer support, so they can resolve their concerns efficiently.

9. As a user, the customer wants the app to load quickly and respond smoothly, so they can browse and purchase without delays.

10. A user wants their personal and payment information to be secure, so they can shop with confidence.

11. A business wants the app to comply with data privacy regulations (e.g., DPDP), so it can maintain customer trust and legal compliance.

12. A user wants personalized notifications for order updates, promotions, and new arrivals to stay informed without feeling overwhelmed.

Continuing on the theme of deprioritization, so the focus is on what minimal can be built to achieve the goals of the MVP, Tara and Scully de-prioritize the following features for the customer-facing app for the purpose of scrum development:

- As a business, I want the mobile app to handle increasing users and transactions efficiently, so the experience remains seamless even during high traffic.

- As a user, I want to continue browsing and adding items to my cart even with limited or no internet connectivity, so I do not lose progress.

- As a user, I want my browsing history, cart, and wish list to sync across devices, so I can switch between them seamlessly.

- As a user with disabilities, I want the app to support screen readers, voice commands, and high-contrast modes, so I can navigate easily.

- As a user, I want to receive regular updates with minimal disruption, so I can always access the latest features and security patches.

- As an Indian user, I want the app to support multiple languages, so I can shop comfortably in my preferred language.

- As a user, I want the app to be optimized for battery and data usage, so I can shop without draining my phone's resources.

The prioritized backlog can now be taken up by a software development team.

To further facilitate them, Scully broke the 12 prioritized epics further into user stories that can be picked during a sprint.

Here are the user stories grouped by the capability:

- **Product discovery and navigation**:

  o A user wants to search for handmade products by category, price, and artisan, so they can quickly find items that match their preferences.

  o A user wants to apply multiple filters simultaneously, so they can refine their search results efficiently.

  o A user wants to sort products by relevance, popularity, or price, so they can browse in a way that suits their shopping style.

- **Authenticity and artisan storytelling**: A user wants to view artisan profiles and their stories, so they can feel confident that the product is genuine and handmade.

- **Seamless and secure checkout**:

  o A user wants a fast and intuitive checkout process, so they can complete their purchase without unnecessary steps.

  o A user wants to save their payment details securely, so they can check out faster for future purchases.

- **Order tracking and delivery updates**:

  o A user wants to track my order in real-time, so they know its exact location and estimated delivery date.

- o A user wants to receive push notifications and email updates about their order status, so they stay informed of any changes.

- **Reviews and ratings**:

  - o A user wants to leave a rating and review after receiving their order, so they can share their experience with other buyers.

  - o A user wants to read verified buyer reviews, so they can make informed purchasing decisions.

- **Social sharing and engagement**: A user wants to share the review on social media, so I can spread awareness about artisan-made products.

- **Transparent pricing and cost breakdown**: A user wants to see a detailed price breakdown, including taxes and shipping fees, so they can avoid unexpected charges at checkout.

- **Customer support and assistance**:

  - o A user wants to access customer support via chat, email, or phone, so they can resolve their concerns quickly.

  - o A user wants to browse a self-service help center with FAQs, so I can find answers without waiting for support.

- **Performance and security**:

  - o A user wants the app to load quickly and respond smoothly, so they can browse and shop without frustration.

  - o A user wants their personal and payment information to be securely encrypted, so they can shop with confidence.

- **Compliance and data privacy**: A business wants the app to comply with data privacy regulations (e.g., DPDP), so it maintains customer trust and legal compliance.

- **Personalized notifications and engagement**:

  - o A user wants to receive personalized notifications for order updates, promotions, and new arrivals, so they stay informed without feeling overwhelmed.

  - o A user wants to customize their notification preferences, so they receive only the updates that matter to them.

Scully made a big difference by converting a series of high-level expectations into an actionable list for a software development team. This time again, he de-prioritized a few user stories to do away with user stories that would not bring additional value to the MVP:

- **Authenticity and artisan storytelling**: As a user, I want to see details about the craftsmanship and materials used, so I can better understand the uniqueness of each product.

- **Seamless and secure checkout**: As a user, I want to apply discount codes or promotions at checkout, so I can avail special offers easily.

- **Reviews and ratings**: As a user, I want to upload photos and videos with my review, so I can showcase the actual product to potential buyers.

- **Social sharing and engagement**: As a user, I want to share a product on social media or with friends, so I can get their opinions before buying.

- **Transparent pricing and cost breakdown**: As a user, I want to choose from multiple shipping options with clear costs and delivery times, so I can make the best decision based on my needs.

Now, Tara must figure out how to build a software development team.

Team development

For non-technical entrepreneurs, building a software development team can feel like a daunting task, as it involves navigating unfamiliar territory. Similarly, technical entrepreneurs often find it challenging to hire the right people and establish an effective organizational structure for operations, sales, and support. Let us explore the approaches entrepreneurs can take to tackle these challenges with confidence.

For an entrepreneur, building a capable software development team is a critical strategic decision that can determine the success or failure of their MVP and long-term growth. Unlike other business decisions, team-building is not something that can be easily backtracked or pivoted without significant disruption. To ensure the best possible outcome, entrepreneurs must approach this process thoughtfully and strategically. Here is a structured approach.

Collaborate with trusted advisors

The first and most important step is to seek guidance from experienced mentors, industry experts, or trusted advisors. No entrepreneur is an expert in every domain, and leaning on seasoned professionals can provide invaluable insights into hiring decisions, technology choices, and team structure. Advisors can help evaluate potential candidates, recommend best practices for team management, and ensure that the entrepreneur avoids common pitfalls in software development.

Hire key roles first

Once the development needs are well-defined, the next crucial step is hiring key roles that will shape the success of the team. Entrepreneurs should collaborate with trusted advisors to identify the most critical hires—these could include a CTO, sales lead, technical lead, or an experienced software developer who can lay the foundation for a strong development team.

To find the right candidates, entrepreneurs can explore various sourcing channels. Specialized staffing agencies that focus on software development recruitment can be valuable in identifying highly qualified professionals. Freelance platforms such as *Toptal, Upwork,* or *Fiverr* provide access to skilled independent contractors who can take on temporary or specialized roles. Entrepreneurs can also leverage their personal and professional networks, including *LinkedIn* connections, alumni groups, and industry meetups, to uncover top talent. Additionally, industry referrals from peers in the startup ecosystem can be an effective way to find skilled developers who are actively seeking new opportunities.

Tara took the help of Prabjot and Scully to identify key roles to make her MVP possible. It was clear to her that one person would play more than one role. The three sat together and built the following roles and responsibilities map:

Role	Responsibility
CEO/founder	Oversees overall strategy, partnerships, and business growth.
Chief operating officer (COO)	Manages end-to-end operational efficiency, artisan network, and logistics.
Chief technology officer (CTO)	Leads tech infrastructure, platform development, and system integrations.
Chief marketing officer (CMO)	Drives branding, digital marketing, and customer engagement.
Chief financial officer (CFO)	Handles financial strategy, payment processing, and compliance.
Head of product	Leads product strategy, roadmap, and UX/UI design.
Product manager	Own specific areas like customer experience, artisan experience, and order management.
Engineering manager	Develops and maintains the platform, integrations, and mobile app.
Data and analytics manager	Works on performance tracking, customer insights, and optimization.
Cybersecurity and compliance manager	Ensures platform security and regulatory compliance (e.g., DPDP).
Head of artisan relations	Manages artisan engagement and quality control.
Artisan onboarding specialists	Train and onboard new artisans.
Product documentation and photography manager	Assists artisans in listing high-quality products.

Inventory and replenishment manager	Ensures stock levels are updated, and artisans restock as needed.
E-commerce operations manager	Manages the platform's day-to-day operations.
Order and fulfillment manager	Oversees order processing and artisan notifications.
Shipping and logistics manager	Ensures smooth product packaging, shipping, and delivery.
Digital marketing manager	Runs advertising, email campaigns, and SEO efforts.
Social media and influencer marketing manager	Manages brand presence and partnerships.
Head of customer support	Manages customer service strategy and escalation.
Customer feedback and review manager	Collects insights to improve the platform.
Payments and settlements manager	Ensures timely artisan payments and order processing.
Financial analyst	Monitors revenue, expenses, and pricing models.

Table 9.2: Tara's roles and responsibilities map

Realizing it is the right time to commit as an entrepreneur, Tara puts a team together. Some are doing this part-time, and a few have decided to join based on ownership. She assigned various roles to the small team that had come together with her to build the MVP for IndicOcean. Here is what the allocation looked like:

Role	Person
CEO/founder	Tara
COO	Tara
CTO	Kalhan (a technologist)
CMO	Tara
CFO	Chaaya (a chartered accountant)
Head of product/product owner	Tara
Product manager	Scully (a scrum expert)
Engineering manager/scrum master	Scully
Data and analytics manager	Kalhan
Cybersecurity and compliance manager	Kalhan
Head of artisan relations	Tara
Artisan onboarding specialists	Pema (a marketing expert)
Product documentation and photography manager	Danish (a customer support specialist)
Inventory and replenishment manager	Pema

E-commerce operations manager	Pema
Order and fulfillment manager	Pema
Shipping and logistics manager	Pema
Digital marketing manager	Danish
Social media and influencer marketing manager	Danish
Head of customer support	Tara
Customer feedback and review manager	Danish
Payments and settlements manager	Tara
Financial analyst	Chaaya
Trusted advisor	Prabjot

Table 9.3: Tara's roles allocation

Now Tara has the daunting task of putting together a software development team. Thankfully, she has Prabjot and Kalhan to support her.

Deciding between in-house development and outsourcing

Entrepreneurs must carefully evaluate whether to build an in-house development team or outsource the work based on factors such as project complexity, budget, and long-term vision. Each approach has its advantages, and the right choice depends on the specific needs of the business.

In-house development is ideal for long-term projects that require deep product knowledge, continuous iteration, and close collaboration. Having an in-house team provides entrepreneurs with full control over product development and prioritization while ensuring faster communication and alignment with business objectives. Additionally, it fosters long-term team stability and institutional knowledge, which can be invaluable as the product evolves.

Outsourcing development works well for short-term projects or when technical expertise is limited. This approach enables entrepreneurs to develop an MVP quickly without the commitment of hiring a full-time team. Engaging a small or mid-sized software development agency can be beneficial, as these firms often provide a full team, including project managers, developers, and designers, to execute the project efficiently. Alternatively, hiring freelancers or contract developers is a viable option for projects with a well-defined scope and deliverables.

A hybrid approach is common among entrepreneurs. Many choose to outsource the initial MVP development to accelerate time-to-market and reduce upfront costs. Once product-market fit is achieved, they transition to an in-house team to scale and refine the product further. This approach balances speed, flexibility, and long-term sustainability.

Outsourcing MVP development

While some entrepreneurs choose to build their MVPs in-house, outsourcing development to an external team can be a cost-effective and time-efficient approach—if managed correctly. For startups looking to move fast and optimize their resources, outsourcing provides access to skilled professionals, proven processes, and industry best practices without the complexities of assembling an in-house team from scratch.

Need for outsourcing

Outsourcing allows entrepreneurs to leverage specialized talent, reduce development costs, and accelerate time to market. Hiring a full-time, in-house development team can be expensive and time-consuming, requiring months of recruitment, onboarding, and training. In contrast, outsourcing provides immediate access to experienced professionals who have worked on similar projects before, eliminating the need for a long-term commitment. This flexibility enables startups to focus on core business strategies while ensuring that development progresses efficiently.

One of the biggest advantages of outsourcing is speed to market. Development agencies and specialized teams have built MVPs multiple times, refining their processes along the way. They understand common challenges, have ready-to-use templates, and leverage accelerators to speed up development. Their experience allows them to anticipate roadblocks, optimize workflows, and deliver a functional product in a shorter timeframe than an in-house team starting from scratch.

Cost efficiency is another major benefit. Since an outsourced team is hired for a specific duration, startups avoid the high salaries, benefits, and overhead costs associated with full-time employees. Entrepreneurs can scale resources up or down based on their development phase, ensuring they pay only for the expertise they need. This flexible engagement model helps startups preserve capital while still gaining access to top-tier talent.

Outsourcing also provides access to specialized skills that may not be available in-house. Whether it is UI/UX design, backend development, mobile app expertise, or cybersecurity, outsourced teams bring in domain-specific professionals at the right stages of development, minimizing waste and maximizing efficiency. Instead of hiring multiple full-time specialists, startups can engage on-demand experts to handle critical aspects of the product, ensuring high-quality results while keeping costs manageable.

However, outsourcing is not without its challenges. Communication gaps, quality control issues, and misalignment with business goals can arise if the process is not managed effectively. The key to a successful outsourcing partnership lies in choosing the right development partner, setting clear expectations, and maintaining active involvement throughout the project. By carefully selecting a team with proven experience, strong communication skills, and a structured approach to Agile development, entrepreneurs can ensure that their MVP is built efficiently, meets user expectations, and sets the foundation for future growth.

Choosing a development partner

Selecting the right outsourcing partner is one of the most critical decisions in MVP development. A poor choice can lead to missed deadlines, budget overruns, and a subpar product that fails to meet market needs. Since the MVP phase is all about validating an idea quickly and efficiently, choosing a development team that aligns with your business goals and working style can significantly impact the outcome.

When evaluating potential partners, entrepreneurs should focus on whether the team has experience building MVPs for startups at a similar stage. Agencies, freelancers, or offshore teams that have worked with early-stage companies understand the constraints of speed, budget, and flexibility, making them better suited for the challenges of startup development. Looking at past work, case studies, and product launches can provide insights into their ability to deliver functional and scalable MVPs.

Client references and reviews are another crucial factor in assessing a potential partner. Entrepreneurs should seek feedback from past clients to understand the strengths and weaknesses of the development team. While no partner will be a perfect match, the goal is to find a team whose expertise, approach, and work ethic align most closely with the startup's needs. Reviews and testimonials often highlight how well the team handles deadlines, problem-solving, and unexpected challenges, giving valuable insight into what working with them would be like.

Technical expertise is also essential. The outsourcing partner should be skilled in the required tech stack to ensure they can build and scale the MVP effectively. Additionally, compatibility in time zones and responsiveness during initial discussions can be strong indicators of how smooth communication and collaboration will be throughout the engagement. A team that is proactive and responsive early on is more likely to maintain transparency and accountability during the development process.

Entrepreneurs should prioritize teams with startup experience who understand the lean development mindset and are comfortable with changing requirements and iterative improvements. Startups often refine their MVP based on real-time user feedback and evolving business strategies, so working with a development team that is adaptable and flexible can make a significant difference. The best outsourcing partner is not just a service provider but a collaborator who understands the fast-paced nature of building a startup and is invested in its success.

Managing the outsourced team

Outsourcing development does not mean simply handing over your idea and waiting for a finished product to arrive. Active involvement is essential to ensure alignment, maintain quality, and achieve timely delivery. Without proper engagement, miscommunication, delays, and mismatched expectations can derail progress. By establishing clear processes, maintaining open communication, and setting structured milestones, entrepreneurs can ensure that their outsourced team functions as an extension of their vision rather than just a third-party vendor.

One of the most critical aspects of managing an outsourced team is establishing clear communication channels. Regular interaction ensures that expectations remain aligned and roadblocks are addressed promptly. Tools such as Slack or Microsoft Teams facilitate daily communication, while Trello, Jira, or Asana help track tasks and manage the development process efficiently. Platforms like Google Docs or Notion ensure that documentation and product requirements are well-organized and easily accessible. Holding weekly check-ins allows the team to review progress, discuss challenges, and incorporate feedback, ensuring that development remains on track.

Even when outsourcing, it is crucial to assign a product owner—someone from your team (or yourself) who takes responsibility for overseeing the project, prioritizing tasks, and serving as the main point of contact for the outsourced team. The product owner plays a key role in clarifying priorities, answering technical and business-related questions, and approving features before they move to the next stage of development. Without this structured leadership, decision-making can become slow and uncoordinated, leading to inefficiencies and potential misalignment between business goals and development execution.

To ensure smooth execution, setting milestones and deliverables is essential. Breaking the MVP development into smaller, well-defined phases provides clarity and accountability.

Example:

- **Week 1–2**: Wireframes and UI design finalized.
- **Week 3–4**: Core backend functionality developed.
- **Week 5–6**: Frontend integration with backend.
- **Week 7–8**: Alpha testing and user feedback.

By structuring development in an iterative and incremental manner, potential risks can be identified early, avoiding last-minute surprises and costly delays.

Another crucial aspect of managing an outsourced development team is ensuring code ownership and proper documentation. Before engaging with an external team, it is advisable to define clear contractual agreements that secure full ownership of the codebase, detailed documentation, and access to repositories from day one. This prevents vendor lock-in, where a startup becomes overly dependent on an external team and struggles to transition development in the future. Signing a **non-disclosure agreement** (**NDA**) protects intellectual property while ensuring that repositories are maintained in GitHub, GitLab, or Bitbucket, which guarantees transparency and control over the project's source code.

By proactively managing these aspects, entrepreneurs can foster a strong, collaborative relationship with their outsourced team while maintaining control over their product's development. A structured approach not only mitigates risks but also ensures that the MVP is built efficiently, meets business objectives, and sets a strong foundation for future growth.

Understanding pricing models

Outsourcing development costs can vary significantly depending on location, expertise, and project complexity. Understanding different pricing models helps entrepreneurs choose one that fits their budget, development needs, and risk tolerance. The right pricing structure depends on factors such as how well-defined the scope is, the level of flexibility required, and the need for long-term engagement.

Time and material

One of the most used models is the T&M approach, where businesses pay for actual hours worked based on an hourly or daily rate. This model offers high flexibility, making it ideal when the MVP scope is evolving and not fully defined. Since changes and iterations are common in early-stage startups, T&M allows teams to adjust priorities as they learn from user feedback. However, costs can fluctuate if not monitored properly, so regular progress tracking is essential to prevent budget overruns.

Many non-technical entrepreneurs view this model as risky, fearing that a development partner might overcharge or extend timelines unnecessarily. Without a deep understanding of the technical aspects, they worry about being misled or paying for inefficiencies.

Fixed bid

For entrepreneurs who have a clearly defined MVP scope, the fixed bid (fixed scope) model provides a predefined cost for the entire project. This approach is best suited for projects with minimal expected changes, as it offers predictable costs and reduced financial risk. While fixed pricing ensures better budget control, it lacks flexibility—any changes or feature additions after the contract is signed can lead to expensive scope adjustments.

This model is ideal when product requirements have been thoroughly researched and are unlikely to change significantly during development. However, it runs counter to an iterative learning and improvement approach, as it limits flexibility for incorporating new insights, user feedback, or market-driven adjustments once development is underway.

Capped time and material

A hybrid approach, **capped time and material** (**Capped T&M**), combines the benefits of both models. It works similarly to T&M but with an agreed-upon spending limit, balancing flexibility with cost control. This model prevents excessive budget overruns while still allowing room for iteration and refinement as development progresses. However, it requires active monitoring of budget utilization, ensuring that the cap is not reached too soon, which might require additional negotiations.

This approach is particularly useful for entrepreneurs who want flexibility without the risk of unlimited spending.

Dedicated team model

For businesses looking for a long-term development relationship, the dedicated team model offers a fixed monthly cost to hire a development team or specific roles. This model provides more control and dedicated resources, making it a great fit for startups that need continuous development post-MVP. While this model ensures consistent access to skilled developers, it requires higher commitment and active management to keep the team aligned with business goals. This model is often used when a company is preparing for growth and scaling beyond the initial MVP phase.

Each pricing model has its advantages and trade-offs, and the right choice depends on the startup's financial constraints, level of uncertainty in the product roadmap, and need for adaptability. By carefully selecting the appropriate pricing structure, entrepreneurs can ensure efficient development, cost optimization, and a successful MVP launch without unnecessary financial risks.

Tara decided to go with the CT&M model, allowing her to maintain flexibility in development while keeping costs under control. This approach ensured that she could iterate based on feedback without exceeding her budget.

For the artisan-facing app, Prabjot initially estimated the development cost to be around ₹12,00,000. However, after factoring in additional features Tara wanted to incorporate, the estimated cost was adjusted to ₹14,00,000. Similarly, for the customer-facing app, Prabjot estimated the cost at ₹15,00,000, which was later revised to ₹17,00,000 based on Tara's specific requirements.

Tara found an outsourcing partner *Singaji Software Solutions*, based in a rural area near Indore, Madhya Pradesh, which aligned well with her budget and operational needs. They offered to assign nine of their best talent using the following distribution:

Role	Team size	Allocation	Responsibility
Scrum master	1	Shared across both apps	Facilitates Agile process, removes roadblocks, ensures smooth execution
UI/UX designer	1	Shared across both apps	Designs user interface, enhances user experience, ensures visual consistency
QA specialist	1	Shared across both apps	Conducts testing, ensures quality control, identifies and fixes bugs
Developers	6	3 for artisan-facing app, 3 for customer-facing app	Builds application features, implements backend logic, integrates APIs
Total team size	9	Across both applications	Ensures structured development and parallel progress

Table 9.4: Role allocation for MVP development team

The firm offered to complete the scope of work in two months at a competitive rate of ₹1,200 per hour per person:

Application	Estimated cost	Development timeline
Artisan-facing app	₹14,00,000	2 Months
Customer-facing app	₹17,00,000	2 Months

Table 9.5*: Estimated cost for MVP development team*

Tara was pleased that the team structure, development scope, and cost estimates aligned well with her budget expectations, ensuring a structured and efficient outsourcing partnership. Given the affordability and expertise they brought to the table, Tara felt confident moving forward with them.

Actions for the entrepreneur

1. Assemble the core team needed for execution.
2. Develop the development backlog for MVP implementation.
3. Decide whether to build an in-house team or outsource development to a partner.

Conclusion

Iterative MVP development empowers entrepreneurs to build products that evolve based on real-world feedback and changing market conditions. Unlike traditional development methods that require rigid, upfront planning, an iterative approach ensures that products are continuously refined, improved, and aligned with customer needs. By embracing this methodology, entrepreneurs minimize risk, optimize resource allocation, and accelerate time to market—critical factors in today's fast-paced business environment.

At the core of this approach lies Agile methodology, with frameworks such as scrum providing structure for development cycles that emphasize incremental progress and continuous learning. Through well-defined roles, ceremonies, and artifacts, Agile enables teams to remain adaptable while ensuring efficient execution. Entrepreneurs who actively engage in the development process—whether through collaboration with their teams, defining priorities, or participating in sprint reviews—gain better control over the direction and success of their MVP.

Equally important is the team composition and development strategy. Entrepreneurs must make informed decisions about hiring in-house talent or outsourcing development based on factors such as budget, expertise, and scalability needs. While outsourcing offers access to specialized skills and flexibility, insourcing provides greater control and long-term alignment with the company's vision. Understanding the advantages, risks, and pricing models of outsourcing ensures that entrepreneurs can establish productive partnerships and maintain oversight over their product's development.

Ultimately, iterative MVP development is not just about building a functional product—it is about building the right product. By adopting an incremental, feedback-driven, and collaborative approach, entrepreneurs can navigate the complexities of product development with confidence.

In the next chapter, the entrepreneur will learn how to test and validate that the MVP is really addressing the stated problem statement.

Join our Discord space

Join our Discord workspace for latest updates, offers, tech happenings around the world, new releases, and sessions with the authors:

https://discord.bpbonline.com

CHAPTER 10
Iterative MVP Testing

Introduction

Building an MVP is only the beginning of the journey. The true power of an MVP lies in iterative testing, a process that ensures the product evolves based on real user behavior, feedback, and data-driven insights. Unlike traditional product development, where extensive features are built before launch, iterative MVP testing enables entrepreneurs to validate assumptions early, minimize wasted effort, and optimize for product-market fit.

At the heart of iterative MVP testing is the build-measure-learn framework. While the previous chapter focused on the Build phase—creating an MVP with essential features—this chapter shifts the focus to measure and learn. Measuring how users interact with the MVP provides critical insights into what works, what does not, and where improvements are needed. Learning from this data allows for rapid iterations, ensuring the product remains aligned with customer needs and market realities.

Successful iterative testing relies on a combination of qualitative and quantitative methods. A/B testing, multivariate testing, and feature flagging help measure user behavior through controlled experiments, while usability testing, heatmaps, and session recordings offer deep insights into user interactions. Additionally, cohort analysis and customer feedback loops provide a structured way to refine and enhance the MVP over time.

By embracing iterative testing, entrepreneurs can make data-backed decisions, prioritize features that drive the most value, and pivot when necessary. This approach not only accelerates learning but also ensures the product is continuously optimized for user satisfaction and business success.

Structure

In this chapter, we will cover the following topics:

- Common MVP testing methods
- Gathering and synthesizing user feedback
- Guidance metrics

Objectives

By the end of this chapter, entrepreneurs will gain a comprehensive understanding of how to test and iterate on an MVP effectively, using data-driven insights to refine their product and optimize for product-market fit. They will learn how to implement iterative testing methodologies, ensuring continuous improvement through structured experimentation and user feedback.

Entrepreneurs will explore key testing frameworks such as A/B testing, multivariate testing, feature flagging, and cohort analysis, equipping them with practical tools to validate product decisions. They will also understand how to leverage qualitative feedback methods such as exploratory usability testing, heatmaps, session recordings, and clickstream analysis to uncover hidden user insights.

The chapter will also provide insights into incorporating user feedback into MVP iterations, enabling entrepreneurs to establish feedback loops, implement feature voting, and leverage customer advisory boards for prioritizing feature development. Additionally, they will learn how to monitor **key performance indicators (KPIs)** such as retention, engagement, conversion, and churn to assess the effectiveness of their MVP.

Through these topics, entrepreneurs will be empowered to build a data-backed iteration process that minimizes risk, accelerates learning, and enhances user satisfaction—ultimately enabling them to make informed decisions on whether to pivot, persevere, or scale their product.

Common MVP testing methods

The success of an MVP relies not just on building a minimal version of the product but also on continuously testing and refining it based on real-world user interactions. MVP testing methods help entrepreneurs validate assumptions, optimize features, and ensure that their product evolves in the right direction. By leveraging both qualitative and quantitative approaches, startups can uncover usability issues, improve conversion rates, and make data-driven decisions.

Let us look at various testing techniques that help measure user behavior, collect actionable insights, and refine the MVP through iteration. By following these testing methods, entrepreneurs can reduce guesswork, minimize risks, and optimize for product-market fit while maintaining agility in their development process.

A/B testing

A/B testing is an experiment-based approach used to compare two variations of a webpage, feature, email, or any other digital experience to determine which one performs better based on predefined metrics. The goal is to use data-driven insights to optimize conversions, engagement, or any other KPI.

In an A/B test, the user group is split into two segments:

- Group A (control group) experiences the existing version of the feature or design.

- Group B (test group) is exposed to the new variation with a single modified element (e.g., a different button color, headline, pricing format, or call-to-action).

User interactions with each version are measured and analyzed, with the winning variation being implemented based on statistical significance.

Example: An e-commerce store wants to see if a red CTA button converts better than a blue CTA button on the checkout page. They run an A/B test where half of the visitors see version A (red button) and the other half see version B (blue button). The test helps determine which button color results in more purchases.

A/B testing is ideal in scenarios where small, incremental changes can significantly impact user behavior. Let us look at common scenarios when A/B testing should be used:

- **Optimizing conversion rates**: If a landing page has a high bounce rate, A/B testing can be used to experiment with different headlines, CTA placements, form lengths, or layouts to see which version encourages more users to take an action.

- **Enhancing user engagement**: When testing elements such as navigation, content structure, or personalization, A/B testing can identify which changes improve time spent on the platform, scroll depth, or interaction rates.

- **Improving email marketing performance**: Testing variations of subject lines, email copy, CTA buttons, or sending times can help determine what drives higher open and click-through rates.

- **Refining product features and UI/UX elements**: A/B testing can be used to validate changes in onboarding flows, checkout processes, or search functionality, ensuring that updates positively impact user behavior.

- **Validating pricing strategies**: Businesses can test different pricing models, discount structures, or bundling options to determine what maximizes revenue without negatively affecting conversions. We have covered more on validating pricing in *Chapter 8, Business Model Validation*.

- **Running A/B tests**: Entrepreneurs are constantly experimenting to refine their products, marketing strategies, and user experiences. However, if these experiments are conducted haphazardly, the learning process can become unstructured and ineffective. When multiple factors contribute to the success or failure of an experiment, it becomes impossible to determine which specific change was responsible for the outcome. This lack of clarity can lead to misguided decisions and wasted resources.

To ensure meaningful insights, A/B testing must be conducted with a disciplined approach. A key principle when running an A/B test is that option B should be a single, clearly identifiable, repeatable, and measurable variation of the control (option A). This allows entrepreneurs to isolate the impact of a single change and confidently attribute any differences in performance to that specific variation. Testing multiple changes at once introduces too many variables, making it difficult to pinpoint the real reason behind the results.

Another crucial consideration is user segmentation. Results may vary based on device type, geography, user behavior, or demographics. A test that performs well for desktop users might not yield the same results for mobile users, and a variation that succeeds in one region may not work in another. Entrepreneurs should analyze results across different segments to ensure that decisions are based on a comprehensive understanding of user behavior.

Additionally, test duration plays a critical role in obtaining reliable data. Running an experiment for too short a period can lead to misleading conclusions based on temporary fluctuations. For example, if an A/B test is launched and an enthusiastic employee shares the link to Option B with a large group of friends, it might experience a sudden spike in engagement. If the test is stopped too early, this temporary surge could falsely suggest that Option B is the better choice. However, by running the test for a sufficient duration—typically at least 14 to 15 days—these temporary anomalies normalize over time, revealing a more accurate picture of user preference.

Split testing

Split testing, on the other hand, is used when testing significantly different versions of an experience, such as two completely different landing pages, product flows, or website layouts. Instead of just tweaking a single element, split testing evaluates entirely different designs, structures, or functionalities.

During split testing, users are directed to entirely different pages or experiences. Tests large-scale changes like different layouts, navigation, or checkout processes. Requires more development effort to build and maintain multiple versions.

Example: A SaaS company wants to test two completely different onboarding flows for new users. Version A takes users through a step-by-step walkthrough, while version B offers an interactive tutorial with tooltips. Instead of just tweaking a single feature, the test evaluates which onboarding experience leads to higher activation rates.

Multivariate testing

Multivariate testing (**MVT**) is an advanced experiment-based optimization technique that evaluates multiple elements on a page or user experience simultaneously to determine which combination performs best. Unlike A/B testing, which compares two variations with a single isolated change, or split testing, which compares entirely different experiences, multivariate testing allows businesses to analyze the interaction between multiple changes at once.

By running an MVT experiment, entrepreneurs can test different combinations of elements, such as headlines, images, CTA buttons, layouts, and colors, all at the same time. The key benefit of this approach is that it does not just show which individual change improves performance but also reveals how different elements work together to create an optimal user experience. This deeper insight helps businesses refine their digital experiences with greater precision, ensuring that they optimize not just individual elements, but their entire conversion strategy.

Using multivariate testing

Following is a structured approach to running a successful MVT experiment—from identifying key elements to analyzing performance:

- **Identify multiple elements to test**: The first step in setting up an MVT experiment is to determine which elements of a webpage, app interface, or marketing experience you want to optimize. Unlike A/B testing, which focuses on changing just one component, MVT modifies several elements at the same time.

  Example: An e-commerce store might want to test:
  - ○ Three different headlines
  - ○ Two product images
  - ○ Two CTA button colors

  This results in a total of $3 \times 2 \times 2 = 12$ different variations that need to be tested to determine which combination delivers the best conversion rate.

- **Create all possible variations**: Once the key elements have been identified, MVT requires creating different variations for each element and combining them in every possible way. Each unique combination forms a distinct version of the webpage or app screen, allowing entrepreneurs to analyze not only the individual impact of each element but also how different changes interact with one another.

Example: If an entrepreneur tests three headlines, two images, and two CTA button colors, the MVT system will generate all possible combinations of these elements and present them to different users.

- **Split traffic equally among variations**: Once the variations are created, users are randomly assigned to different test versions, just like in an A/B test. However, because there are more variations in an MVT experiment, the total traffic needs to be divided among several combinations rather than just two versions. This means that multivariate testing requires significantly higher traffic volume than A/B testing to achieve statistically significant results.

Example: If a website receives 100,000 visitors per week and is running a test with 10 variations, each version will receive around 10,000 visitors if traffic is distributed evenly. This ensures that each variation gets enough data to produce reliable insights.

- **Analyze performance of each combination**: After the test runs for an adequate duration, the results are analyzed to determine which individual elements perform best and which combinations work most effectively together.

Unlike A/B tests, where the focus is on a single change, MVT allows entrepreneurs to identify:

  o   Which individual element (headline, image, CTA) contributes most to improved performance

  o   How certain combinations work together to drive higher engagement and conversions

  o   Whether some elements negatively impact performance when paired with others

By analyzing these insights, businesses can refine their website, landing page, or marketing funnel with a deeper understanding of how different components interact to influence user behavior.

Running multivariate testing

Multivariate testing is best suited for complex experiments when multiple elements impact user behavior. Businesses should consider using MVT in the following scenarios:

- **Testing multiple elements at once**: When there are multiple variables influencing user behavior, and you need to determine how different elements interact with each other, MVT is the ideal testing approach. For example, optimizing a landing page layout, where headline, images, CTA, and form fields all impact conversion rates, requires testing how these elements work together rather than in isolation.

- **Optimizing combinations instead of individual changes**: A/B testing tells you whether a single change improves performance, but it does not show how multiple changes interact. If you want to identify the best combination of changes, MVT is the better approach.

Example: An online learning platform might want to test:

- o Different course preview images

- o Various instructor introductions

- o Alternative CTA wording (Start Learning vs. Join for Free)

Instead of running separate A/B tests for each element, MVT can determine which combination of image, introduction, and CTA performs best overall.

- **Testing requires large sample sizes**: As multivariate testing involves multiple variations, it requires a high volume of traffic to generate statistically significant results. Businesses with steady, high traffic (e.g., established e-commerce sites, SaaS platforms, and media publishers) can leverage MVT effectively.

If a website or app has limited traffic, MVT may take too long to produce reliable insights, and an A/B test or split test might be a better alternative.

In summary, here is a quick look at how multivariate testing, A/B testing, and split testing compare:

Feature	A/B testing	Split testing	Multivariate testing
Scope	Tests one change at a time	Tests entirely different versions	Tests multiple elements and combinations at once
Best for	Small optimizations	Testing different designs or user flows	Understanding how multiple elements interact
Traffic requirement	Low to moderate	Moderate to high	High (needs significant traffic volume)
Complexity	Simple	Moderate	High
Example	Testing button color: Red vs. Blue	Comparing two different homepage layouts	Testing multiple headlines, images, and CTA buttons together

Table 10.1: Multivariate testing vs. A/B testing vs. split testing

Heatmaps and click tracking

While the above-mentioned methods provide numbers on traffic, conversions, and bounce rates, they often fail to explain why users behave a certain way. This is where heatmaps and click tracking come into play. By visually mapping out user interactions, heatmaps offer a clear, intuitive representation of engagement patterns, helping entrepreneurs optimize their MVPs' user experience, layout, and conversion funnels.

Heatmaps help visualize user engagement patterns

Heatmaps work by tracking and visualizing user behavior on a website, mobile app, or digital product. They use color-coded overlays to represent areas of high and low engagement—

typically, warmer colors like red and yellow indicate areas where users interact the most, while cooler colors like blue and green signify less activity.

This visualization provides instant clarity on which parts of a page attract the most attention, where users hesitate, and which elements they ignore completely. By analyzing these patterns, entrepreneurs can identify friction points and opportunities for improvement, ensuring that the design aligns with how users naturally navigate and interact with the platform.

Example: If a checkout page has a high drop-off rate, a heatmap can reveal whether users are hesitating on the payment form, struggling to find the CTA button, or abandoning the process due to unnecessary distractions. Such insights make it easier to adjust the design and layout for better usability and increased conversions.

Types of heatmaps

Different types of heatmaps offer unique insights into user behavior. Click heatmaps show where users are clicking, helping entrepreneurs determine whether CTAs, links, and navigation elements are positioned effectively. If users frequently click on a non-clickable element, it may indicate confusion, suggesting that the design needs improvement.

- **Scroll heatmaps**: Scroll heatmaps track how far users scroll down a page before dropping off. This is especially useful for long-form content, landing pages, and product descriptions. If a large portion of users never scrolls past the first third of a page, important content placed further down may go unnoticed. This insight helps entrepreneurs restructure layouts, ensuring that key messages, CTAs, and engagement points are positioned where users are most likely to see them.

- **Movement-based heatmaps**: Movement-based heatmaps, sometimes referred to as **hover maps**, track cursor movements to estimate where users focus their attention. These are particularly useful for desktop experiences, where cursor movement often corresponds to eye-tracking behavior. If users hover over a certain section but do not engage, it might indicate unclear messaging or an ineffective design element.

Each type of heatmap plays a valuable role in diagnosing usability issues and optimizing the overall user experience. Entrepreneurs can use these insights to adjust page structure, CTA placement, and content hierarchy, ensuring that the most important elements receive the attention they deserve.

Identifying high and low engagement areas

Once heatmaps are generated, the next step is interpreting the data effectively. Areas with frequent clicks, heavy scrolling, or prolonged cursor activity indicate high engagement and suggest that users find those elements useful or compelling. Conversely, areas that receive little to no interaction may indicate that users either do not notice those elements, do not find them valuable, or do not understand their purpose.

For instance, if a signup button is in an area with low interaction, it might not be in an intuitive position, and relocating it could improve conversion rates. Similarly, if users frequently scroll past a key section without engaging, the content may not be relevant or compelling enough to hold their attention.

By regularly reviewing heatmap data, entrepreneurs can refine their MVP's design to create a smoother, more intuitive experience, reducing friction and increasing user engagement.

Popular tools for heatmaps and click tracking

Several tools make it easy to generate and analyze heatmaps, with Hotjar, Crazy Egg, and Microsoft Clarity among the most widely used options. These platforms record real user interactions, provide visual analytics, and allow entrepreneurs to test design changes with real-world data.

Hotjar is known for its all-in-one approach, combining heatmaps, session recordings, and user feedback tools, making it ideal for startups that want to gain holistic insights into user behavior. Crazy Egg provides detailed heatmaps and A/B testing capabilities, enabling entrepreneurs to compare how different design variations affect engagement. Microsoft Clarity, a free alternative, offers scroll heatmaps, session replays, and AI-driven insights, helping entrepreneurs identify usability issues at scale.

Choosing the right tool depends on factors such as budget, traffic volume, and specific insights needed. Regardless of the platform, integrating heatmaps into an MVP testing strategy ensures that user behavior is not just measured but truly understood.

Using heatmaps

Heatmaps become especially powerful when used in conjunction with conversion funnel optimization. By tracking how users navigate from landing pages to signups, purchases, or key interactions, entrepreneurs can pinpoint where drop-offs occur and refine those touchpoints accordingly.

For example, if a product page has a high bounce rate, a heatmap might reveal that users are losing interest before reaching key information like pricing, reviews, or CTAs. By repositioning those elements higher on the page or making them more visually prominent, conversion rates can be significantly improved.

Similarly, if users frequently abandon a signup form midway, a heatmap can reveal whether certain fields are confusing, unnecessary, or too time-consuming. Simplifying the form based on these insights can reduce friction and increase completion rates.

Session recordings and behavior flow analysis

Session recordings and behavior flow analysis provide a direct way to observe how users interact with a product in real-time. Unlike heatmaps, which offer a static overview of engagement patterns, session recordings capture live user interactions, replaying how users navigate, click, scroll, and engage with various elements of an app or website. By reviewing these recordings, entrepreneurs can uncover hidden usability issues, unexpected friction points, and patterns that influence user retention and conversion rates.

Behavior flow analysis takes this a step further by visualizing how users move through a product, identifying common paths, drop-off points, and areas where they struggle. Together, these tools offer a powerful way to refine an MVP based on real-world usage rather than assumptions or generic analytics data.

Benefits of watching real user interactions

Traditional analytics provide numbers—bounce rates, conversion rates, and time spent on a page—but they rarely explain why users behave a certain way. Session recordings bridge this gap by offering a first-person view of user experiences, allowing product teams to see exactly how users engage with an MVP. This firsthand insight makes it easier to spot pain points, inefficiencies, and unexpected behaviors that may not be evident through quantitative data alone.

By observing actual user interactions, entrepreneurs gain a clearer understanding of how intuitive the user experience is, which features attract attention, and where confusion or hesitation occurs. For example, if a significant number of users hover over an element but do not click, it may indicate uncertainty about its functionality. Similarly, if users frequently retrace their steps or abandon a form mid-way, it could suggest friction in the process that needs to be addressed.

Identifying UX friction points through session recordings

One of the most valuable applications of session recordings is the ability to identify UX friction points—areas where users struggle, hesitate, or abandon the product experience. These friction points can take many forms:

- Confusing navigation that leads users to click around aimlessly in search of relevant content.

- Forms that users abandon halfway through, indicating that the process is too lengthy, complex, or intrusive.

- Slow-loading pages or broken elements that result in frustration and premature exits.

- Call-to-action buttons that are overlooked reveal potential issues with visibility or wording.

By reviewing these recordings, teams can pinpoint exactly where users are experiencing issues and make informed decisions on how to improve usability, optimize workflows, and streamline interactions. Addressing these pain points ensures that users encounter fewer barriers, making it easier for them to achieve their goals and increasing overall engagement and retention.

Using behavior flow

Behavior flow analysis provides a visual representation of how users move through an MVP, mapping out the steps they take from entry to exit. This analysis helps teams answer crucial questions:

- *Which paths lead to conversions, and which result in drop-offs?*

- *Are users navigating in the way the product was designed, or are they getting lost?*

- *Are there recurring detours or dead ends that indicate frustration?*

By studying these movement patterns, product teams can optimize the placement of CTAs, improve menu structures, and streamline key interactions to encourage seamless navigation. If a large percentage of users drop off after reaching a particular page, it may suggest that critical information is missing, the content is not engaging, or a technical issue is preventing progress.

For example, if users frequently return to a previous step before completing an action, it might indicate that they lack confidence in their choices or are confused about what happens next. Behavior flow analysis helps teams identify these roadblocks and implement iterative improvements, ensuring that users move smoothly through the experience rather than abandoning it out of frustration.

Extracting meaningful insights

To get the most value from session recordings and behavior flow analysis, it is important to follow a structured approach rather than reviewing data randomly. Teams should:

- **Focus on key user journeys**: Instead of watching every recorded session, prioritize those that correspond to critical conversion paths, sign-ups, purchases, or onboarding flows.

- **Look for patterns, not one-off anomalies**: A single frustrating session may not be representative of all users. Instead, teams should look for consistent friction points that multiple users encounter.

- **Combine qualitative insights with quantitative data**: Using session recordings alongside heatmaps, surveys, and analytics dashboards ensures a well-rounded understanding of user behavior.

- **Iterate and re-test**: Making changes based on insights is only half the process. Running follow-up tests to measure improvements ensures that adjustments actually enhance user retention and engagement.

Funnel analysis for identifying bottlenecks

A well-designed MVP should guide users seamlessly through key actions, whether that means signing up, making a purchase, or completing an onboarding process. However, many users drop off before reaching the intended goal, leaving behind abandoned carts, incomplete forms, or disengaged sessions. Funnel analysis helps entrepreneurs pinpoint exactly where and why users are leaving so that they can refine their MVP to improve conversions and user retention.

Funnel analysis is the process of mapping out the user journey step by step and identifying where significant drop-offs occur. Each step in the funnel represents a critical interaction or decision point—from landing on the homepage to completing a purchase or subscribing to a service. By tracking these steps and analyzing where users abandon the process, businesses can identify bottlenecks, friction points, and opportunities for improvement.

Tracking user drop-off rates

One of the most important aspects of funnel analysis is identifying drop-off points—the steps where users exit before completing an intended action. These drop-offs signal areas where the user experience is unclear, frustrating, or not compelling enough to encourage continuation.

For example, if an e-commerce MVP has a four-step checkout process, but 60% of users abandon the process at the payment page, this suggests an issue that needs to be addressed. The problem could stem from a lack of payment options, an unexpected additional charge, or a confusing layout. Similarly, if a SaaS platform sees users signing up but not completing onboarding, it may indicate that the process is too long, complex, or lacks immediate perceived value.

Tracking drop-off rates at these key conversion points allows teams to focus on fixing the areas that will have the most impact, rather than making changes based on assumptions.

Understanding micro vs. macro funnel optimization

Funnel optimization can be approached at two levels: micro funnels and macro funnels.

A macro funnel represents the entire customer journey from awareness to retention. This could include steps such as a user discovering a product through an ad, signing up for a free trial, using the product, and eventually converting into a paid user. Optimizing a macro funnel involves improving overall engagement and ensuring a smooth transition from one major stage to the next.

On the other hand, a micro funnel focuses on a specific interaction within a product or marketing flow. This could include an email campaign funnel, where the goal is to optimize open rates, click-through rates, and conversions. Another example is an onboarding funnel, where users move through a series of setup screens before fully activating their account.

Understanding both levels of funnel optimization is essential for building a product that not only acquires users effectively but also keeps them engaged in the long run. Entrepreneurs need to evaluate which part of the funnel is underperforming and whether the issue is attracting new users, converting them, or retaining them over time.

Fixing high-exit pages and reducing bounce rates

Once drop-off points have been identified, the next step is addressing high-exit pages and bounce rates. A high-exit page is where users consistently leave without completing the next step, while a bounce rate measures how many users abandon a page without interacting further.

A checkout page with a high exit rate could indicate unexpected costs, confusing payment options, or a lack of trust signals, such as security badges or customer testimonials. Improving these aspects—adding clear pricing breakdowns, simplifying the form, and providing alternative payment methods—can significantly reduce exits.

For content-driven pages, a high bounce rate may suggest that the content is not engaging, relevant, or structured effectively. Optimizing page layouts, improving copy, and including clear CTAs can help keep users engaged.

Testing changes through A/B testing and multivariate testing ensures that optimizations are backed by data rather than guesses.

Using cohort-based funnel analysis for long-term trends

While traditional funnel analysis provides a snapshot of user behavior, cohort-based analysis helps track long-term engagement trends. A cohort is a group of users who started using a product at the same time or share a common characteristic.

By analyzing how different cohorts behave over weeks or months, businesses can identify whether changes to the product improve retention over time.

For example, if an MVP introduced a redesigned onboarding process, cohort analysis can compare user engagement before and after the change. If the newer cohort shows higher activation rates and lower churn, it validates that the redesign had a positive impact.

Cohort analysis is particularly useful for subscription-based products, where long-term engagement and repeat usage determine success. Tracking how many users from each cohort return and continue using the product offers deeper insights into customer retention and lifetime value.

Retention cohort analysis

In the early stages of an MVP, much of the focus tends to be on acquisition—getting users to sign up, download the app, or make an initial purchase. While acquiring users is essential, long-term success is determined by how many of those users stay engaged over time. This is where retention cohort analysis becomes a crucial tool. By tracking how users behave after their initial interaction with a product, entrepreneurs can gain valuable insights into engagement patterns, repeat usage, and churn signals, allowing them to refine their MVP iteratively.

Retention analysis helps answer a critical question: *Are users finding enough value in the product to continue using it over time?* A well-designed MVP should not only attract users but also retain them by delivering continuous value. If retention rates are low, it often signals that the product is not yet meeting user expectations, lacks engagement hooks, or has usability issues that lead to early drop-offs. By tracking retention across different time frames and cohorts, businesses can identify patterns of user behavior and make data-driven decisions to improve engagement and long-term success.

Importance of retention

Many entrepreneurs make the mistake of focusing heavily on user acquisition while neglecting retention. However, attracting new users without a strong retention strategy often leads to high churn rates, making customer acquisition expensive and unsustainable. Retention is far more cost-effective than acquisition because keeping an existing customer engaged requires less marketing spend compared to acquiring new users.

Moreover, a high retention rate is a strong indicator of product-market fit. When users keep coming back, it suggests that the product is delivering real value. Conversely, if users drop off quickly, it signals that something is missing—whether it is usability, relevance, or overall experience. Entrepreneurs who prioritize retention gain a competitive edge because loyal users drive organic growth through word-of-mouth, referrals, and repeat purchases, reducing the dependency on paid marketing efforts.

Analyzing day 1, week 1, and month 1 retention rates

To measure retention effectively, businesses track how many users return and engage with the product after their first interaction. This is typically broken down into three key retention time frames:

- **Day 1 retention**: This metric tracks how many users return the day after their first visit or signup. A low day 1 retention rate often indicates poor onboarding, lack of immediate value, or unclear product experience. Successful MVPs ensure that users experience an early *aha moment* that hooks them into returning.

- **Week 1 retention**: At this stage, retention reflects whether users see enough value to continue engaging beyond the initial novelty phase. A drop-off between day 1 and week 1 suggests that while users were intrigued at first, they did not find lasting value or were not given a compelling reason to return. Iterations at this stage often focus on improving engagement loops, notifications, and feature discoverability.

- **Month 1 retention**: This longer-term metric helps determine how deeply the product fits into users' habits and routines. A high month 1 retention rate indicates that users see the product as a core part of their workflow or lifestyle, while a steep decline suggests that the product fails to create long-term stickiness. If users are not returning after a month, it may indicate a lack of ongoing value, insufficient differentiation from competitors, or failure to build long-term engagement mechanics.

By tracking retention across these time frames, entrepreneurs can diagnose where engagement drops off and refine their product strategy accordingly.

Understanding repeat usage vs. churn signals

A core goal of retention analysis is to differentiate between engaged users and those who are likely to churn. Repeat usage is a strong indicator of a sticky product, meaning users return frequently and engage deeply with its features. However, not all retained users are necessarily active—some may return sporadically without making meaningful contributions to engagement, revenue, or community growth.

Churn signals, on the other hand, indicate when users are at risk of disengaging entirely. These signals can include:

- A sharp decline in feature usage over time.
- Skipping key engagement milestones (e.g., not completing onboarding, not interacting with core features).
- Dropping from daily to weekly, then to monthly usage before stopping altogether.

By monitoring repeat usage trends and churn signals, businesses can take proactive steps to re-engage users before they leave permanently. Strategies such as personalized email campaigns, reactivation incentives, and product enhancements can help bring users back before they disengage for good.

Understanding how retention guides future iterations

Retention data is one of the most powerful indicators of MVP success, as it reveals whether users truly value the product or simply try it and leave. Low retention rates signal the need for improvements in usability, engagement, or overall product positioning. High retention, on the other hand, provides a strong foundation for scaling growth efforts.

By studying which features drive retention, teams can prioritize development efforts around elements that keep users engaged. If certain features correlate with higher long-term retention, those should be refined and highlighted. If new releases negatively impact retention, teams can quickly iterate and fix usability or functionality issues.

Additionally, retention insights guide customer segmentation and marketing efforts. Identifying which user personas have the highest retention allows businesses to target their ideal audience more effectively. If power users tend to come from a specific industry, demographic, or behavioral segment, marketing strategies can be adjusted to attract more of the right users.

Common tools for MVP testing

Successful MVP testing is not just about choosing the right method—it is also about selecting the right tools. The following table summarizes MVP testing methods we have discussed and outlines what makes each one valuable:

Method	Tools	USP
A/B testing	AB Tasty, Optimizely, VWO	Optimizely provides real-time experimentation insights, while VWO is great for A/B testing with personalization features.
Split testing	Adobe Target, Convert.com	Google Optimize is free and integrates well with Google Analytics, while Adobe Target supports AI-driven automated testing.
Multivariate testing	AB Tasty, VWO, Adobe Target	AB Tasty enables AI-powered predictive experiments, while VWO offers intuitive multivariate test setups.
Heatmaps and click tracking	Hotjar, Crazy Egg, Microsoft Clarity	Hotjar is known for its easy-to-use visual analytics, while Crazy Egg offers A/B testing alongside heatmaps.
Session recordings and behavior flow analysis	FullStory, Smartlook, Inspectlet	FullStory captures detailed session replays with AI-powered frustration detection, while Smartlook provides event-based insights.
Funnel analysis for identifying bottlenecks	Mixpanel, Amplitude, Google Analytics	Mixpanel and Amplitude allow deep user segmentation and real-time funnel tracking for precise bottleneck analysis.
Retention cohort analysis	Amplitude, Mixpanel, Heap.io	Amplitude excels at long-term user behavior tracking, while Mixpanel provides advanced retention segmentation and cohort insights.

Table 10.2: Common tools for MVP testing

Gathering and synthesizing user feedback

Understanding user behavior is essential in the iterative MVP testing process. However, raw data alone is not enough—what matters is how that data is gathered, interpreted, and acted upon. Entrepreneurs must employ both qualitative and quantitative feedback methods to gain a comprehensive understanding of user experiences, pain points, and expectations. This feedback serves as a foundation for data-driven improvements, ensuring that every iteration of the MVP moves closer to meeting customer needs.

Collecting feedback is only the first step. Synthesizing and interpreting insights effectively is what transforms data into actionable decisions. Without proper synthesis, businesses risk making random changes based on isolated feedback, rather than identifying meaningful patterns that truly impact user engagement and retention.

Qualitative and quantitative feedback

Both qualitative and quantitative feedback play a crucial role in shaping product improvements, but they serve different purposes. Quantitative feedback is data-driven, focusing on metrics, analytics, and trends that provide measurable insights. This includes conversion rates, bounce rates, time spent on a page, and retention figures, which help determine where friction points exist.

Qualitative feedback, on the other hand, is experience-driven, capturing users' emotions, frustrations, motivations, and expectations through direct communication. This includes surveys, user interviews, usability tests, and open-ended feedback collected via support channels or community forums.

The most effective product teams combine both approaches to get a balanced perspective. For example, if quantitative data shows that a checkout process has a high abandonment rate, qualitative research can help uncover why users are dropping off—perhaps they found the form too long, the payment options unclear, or the interface confusing.

There are also times when user feedback should take priority over data trends. If multiple users provide consistent complaints or suggestions, even if analytics do not immediately reflect a major issue, their feedback can be a leading indicator of future engagement problems. Testing these insights through A/B testing or usability studies ensures that adjustments are data-backed rather than purely reactive.

Balancing objective analytics with subjective user experience helps entrepreneurs make more informed, thoughtful decisions, rather than relying on assumptions or incomplete data.

Surveys and user interviews

Surveys and interviews are direct methods of gathering user feedback, providing valuable insights into customer needs, expectations, and frustrations. However, the effectiveness of these methods depends on how well they are designed and executed.

User interviews provide deeper, context-rich insights but require careful structuring. Structured interviews follow a predefined set of questions, making it easier to compare responses across users, while open-ended interviews allow for more flexible, exploratory discussions. The right approach depends on whether the goal is to validate assumptions or uncover new, unexpected pain points.

Long-term tracking of survey responses helps identify trends over time, rather than relying on one-off feedback cycles. If a feature that was once popular starts receiving increasingly negative feedback, it signals a need for re-evaluation and improvement.

We have covered topics of surveys and user interviews in *Chapter 2, Market Analysis and Validation*, extensively.

Usability testing

Usability testing provides direct, real-world insights into how users interact with an MVP. It goes beyond asking users for opinions by observing their actual behavior when completing tasks within the product. This method uncovers hidden friction points, such as confusing navigation, unintuitive UI elements, or inefficient workflows, which users may not articulate through surveys alone.

There are three main types of usability testing:

- Moderated usability testing involves real-time interaction between a user and a facilitator who asks questions and observes behaviors.

- Unmoderated usability testing allows users to complete tasks on their own, with tools recording their actions for later analysis.

- Remote usability testing enables participants to test from their own environment, offering a more natural and scalable approach to gathering feedback.

To ensure usability tests produce actionable insights, businesses should set clear objectives, recruit participants that match the target audience, and observe without interference. Encouraging users to think aloud while completing tasks helps researchers understand their thought processes and pain points in real time.

Synthesizing feedback

Collecting user feedback is only valuable if the insights are effectively synthesized. Synthesis refers to the process of organizing, analyzing, and drawing meaningful conclusions from raw user data, transforming scattered feedback into a structured, actionable roadmap for product improvement.

Without proper synthesis, teams risk making reactive changes based on isolated feedback rather than identifying patterns and underlying issues. A single complaint may not indicate a major problem, but if multiple users express the same frustration, it signals a broader issue that needs attention.

Synthesizing feedback also prevents decision paralysis—when faced with a large volume of user suggestions, teams may struggle to determine which improvements to prioritize. Using structured methods, such as affinity mapping or thematic analysis, helps group similar feedback points and highlight the most critical areas for iteration.

Synthesizing for iterative improvements

Iterative MVP testing relies on continuous learning and refinement, making it essential to systematically process and act on user feedback. By synthesizing insights, businesses can:

- Identify the root causes of usability issues, rather than just surface-level symptoms.

- Distinguish between high-impact improvements and minor preferences, ensuring that development efforts focus on changes that drive meaningful results.

- Align feedback with business goals, prioritizing optimizations that enhance both user experience and key performance metrics.

Effective synthesis starts with organizing feedback into categories, such as usability, functionality, performance, and engagement. Teams should look for recurring themes, grouping similar comments together to reveal patterns. For instance, if multiple users mention difficulty finding a feature, it may indicate that navigation or onboarding needs improvement.

Visual tools like Miro or FigJam can be used to create affinity diagrams, mapping out common pain points and potential solutions. Additionally, quantitative data should be integrated with qualitative insights to validate findings. If session recordings show that many users abandon a form at the same step, and survey responses mention frustration with the form's length, it confirms the need for simplification.

Synthesized feedback should be translated into clear action steps, with prioritized improvements documented in the product backlog. Ensuring that feedback is not just collected, but continuously revisited and acted upon, keeps the MVP evolving in alignment with user needs and market demands.

Tara has now launched IndicOcean, her artisan marketplace, to a limited audience, marking a crucial phase in her MVP journey. Rather than assuming what works, she has embraced iterative testing to validate features, understand user behavior, and refine the platform based on real-world data.

Over the course of several weeks, Tara engaged in user interviews and surveys to gather direct feedback. In addition, she leveraged data-driven testing methods such as A/B testing, heatmaps, click tracking, session recordings, behavior flow analysis, and retention tracking at key milestones (day 1, week 1, and month 1).

One of the most valuable insights from this iterative testing phase was that users were deeply engaged with artisan profiles and their stories, often sharing them widely. However, despite initial expectations, users were not leaving ratings and reviews after receiving their orders.

During user interviews, Tara uncovered a crucial behavioral trend: users found artisan stories more authentic and compelling than traditional ratings and reviews. Many expressed skepticism toward reviews, viewing them as easily manipulated or gamed, whereas hearing directly from artisans felt more genuine and relatable.

This learning challenged the team's initial assumptions and led to a strategic decision—de-prioritizing further development of the ratings and reviews features. Instead of investing time and effort into enhancing a feature that did not provide much value, the team redirected resources toward initiatives that aligned with user behavior and engagement patterns.

By focusing on what users truly valued, Tara's team not only avoided unnecessary development work but also created space for higher-impact improvements, ensuring that IndicOcean evolved in a way that resonated with its audience. This data-driven, user-centric approach highlights the power of iterative MVP testing in refining a product efficiently and effectively.

Guidance metrics

A key aspect of iterative learning is consistently monitoring metrics to evaluate whether the changes made are positively impacting the MVP and moving it toward the desired outcome. Without tracking measurable progress, it becomes difficult to determine if improvements are truly effective or if further adjustments are needed.

For entrepreneurs, this means keeping a close eye on well-chosen outcome metrics that align with business goals and user needs. These metrics serve as a compass, guiding the next steps in product development based on real-world performance rather than assumptions.

The following is a list of common outcome metrics that entrepreneurs can use to assess the impact of improvements and gain valuable insights on what to iterate, refine, or pivot next:

A/B test conversion rate	The percentage of customers who convert in different variations of A/B tests.
App install rate	The number of customers who install the product's application over a period of time.
App uninstalls	The number of customers who uninstall the product's application from their devices over a period of time.
Average order processing time	The average time taken to process and fulfill customer orders.
Average order value	The average value of orders placed by customers.
Average resolution rate	The rate at which customer issues or support tickets are resolved successfully.
Average response time	The average time taken by the product to respond to customer actions or requests.
Average revenue per customer (ARPU)	The average revenue generated per customer or customer.
Average session duration	The average duration of customer sessions within the product.
Average time between purchases	The average time interval between consecutive customer purchases.
Cart abandonment rate	The number of carts or orders that are left abandoned without completing the purchase.
Customer acquisition cost (CAC)	The cost incurred to acquire a new customer.
Customer activation rate	The rate at which customers activate or start using the product after signing up.

Customer bounce rate	The percentage of customers who leave the product or website without taking any further action.
Customer churn rate	The rate at which customers discontinue or cancel their subscription or contract.
Customer effort score (CES)	A metric that measures the effort customers have to put into using the product or resolving issues.
Customer feedback sentiment analysis	The analysis of customer feedback to determine sentiment (positive, negative, neutral).
Customer growth rate	The rate at which the customer base of the product is growing.
Customer lifetime value (CLTV)	The predicted revenue a customer will generate over the entire relationship with the product.
Customer loyalty rate	The rate at which customers exhibit loyalty and repeat purchases of the product.
Customer onboarding drop-off rate	The rate at which customers drop off or abandon the onboarding process.
Customer onboarding time	The time taken to onboard customers and make them fully operational with the product.
Customer referral rate	The rate at which customers refer others to use the product.
Customer satisfaction score (CSAT)	A metric that measures customer satisfaction with the product on a scale.
Daily active users (DAU)	The number of unique customers who engage with the product on a daily basis.
Funnel conversion rate	The percentage of customers who progress through each stage of the conversion funnel.
Monthly active users (MAU)	The number of unique customers who engage with the product on a monthly basis.
Net promoter score (NPS)	A metric that measures customer satisfaction and loyalty on a scale.
Social media conversion	The number of customers who convert or make a purchase through the product's social media presence.
Subscription renewal rate	The percentage of customers who renew their subscription after it expires.
Time between sessions	The average time elapsed between consecutive customer sessions within the product.
Time to achieve key milestones	The time taken for customers to reach key milestones or desired outcomes within the product.
Time to first value	The time taken for customers to experience the first tangible value or benefit from using the product.

Table 10.3: Common MVP outcome metrics

Actions for the entrepreneur

1. Post-launch, initiate MVP testing to track real-world performance.

2. Gather and synthesize user feedback to drive improvements.

3. Based on metrics defined in *Chapter 7, Building Successful MVP*, establish outcome metrics to measure MVP success and inform future iterations.

Conclusion

Iterative MVP testing is the foundation of building a product that continuously evolves based on real-world feedback and user behavior. Unlike traditional development approaches that rely on assumptions and extensive pre-launch planning, iterative testing ensures that every improvement is driven by measurable data and validated insights. By leveraging structured experimentation—through methods such as A/B testing, multivariate testing, heatmaps, and session recordings—entrepreneurs can refine their MVP to better align with customer needs and market demands.

At the heart of this process lies the build-measure-learn framework. While previous chapters emphasized building an MVP, this chapter reinforced the importance of measuring and learning from user interactions. Entrepreneurs who systematically analyze conversion rates, engagement trends, retention metrics, and customer feedback loops gain a competitive advantage by making informed, data-backed decisions. Instead of blindly investing resources into features that may not drive value, iterative testing enables teams to prioritize improvements that enhance user satisfaction and business outcomes.

An essential takeaway from this approach is that not all feedback is created equal. Balancing qualitative and quantitative insights ensures that product decisions are guided by both hard data and real user sentiment. While analytics tools provide objective measurements, direct user feedback, gathered through surveys, interviews, and usability testing, uncovers deeper motivations, pain points, and expectations. Entrepreneurs who synthesize these inputs effectively can make high-impact refinements that foster long-term engagement and retention.

Ultimately, iterative MVP testing is not just about fixing issues or optimizing performance—it is about creating a continuous learning culture that allows businesses to adapt, experiment, and innovate with confidence. Entrepreneurs who embrace this methodology minimize risk, accelerate time to market, and develop products that truly resonate with their target audience.

In the next chapter, the entrepreneur will learn how to identify various risks early and manage them.

CHAPTER 11
Fail-fast

Introduction

Failure is an inevitable part of the entrepreneurial journey, but what differentiates successful ventures from those that struggle is how quickly they recognize, adapt to, and learn from failure. The Fail-fast approach embraces this mindset by encouraging entrepreneurs to identify risks early, test assumptions rapidly, and pivot before excessive resources are wasted. Instead of fearing failure, entrepreneurs can treat it as a learning mechanism, allowing them to refine their approach, validate their product direction, and ensure they are solving the right problem in the most efficient way possible.

Failing fast is not about being reckless or giving up at the first sign of trouble; it is about minimizing risk, reducing uncertainty, and making informed decisions. By proactively addressing technical, market, and execution risks, businesses can avoid falling into the sunk cost fallacy—where resources continue to be invested in a failing idea simply because of past commitments. Recognizing when to pivot, persevere, or abandon an idea is a critical skill that can save time, money, and effort.

This chapter introduces practical frameworks and tools for risk assessment and mitigation. Entrepreneurs will learn how to apply the Fail-fast Canvas, risk response planning, risk assessment matrix, and contingency planning to anticipate and address challenges before they escalate. Additionally, techniques such as threat modeling, pre-mortem analysis, and scenario planning will help teams think ahead and build resilience against potential failures.

By implementing structured crisis management plans and Agile retrospectives, businesses can recover from failures quickly and efficiently, ensuring that setbacks become stepping stones for future growth. The Fail-fast approach is not just about avoiding failure—it is about embracing failure as a necessary step toward innovation, allowing entrepreneurs to iterate faster, smarter, and with greater confidence in their MVP journey.

Structure

In this chapter, we will cover the following topics:

- Risk mitigation
- Fail-fast Canvas
- Crisis management

Objectives

By the end of this chapter, entrepreneurs will gain a comprehensive understanding of the Fail-fast approach and how it can be leveraged to identify, assess, and mitigate risks early in the MVP journey. They will learn how to minimize wasted resources, avoid the sunk cost fallacy, and make data-driven decisions about whether to pivot, persevere, or abandon an idea before excessive investments are made.

Entrepreneurs will explore key risk assessment and mitigation frameworks, including the Fail-fast Canvas, risk response planning, risk assessment matrix, and contingency planning. These tools will help them proactively address technical, market, and execution risks, ensuring they can anticipate and respond to challenges before they become costly obstacles.

The chapter will also introduce techniques that will equip entrepreneurs with structured methods to identify potential failure points and build resilience into their MVP strategy. Additionally, they will learn how to implement Lessons Learned Documentation and Agile Retrospectives to create a culture of continuous improvement, where failure is seen as a stepping stone to innovation rather than a setback.

By integrating crisis management planning into their MVP strategy, entrepreneurs will develop the ability to recover quickly from failures, iterate with confidence, and ensure that every misstep leads to valuable learning. Through these strategies, they will be empowered to build a more adaptable, efficient, and risk-aware approach to product development, setting their startup on a path to long-term success.

Risk mitigation

Risk mitigation in MVP development refers to the strategic process of identifying, assessing, and minimizing potential risks that could hinder the successful launch and growth of an MVP. Every MVP is built with assumptions about technology, market demand, and execution capabilities. However, these assumptions carry inherent uncertainties, making risk management a critical discipline for entrepreneurs aiming to create a viable and scalable product.

By implementing proactive risk mitigation strategies, entrepreneurs can avoid costly setbacks, wasted resources, and unnecessary delays while ensuring their MVP remains aligned with market needs. Managing risk does not eliminate uncertainty, but it equips teams with the agility to adapt, pivot, or resolve issues quickly when challenges arise.

MVP development involves a complex interplay of technology, market demand, and execution feasibility. Each of these dimensions presents unique risks that must be identified and addressed early to prevent failure.

Technical risks

Technical risks stem from uncertainties in technology feasibility, scalability, performance, and security. Many startups make the mistake of assuming that if a feature can be imagined, it can be built easily, but technical complexity often introduces unexpected challenges.

Some common technical risks include:

- **Integration challenges**: *Will third-party APIs or external services work seamlessly?*
- **Security vulnerabilities**: *Does the product protect user data and comply with regulations?*

Mitigating technical risks involves choosing the right technology stack, conducting feasibility tests, and implementing robust security and performance measures before scaling.

Market risks

Market risks arise when there is uncertainty about user demand, competition, and product-market fit. Even the most technically sound product can fail if it does not resonate with customers.

The common market risks include:

- **Lack of user adoption**: *Will customers see enough value in the MVP to use or pay for it?*
- **Competitive threats**: *Are there existing solutions that already dominate the market?*
- **Pricing misalignment**: *Will the pricing model support both customer acquisition and business sustainability?*
- **Regulatory challenges**: *Are there legal or compliance barriers to launching the product?*

To mitigate market risks, entrepreneurs must validate assumptions early through user research, competitive analysis, and pilot testing. The faster an entrepreneur gathers real-world feedback, the better they can refine their product and reduce uncertainty before scaling efforts.

Execution risks

Execution risks pertain to operational, financial, and team-related challenges that can prevent an MVP from reaching its intended outcome. These risks often emerge when teams lack experience, resources, or alignment on business goals.

The key execution risks include:

- **Lack of expertise**: *Does the team have the right skill set to execute the vision?*
- **Budget overruns**: *Are development and operational costs exceeding initial estimates?*
- **Poor project management**: *Are sprints and milestones being completed on time?*
- **Inadequate marketing and distribution**: Even the best MVP will fail if it does not reach the right audience.

Addressing execution risks requires building a capable team, maintaining lean operations, setting realistic milestones, and aligning development efforts with market readiness.

Importance of mitigating risks early

Many entrepreneurs make the mistake of assuming that risks can be handled reactively—only addressing them once they surface. However, risk mitigation is most effective when integrated into the early stages of MVP development. By identifying risks proactively, startups can:

- **Avoid costly pivots and redesigns**: Early validation prevents wasted development effort on the wrong features.
- **Improve decision-making**: A clear understanding of potential risks allows teams to make more informed choices about product strategy and investments.
- **Enhance speed to market**: By resolving foreseeable bottlenecks ahead of time, teams avoid delays and maintain momentum.
- **Increase investor and stakeholder confidence**: A well-managed risk strategy reassures investors that the business is resilient and adaptable.

Mitigating risks early does not mean eliminating them entirely. It means reducing uncertainty, preparing for potential setbacks, and enabling faster, more efficient iterations. Entrepreneurs who approach risk management strategically create a strong foundation for building, testing, and scaling their MVP successfully.

Fail-fast Canvas

The *Fail-fast* approach is a fundamental principle for entrepreneurs seeking product-market fit. It encourages early risk identification, rapid iteration, and strategic decision-making to ensure that an MVP evolves efficiently. The Fail-fast Canvas serves as a structured template for implementing this methodology, guiding teams through identifying risks, determining product stages most vulnerable to failure, and taking proactive measures to mitigate uncertainty. This approach allows teams to forecast potential threats, plan risk mitigation strategies, and ultimately decide whether to pivot, persevere, or abandon a given pathway before investing excessive resources.

The Fail-fast Canvas is a practical tool designed to help entrepreneurs pinpoint pivotal capabilities across different phases of product development, highlighting the potential risks involved in transitioning from one phase to the next. This structured framework is divided into distinct sections, each corresponding to a critical stage in the product lifecycle and outlining the key considerations for decision-making.

By using this Fail-fast Canvas, entrepreneurs can anticipate challenges early, refine their product roadmap, and navigate the MVP journey with greater confidence and agility:

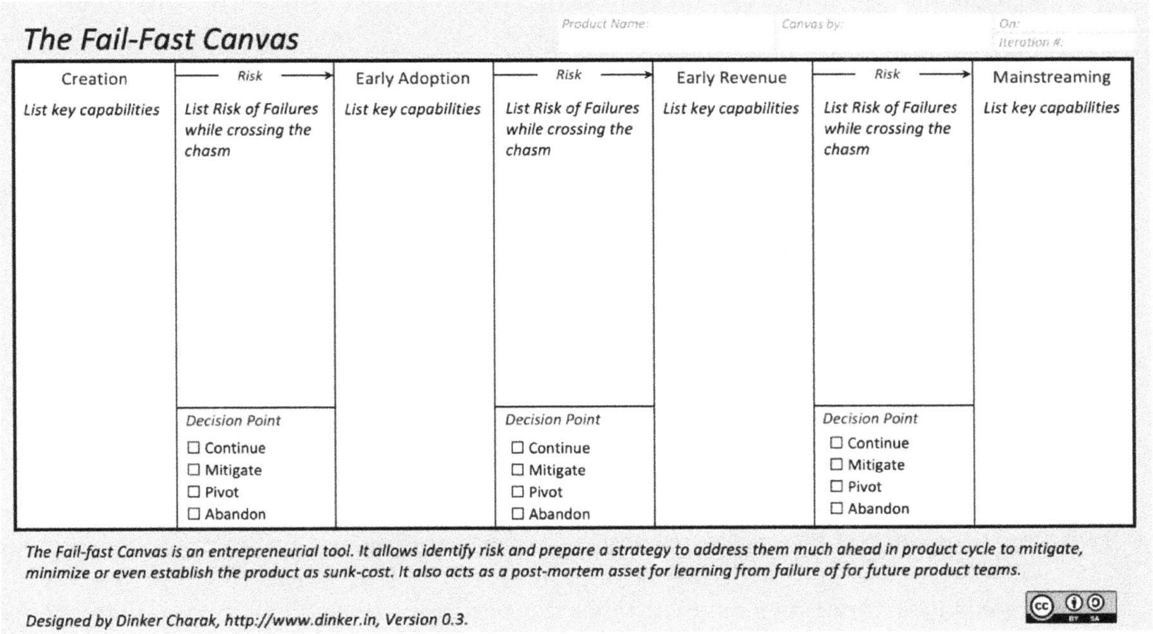

Figure 11.1: The Fail-fast Canvas

The following is an overview of the key sections of this canvas and how they guide risk assessment at different phases of product development:

- **Creation phase**: This phase focuses on defining the essential capabilities that the entrepreneur intends to build during the MVP creation stage. These capabilities set the foundation for product functionality and initial market testing.

- **Risk assessment**: Entrepreneurs evaluate potential challenges that could arise when transitioning from the MVP phase to the early adoption phase. Risks at this stage might include technical feasibility issues, lack of user adoption, or an unclear value proposition.

- **Decision point**: After conducting a thorough risk analysis, the team assesses each capability to determine its viability. At this stage, the team must decide whether to proceed as planned, modify the feature set, pivot toward a different capability, or abandon certain features altogether before moving forward to the early adoption phase.

- **Early adoption phase**: At this stage, the product is introduced to a limited market segment, often comprising early adopters and beta users who provide critical feedback on product usability, desirability, and effectiveness.

- **Risk assessment**: The primary focus here is on identifying potential roadblocks when transitioning from the early adoption phase to the early revenue phase. Common risks include low user retention, misalignment with customer needs, difficulty in scaling, and operational inefficiencies.

- **Decision point**: Based on insights gathered from user feedback and risk evaluations, the team must determine whether to maintain, adjust, pivot, or eliminate specific capabilities. The goal is to ensure that the product is well-positioned to enter the revenue-generation phase while addressing any critical concerns that could hinder adoption at scale.

- **Early revenue phase**: During this phase, the entrepreneur's focus shifts toward monetization and revenue generation. Key capabilities at this stage involve pricing models, payment infrastructure, customer acquisition, and revenue retention strategies.

- **Risk assessment**: The team evaluates challenges associated with scaling revenue operations, sustaining customer engagement, optimizing pricing, and ensuring financial viability as the product moves toward mainstream adoption. This includes analyzing potential churn risks, payment failures, legal compliance, and market competition.

- **Decision point**: Once risks are assessed, the team makes strategic decisions about whether to proceed with the current revenue model, adjust, explore alternative monetization strategies, or pivot toward a new approach. The objective is to ensure a smooth transition from early revenue generation to mainstream market adoption.

- **Mainstreaming phase**: In this final phase, the focus shifts from early traction to long-term sustainability and market dominance. The product has moved beyond early adopters and is now entering the mainstream market, where it must demonstrate reliability, scalability, and competitive differentiation. At this stage, product managers play a crucial role in defining the primary capabilities that will solidify the product's position and drive mass adoption.

By systematically identifying risks, assessing potential pitfalls, and making informed decisions, entrepreneurs can accelerate learning, refine their product roadmap, and allocate resources efficiently.

To Fail-fast, Tara takes the help of the Fail-fast Canvas to identify the risks as early as she can. After discussion with her team and advisors, she also chalks out a plan to mitigate those identified risks. Here is her version of the Fail-fast Canvas:

Phase	Key capabilities	Risk assessment	Decision point
Creation phase (MVP development)	Artisan onboarding, product catalog setup, secure payments, search and filter functionality, artisan storytelling	• **Technical risks**: Payment gateway integration issues, data privacy compliance. • **Market risks**: Artisans hesitant to onboard due to digital literacy barriers. • **Execution risks**: Delays in content creation for artisan profiles.	• Simplify onboarding for artisans. • Conduct training sessions for artisans. • Prioritize payment integration before scaling.
Early adoption phase (beta launch)	Order tracking, social sharing, user reviews, push notifications, early customer support setup	• **Technical risks**: Backend scalability for real-time tracking. • **Market risks**: Low initial user trust, difficulty in generating reviews. • **Execution risks**: Logistics and delivery inconsistencies.	• Focus on artisan storytelling over reviews. • Strengthen logistics partnerships. • Implement basic order tracking with user feedback.
Early revenue phase (scaling monetization)	Subscription for artisans, loyalty programs, expanded artisan categories	• **Technical risks**: Issues with subscription payment processing. • **Market risks**: Low customer retention beyond first purchase. • **Execution risks**: High CAC.	• Test subscription model with a limited group of artisans. • Introduce early adopter discounts and referral rewards. • Optimize organic growth channels to reduce CAC.
Mainstreaming phase (market expansion)	Global expansion, AI-powered recommendations, B2B offerings	• **Technical risks**: Handling multi-currency, multi-language transactions. • **Market risks**: Artisan supply struggling to meet rising demand. • **Execution risks**: Need for compliance with diverse regulations.	• Pilot international expansion in select regions. • Implement automated supply-demand balancing for artisans. • Establish regional compliance and support teams.

Table 11.1: Tara's Fail-fast Canvas

Crisis management

Unexpected challenges, whether technical failures, market shifts, or execution missteps, can threaten the success of an MVP if not handled effectively. Entrepreneurs must anticipate these potential challenges early and implement structured contingency plans to ensure that failures become learning opportunities rather than catastrophic setbacks.

By preparing for crises, analyzing risks, and institutionalizing continuous learning, teams can build a culture of resilience and adaptability—two critical traits for a startup's long-term success. The following strategies help in mitigating risks and ensuring that any disruptions are handled efficiently while keeping customer trust intact.

A crisis can take many forms—system outages, security breaches, PR issues, or major operational failures. The key to handling these situations effectively is having a well-defined contingency plan that enables quick response, clear communication, and structured resolution.

Setting up a response team

A dedicated crisis response team should be identified before an issue arises. This team should consist of representatives from engineering, product management, customer support, and communications. Each member should understand their role in diagnosing the issue, mitigating impact, and keeping internal and external stakeholders informed.

Response communication strategy

Clear and transparent communication during a crisis builds trust and helps prevent misinformation. The team should designate a **single point of contact** (**SPOC**) for all external and internal communications. This person is responsible for:

- Announcing the issue openly, detailing what went wrong without speculation.
- Providing frequent updates on the resolution progress.
- Managing media and customer communication in a consistent and professional manner.
- Coordinating internal updates to ensure all teams are aligned on the status of the issue.

The goal is not only to resolve the issue swiftly but also to ensure that customers and stakeholders feel informed and reassured throughout the process.

Common contingencies

Failures are inevitable, but how a team anticipates, monitors, and responds to them makes all the difference. Entrepreneurs should focus on identifying common failure modes and implementing tools to detect and resolve them quickly.

System outages and downtime

Unexpected downtimes can severely impact customer trust and revenue. Using monitoring solutions such as Pingdom, UptimeRobot, or New Relic helps track website and API uptime, ensuring a quick response to any unexpected outages.

Application errors and bugs

Bugs and application errors can degrade user experience and reduce retention rates. Tools like Sentry, Datadog, or LogRocket allow teams to proactively detect, log, and resolve issues before they impact users.

Denial-of-service attacks

Malicious actors can attempt to flood a system with excessive requests, causing slowdowns or total outages. Security solutions such as Cloudflare, AWS Shield, or Imperva help mitigate **denial-of-service (DoS)** and **distributed denial-of-service (DDoS)** attacks, ensuring continued service availability.

Non-renewal of licenses and SSL certificates

Failure to renew software licenses, domain registrations, or SSL certificates can lead to security vulnerabilities, website downtime, or loss of critical business functionalities. Automated tracking and renewal reminders using tools like Let's Encrypt, SSL Monitor, or StatusCake ensure these critical assets remain active and up to date.

Password breach and unauthorized access

Weak passwords or stolen credentials can lead to data breaches, compromising user trust and security. Implementing **multi-factor authentication (MFA)**, password management tools (1Password, LastPass), and breach detection services (Have I Been Pwned, Google Password Checkup) helps mitigate these risks.

Ransomware attack

A ransomware attack can encrypt critical business data and demand payment for decryption keys. Businesses should implement regular backups using solutions like Veeam, Acronis, or AWS Backup, maintain endpoint security solutions such as SentinelOne or CrowdStrike, and educate employees on recognizing suspicious activities.

Phishing attack

Phishing scams trick employees or customers into revealing sensitive information, leading to security breaches. Using email filtering tools like Proofpoint or Mimecast, training teams on recognizing phishing attempts, and implementing Zero Trust security models significantly reduces this risk.

Scaling issues under high traffic load

A sudden spike in user activity, especially during marketing campaigns or product launches, can overwhelm servers, leading to slowdowns or crashes. Using auto-scaling solutions like AWS Auto Scaling, Google Cloud Load Balancer, and Kubernetes Horizontal Pod Autoscaler helps distribute traffic efficiently.

Data loss or corruption

Data corruption or accidental deletions can result in irreversible losses. Implementing automated backups with AWS Backup, Google Cloud Backup, or Veeam ensures data recoverability and continuity.

API or third-party service failures

If an MVP relies on external APIs (e.g., payment gateways, authentication services, shipping providers), outages or disruptions in these services can cause failures in core functionalities. Using API monitoring tools like **Postman**, **Runscope**, or **Statuspage.io** can help detect downtime early and switch to backup services.

Compliance violations

Failure to comply with data privacy regulations can result in hefty fines, legal actions, and reputational damage. Using compliance management tools such as **OneTrust**, **Vanta**, or **Drata** helps automate regulatory checks and maintain adherence to data protection laws.

Vendor or supplier failures

If an MVP relies on third-party vendors for logistics, payment processing, cloud hosting, or customer support, disruptions in their services can impact business operations. Establishing backup vendors, diversifying partnerships, and negotiating **service level agreements** (SLAs) helps mitigate dependency risks.

Delayed or failed product deliveries

For e-commerce or marketplace MVPs, delivery delays can frustrate customers and increase churn. Integrating with multiple logistics partners and implementing real-time order tracking with Shiprocket, ShipBob, or EasyPost ensures smoother operations.

Customer support overload

During major updates or product launches, an influx of support requests can overwhelm small teams. Using AI-powered chatbots like Drift, Intercom, or Freshdesk helps handle common queries while scaling customer support efforts.

Employee turnover in key roles

Losing critical team members, especially in early-stage startups, can stall development. Documenting key processes in Notion, Confluence, or Google Drive, cross-training employees, and maintaining a strong hiring pipeline help ensure business continuity. This is a critical activity both during the MVP development phase and beyond.

Legal and contractual disputes

Early-stage startups often enter agreements with investors, partners, and service providers that may lead to disputes over time. Working with legal advisors, maintaining well-documented contracts, and leveraging contract management tools like **DocuSign** or **PandaDoc** reduces risk exposure.

Competitor moves or market shifts

A sudden launch of a similar product by a major competitor or changes in customer preferences can impact demand for an MVP. Continuously monitoring competitors with tools like **SimilarWeb**, **SEMrush**, or **Brandwatch** allows for Agile adjustments to market strategies.

PR or reputation crises

Negative press or customer backlash can escalate quickly, impacting brand trust. Having a PR crisis response plan, monitoring brand sentiment using *Google Alerts, Meltwater*, or *Brand24*, and responding transparently can help control damage.

By proactively preparing for these contingencies and embedding security measures into their MVP development process, entrepreneurs can minimize disruptions, maintain user trust, and ensure long-term product stability.

Conclusion

The Fail-fast approach is not about avoiding failure—it is about learning from it quickly, minimizing risk, and making strategic, data-driven decisions. By proactively identifying and mitigating technical, market, and execution risks, entrepreneurs can ensure that setbacks do not derail their MVP journey but instead become valuable learning opportunities.

A core principle of the Fail-fast mindset is recognizing failure early, before excessive time, money, and effort are invested in a direction that may not yield results. The ability to pivot, persevere, or abandon an idea based on real insights helps entrepreneurs avoid the sunk cost fallacy and maintain focus on building products that align with customer needs and market demands. Rather than clinging to assumptions, they continuously validate ideas through structured risk assessment tools like the Fail-fast Canvas, ensuring that decision-making remains Agile and informed.

Beyond risk mitigation, contingency planning and crisis management play a crucial role in ensuring business continuity. Technical failures, security breaches, and operational disruptions are inevitable in any startup's journey, but a well-prepared entrepreneur knows how to anticipate and respond to these challenges effectively. Moreover, Agile Retrospectives and Lessons Learned Documentation foster a culture of continuous learning, where every failure serves as a stepping stone toward success.

Ultimately, the Fail-fast methodology empowers entrepreneurs to iterate with confidence, minimize waste, and build resilient, adaptable businesses. By treating failure as an opportunity rather than a setback, startups can accelerate learning, improve decision-making, and increase their chances of achieving product-market fit.

Join our Discord space

Join our Discord workspace for latest updates, offers, tech happenings around the world, new releases, and sessions with the authors:

https://discord.bpbonline.com

Epilogue

Tara made it. Her success in launching IndicOcean was recognized by her peers and the startup community. She shared the following news article published in a popular startup news portal with her family, friends, and team.

A vision realized, a market transformed

How IndicOcean redefined the artisan marketplace

1st October 2027: Today, IndicOcean is a household name among conscious shoppers, but its success was never guaranteed. Tara's journey from concept to market leader is a masterclass in disciplined entrepreneurship—one that closely followed the principles in *Accelerating MVP Development for Entrepreneurs*.

From the outset, Tara resisted the temptation to assume she knew what the market wanted. Instead, she embraced structured validation, conducting in-depth user research, running pre-launch experiments, and iterating based on real data. Early engagement metrics suggested that storytelling was key, but Tara did not stop at intuition—she tested various monetization models before settling on a marketplace approach enhanced with artisan-led live shopping events.

Her rigorous approach paid off. IndicOcean's customers did not just browse—they engaged, purchased, and returned. The platform gained credibility, forming partnerships with influencers and even receiving backing from a major ethical retail fund. Meanwhile, artisans benefited from streamlined logistics and demand forecasting, solving the operational pain points that had plagued similar initiatives before.

By leveraging the structured MVP framework outlined in the book *Accelerating MVP Development for Entrepreneurs*, Tara turned what could have been another failed experiment into a thriving, scalable business—one that not only supports artisans but has reshaped how handmade goods reach the world.

Join our Discord space

Join our Discord workspace for latest updates, offers, tech happenings around the world, new releases, and sessions with the authors:

https://discord.bpbonline.com

Index

www.ingramcontent.com/pod-product-compliance
Lightning Source LLC
Chambersburg PA
CBHW061802210326
41599CB00034B/6848